MANAGING
FOR EXCELLENCE

THE WILEY MANAGEMENT SERIES ON PROBLEM SOLVING, DECISION MAKING, AND STRATEGIC THINKING

MANAGING
FOR EXCELLENCE

THE GUIDE TO DEVELOPING HIGH PERFORMANCE IN CONTEMPORARY ORGANIZATIONS

DAVID L. BRADFORD
Stanford University

ALLAN R. COHEN
Babson College

JOHN WILEY & SONS
New York   Chichester   Brisbane   Toronto   Singapore

This publication is designed to provide accurate and authoritative
information in regard to the subject matter covered. It is sold with
the understanding that the publisher is not engaged in rendering
legal, accounting, or other professional service. If legal advice or
other expert assistance is required, the services of a competent
professional person should be sought. *From a Declaration of
Principles jointly adopted by a Committee of the American Bar
Association and a Committee of Publishers.*

Library of Congress Cataloging in Publication Data:

Bradford, David L.
  Managing for excellence.

  (The Wiley management series on problem solving,
  decision making, and strategic thinking)
  Bibliography: p.
  Includes index.
  1. Management. 2. Leadership. I. Cohen, Allan R.
II. Title. III. Series.

HD31.B722   1984   658.4'092   83-19784
ISBN 0-471-87176-1
ISBN 0-471-85807-2 (paper)

Printed in the United States of America

20 19 18 17 16 15 14

For our children, Jeffrey and Kendra Bradford, and
Megan and Sydney Cohen, who daily test our ability
to use the leadership notions we so blithely
promulgate, and who have taught us that neither
the boss nor the subordinate is always right.

PREFACE

Despite the millions of words on leadership that have assaulted managers, little has been written that truely reflects the world of work. Many theories are too simple for the complexity of dealing in real time with resistant subordinates, changing needs, and conflicting demands. Some are so abstract and narrow that only an armchair academic could love them. And none really fit the conditions we have observed in our work with practicing managers.

As consultants and teachers of managers, we noticed certain patterns common to high-performing departments. These observations led to some strong hunches about the kind of leadership necessary for contemporary conditions. Where excellence prevailed, we saw:

- Tremendous energy and commitment among subordinates. This seemed more significant than a leader doing everything textbook-right.
- A cohesive team. Beyond competent individuals doing remarkable solo work, there was synergistic collective action in the department.
- Rapid-paced, problem-solving meetings. This was different from those too-frequent occasions when we had watched ineffectual groups "keeping minutes but wasting hours."
- A spirited, healthy competition. This was not jockeying for position or nasty undercutting, but competition against a widely shared standard of excellence.

- A belief in the abilities and intentions of subordinates. The leader believed in the subordinates, and they wanted to deliver. Mistakes and failure to come through were not viewed with cynicism about "inadequate subordinates" or seen as attempts to sabotage the boss.

What was the secret? How did some managers create the kind of involvement and cooperation that seemed to make performance soar? How did these outstanding leaders build energy without being overwhelmed? How did they avoid being naive Pollyannas while believing in subordinates and obtaining their commitment?

Our observations plus some key elements of the management literature* served as a base for our theorizing toward a new model of leadership. Long discussion between us (some would describe these as endless arguments!) linked what we had observed of managers in practice with what had been written, and led us to a rough outline of a different approach. This approach was not a radical departure, but a synthesis of what had been developing in management circles. We were starting to put together ideas in a different way.

At this point we had a *normative*, not a *descriptive*, model. We were starting to describe what managers "should be doing," even though we had only seen bits and pieces in different organizations. Since we had not seen many managers using all of what we were advocating, and no one else had conceptualized it the way we did, we needed to see if ordinary mortals could make it work.

Our solution was to set up a leadership training program for middle and upper-middle managers through NTL Institute.

---

*Berlew's theorizing on the need for challenging tasks and charismatic leadership resonated with our own observations about high-performing departments. Miles and Ritchie's distinction between "human relations" and "human resource" approaches to subordinate involvement reflected the problems we had seen when managers used "pseudo-participation" to get others to buy into the leader's predetermined solution (rather than involvement to make full use of employees' abilities and knowledge). Vroom and Yetton's work on decision-making styles provided clues on how best to use a team. Vaill's work on high-performing systems suggested interesting patterns. McClelland's and Kanter's works on power showed vividly that managers could increase the influence of subordinates without having to give up their own power.

We began to try our ideas out with these critical managers from many companies, who wanted education that they could make work for them. The workshop utilized a variety of activities where the managers applied our emerging model to solving critical managerial problems. There were also discussions in which participants raised questions and shared dilemmas from their work experiences. Each time, we further refined our model and tested a new draft of this book on the next attendees.

In order to track the results of the plans for implementation that were made on the last day of each training program, we subsequently mailed a questionnaire to participants asking them what they had tried when they returned—what worked and what didn't. This provided a rich source of examples and illustrated exactly how managers could move their department from where it was to a state of excellence. It demonstrated to us that the model we eventually refined into this book was learnable despite its sophistication, practical despite its newness, and useful to managers facing the toughest complexities of today's organizations.

We are thus indebted to the more than 200 managers who attended this program and let us know when we got too complex or too facile, and to those among them who have taken the model to heart and shown us its potency. We also want to thank the students in our courses who raised critical questions and helped us refine our thinking. There are many professional colleagues and practicing managers who were useful in the numerous informal discussions, but we particularly want to thank David Arella, David Berg, Steve Fink, Frank Friedlander, Fran Hall, Esther Hamilton, Susan Hoffer, Rosabeth Kanter, J. B. Kassarjian, Susan Kominsky, Dwight Ladd, Roy Lewicki, Nancy Roberts, Julien Phillips, Barry Stein, and Rita Weathersby for their helpful comments on earlier drafts of this book.

The nature of this enterprise and the complexities of exchanging drafts across the country meant even more typing and retyping than for the usual book. For typing help far beyond the call of duty, we thank the institutions of Stanford

University, University of New Hampshire, Babson College, and Goodmeasure, Inc., and the tireless individual efforts of Vicky Del Bono, Beri Ellis, Jane Gaskell, Mona Koch, Betty MacNeur, Carol Poirier, Mildred Prussing, Connie Stumpf, and Fritz Winegarden. Jeanne Muller did rapid, accurate indexing.

We are indebted to Allan Kennedy, Tom Peters, Julien Phillips, and Bob Waterman of the McKinsey and Company organization effectiveness task force, with whom David Bradford consulted. Their ideas on superordinate goals served as a stimulus to our thinking.

We are also grateful to the Carter family of Nashua Corp., which funded the James R. Carter Chair of Management at the University of New Hampshire's Whittemore School of Business and Economics. That award helped support Allan Cohen's work on the book, as did a sabbatical year from U.N.H. spent as a visiting scholar at the Harvard Business School.

Although we would like to be consistent with our leadership model and share the responsibility for this book with all those who helped shape it, we unfortunately will have to accept all the blame for its shortcomings. Some responsibilities just can't be passed along, no matter how tempting it is to do so!

Finally, we wish to express our gratitude to our wives, Eva and Joyce, and our children, for their tolerance of our obsessive meetings and extended wrestling with the ideas and drafts. Their support was invaluable.

DAVID L. BRADFORD
ALLAN R. COHEN

Stanford, California
Wellesley, Massachusetts
January 1984

CONTENTS

MANAGING FOR EXCELLENCE

INTRODUCTION: THE CRISIS IN MANAGEMENT

It is no secret that many contemporary American organizations are in trouble. The problem is not so much obsolete factories, backward technologies, or lazy workers as it is outdated leadership practices. Our once-vaunted management methods are being increasingly criticized. Several recent best-selling books have dealt with different aspects of this criticism: Ouchi (1981) described the deficient web of human concerns compared to practices of (at least some) Japanese companies in *Theory Z*; Pascale and Athos (1981) showed how the "soft" management skills have been overlooked in *The Art of Japanese Management*; Deal and Kennedy (1982) argued for the potency of positive *Corporate Cultures*; Kanter (1983) showed in *The Change Masters* how segmented organizations stifle needed innovations; and Peters and Waterman (1982) identified the broad organizational arrangements that appear to produce corporate excellence.

As valuable as these books might be, they focus almost exclusively on the total organization and speak to the chief executive officer, president, and board chairman, who make large-scale decisions, even though the implementation of these plans falls to managers in the next levels down. Thus there lies a great gap between what is known about what organizations ought to be like and what individual managers need to do to achieve excellence. There is little written guidance for individual upper-middle managers in running their departments.

The head of data processing cannot alter his or her organization's total culture, or create lifetime employment practices, or invent a new corporate strategy. Although it is desirable to link the department's activities with the organization's directions and to build on any possible aspects of the existing culture, it is more crucial to find ways to get the best from all subordinates. How can subordinates be led to tie their own interests to the needs of the department and to make the extra effort necessary to perform at an excellent level? Even the visions of supremely enlightened presidents must be translated into action by strong middle managers who can pull their subordinates together to achieve the increasingly difficult tasks necessary for organizational survival.

Where might such a manager turn for help? Contemporary leadership theory offers help in a fragmented, barely usable way. It is probably true that appropriate leadership style depends on the complexity of the task, maturity of the group, relationship of the leader to the group, expertise of the leader, and so forth (Fiedler, 1962; House, 1976; Hersey and Blanchard, 1972). But these generalities don't help much when subordinate A is dragging his feet on finishing a major project, subordinate B is sniping at subordinate C, D is running down a blind alley that is unrelated to what E needs, and none of these subordinates will address the important issues at staff meetings.

It was managers in these kinds of difficulties, working hard but uphill, which led us into the explorations that have resulted in this book. We were trying to help them develop useful ideas for running their departments—ideas that were neither so complicated that managers would be paralyzed into minute analysis of every contingency before they could speak, nor so oversimplified that we would be led into the absurdity of promising one-minute solutions to those who are well aware of the complexities. Getting a department to outstanding performance is sufficient challenge for managers, without the burden of cumbersome theory or insulting oversimplification.

Yet it is the middle and upper-middle managers of contemporary organizations who hold the key to high performance, since they represent the greatest underutilization of human resources. Because of the winnowing of the selection process, managers at this level are typically knowledgeable and competent. They carry great responsibility; having moved past most of the routine and mundane tasks, they translate the lofty long-range plans of top management into successful operation. If they can produce, they have an important impact on much of the organization. Since they often manage managers or skilled professionals, their leadership has a cascading effect on several levels of important subordinates.

Nevertheless, upper-middle managers often feel highly constrained and squeezed from all sides. Buffeted by new demands from outside, high standards from the top, legions of staff specialists from the side, and ambitious, demanding subordinates from below, the manager's responsibility is increased even while independent authority to act is decreased. Government regulations, unions, central personnel, financial and legal departments, all set limits. Top management is also pressured, but frequently has more authority to deal with these demands and is allowed longer time horizons. This imbalance between what is expected and the freedom to act is particularly stressful for this middle group.

Thus, despite the pressing need for excellent work and great potential for moving organizations, the promise is too seldom achieved. In numerous organizations, more problems exist in the middle than at the top or at the bottom.

THE WOES OF MIDDLE MANAGERS

In our work as consultants and teachers to managers in major organizations in the private and public sectors, we have too often seen variations of the situations listed below.

- The middle manager's unit does adequate and sometimes above-average work, but seldom achieves bone-satisfying excellence.
- The manager works hard—50 to 60 hours a week or more —but always with a sense of pushing uphill. Nothing comes easy: Frequently the energy comes more from the manager than from the subordinates.
- The subordinates are usually competent—most are college graduates and many hold advanced degrees—and by and large they are doing good work, yet seldom are they working near their potential.
- The manager complains that subordinates don't initiate enough, don't take on tasks before having to be asked, and

don't anticipate problems, just react to them. When subordinates do take initiative, it is regarding things they are personally interested in—not necessarily what the department needs. Then they resist direction when the leader tries to integrate their efforts with the work of others.

- Furthermore, the subordinates don't seem to have the commitment to the overall unit that the manager has. They focus too much on their narrow domains and seldom share the larger, total department perspective.

- This lesser commitment of subordinates is also manifested in work that lacks quality or promptness. Managers report that they spend excessive time prodding subordinates, usually but not always gently, to be sure that deadlines are met and performance is up to standard.

- Meetings are too often a waste of time. Managers feel that subordinates rarely bring up all the issues; when they do raise problems, they seem more concerned about defending their own turf (and impressing the boss that they are right and the other is at fault) than in striving for a quality solution. They may call themselves a team, but they show very little teamwork.

- Managers often feel that, despite the organization's fancy management information system and their own attempts to gather many sources of information, they are often the last to know. Subordinates do know when problems are proliferating, performance is falling, and costs are creeping up, but they wait for the managers to discover these trouble signs for themselves and refuse to put pressure on each other for improved performance.

- At times subordinates may complain that they want more exciting and challenging work, but the manager is hesitant to delegate such tasks. Since regular work isn't being done to high standards, what guarantee is there that more difficult assignments would be done well?

- When the manager does give feedback on performance, it is often met with defensiveness and denial. Subordinates may say they want to develop, but they ignore the comments and hints their superior gives on substandard aspects of their performance.

These comments are of course not universal, but we have heard variations on these themes with distressing regularity from many of the managers we observe and talk with. Although work does get accomplished (usually at a high enough level of performance so that customers and clients don't consistently complain), there is still a significant gap between what each department produces and its ultimate capacities.

The managers who lead such adequate but not excellent departments often experience a high degree of personal frustration. They feel that if they want something done well, they have to do it themselves. Furthermore, they constantly feel overworked, going from crisis to crisis with too few hours in the day to get everything done. The best moments are described as those when everybody else goes away and the manager is free to "get some real work done." The good old days, when it was possible to solve problems using one's own technical expertise without having to manage anybody else, seem like a golden age, remembered fondly.

THE EXCELLENT DEPARTMENT

If you are a battle-scarred veteran of the middle-management wars, you are probably grimacing with recognition. Hard work is demoralizing when it feels so much like wheel-spinning. Yet is there an option? Isn't life in the trenches just like that, involving plenty of hard work and aggravation, with occasional bright spots?

Let us suggest an alternative. Suppose that a department works close to its potential; instead of the inertia and resistance described above, what characteristics does such a truly excellent unit have? Basically, its members share a commitment to making the unit extraordinarily successful in accomplishing agreed-on organizational objectives. The focus is on quality, on genuinely collaborative team effort, on confronting differences about work without petty infighting, and on continual attention to the development of members as integral to achieving the task.

The concern for excellence in such an operation is not the exclusive property of the leader. Instead, all members share this concern and are prepared to do what is necessary in order to help the unit exceed expectations. Members do not wait for the boss to notice a problem with methods, service, coordination, supplies, and the like, but themselves feel responsible for the unit's success and take initiative when they see a problem. Like the unusually successful paper mill described in a classic Harvard case study (Marshall Co., 1948), when there is a break in the continuous flow and paper starts piling up at a rapid rate, the first person to spot the break leaps in and restarts the process, regardless of rank or job description. Although in most organizations the result of letting precious seconds go by while waiting for the boss to notice a problem would not be so dramatically disastrous, the image of passively working along while up to one's ears in runaway paper has a symbolic truth for many organizational units. In an excellent department, everyone worries about the whole and takes initiative to see that problems are dealt with and objectives met. This does not supersede clear individual responsibilities and accountability, but avoids the passive acceptance of things going wrong because "it's not my job."

The concern for task accomplishment includes a strong emphasis on quality—of products, services, and members themselves. The unit strives to be at the forefront of its field. As a result, doing the work well is the central focus, rather than personal or political issues. Deliberations aim for problem solving instead of personal dominance, winning, or individual point-scoring at others' expense. In order for such a clear focus on work to exist, there must be clarity about the department's and organization's goals. These goals are accepted by all and used as a basis for making decisions and guiding action; they serve as important guideposts that influence individual behavior and department operations, rather than empty statements filed away in the drawer to be pulled out and dusted off on ceremonial occasions.

This dedication to quality work means that careful attention is paid to the quality of people in the unit and therefore to personnel decisions. Members are recruited for their qualifications, not for similarity of social class, race, sex or religion. Unit managers make tough decisions about promotion (with seniority and loyalty given lower priority than competence). People are directly told about poor performance and helped to improve, not treated ambiguously. Continued mediocre work leads to the search for a better job fit, demotion or dismissal, not to a sideways shunt to a safe but useless position. An excellent department has a minimum of deadwood.

It would be easy for this emphasis on quality work and on performance to lead to exploitation of the members, to their being kept as long as they performed well and discarded the moment they started to slip. But that orientation actually prevents excellence from developing; members will not give the requisite effort if they feel they are being used or if they are managed by threats of dismissal at the first sign of mediocre performance. There must be the commitment to help people reach their potential and to support their efforts to improve, although an employment contract cannot be automatically permanent. Over time it might become clear that an individual no longer could or would deliver.

In this type of organization, information is freely transmitted among members as well as between members and the boss. It's true that such sharing increases the probability of open conflict, but about work-related issues, not in defense of turf or toward a goal of empire building and conquest. Genuine disagreements can be acknowledged upward as well, since the manager encourages members to speak their minds and does not kill the messengers for bringing bad news. Similarly, the manager encourages members to be open with each other, not with the goal of pitting subordinate against subordinate, but in order to reveal task disagreements so that they may be resolved. Furthermore, the manager supports members working as a team, without fearing that they will coalesce in opposition to the superior's authority. No one, boss or subordinate, holds back from using strength, since the others are strong as well and have learned to prefer direct dealings, especially when aimed at successful work accomplishment rather than individual ascendance over others. Thus, outstanding performers are encouraged to set even higher goals rather than being pulled down to a safe average. Such increased efforts mean that the individual's talents are used in the service of the unit's overall performance.

Finally, value is placed on diversity. Cohesion is produced by the commitment to a common goal toward which all work, not by everybody's thinking and acting the same. Different viewpoints about how the goal is attained surface and various approaches are encouraged; conformity in thought and style is discouraged.

Sound utopian? Although we have painted an idealized state rather than an actual organization, we have observed all of these conditions to some degree in occasional pockets of excellence, led by middle managers who do things in special ways. Favorable conditions most frequently occur when a department is faced with a challenge, such as developing a new product or service or starting up a new operation. Necessity is often the mother of excellence, bringing with it challenge, excitement, and unusual ways of doing things. But we think such accomplishments can be much more widespread and can be brought into existence under nonemergency conditions. And departmental excellence can be achieved even when the total organization does not have all of the desirable supporting conditions in place.

DISCREPANCY BETWEEN PERFORMANCE AND POTENTIAL: THE PITFALLS OF HEROISM

What causes discrepancy between actual and potential performance? The problem, we believe, lies with the model of leadership used by most managers—a model appropriate to a previous era, but now outdated and inadequate in eliciting the best performance in complex, contemporary organizations.

Theories of leadership and management, irrespective of what label is used or how participatory they claim to be, contain core assumptions that actually *prevent* excellence from being obtained in contemporary organizations. These assumptions place managers in the center of the action, with the burden of responsibility squarely on their shoulders. It is the manager who must parcel out the work, set the objectives, monitor the performance, see that work is done, and fix whatever is wrong. Even though these managers may solicit subordinate input and delegate important tasks, the underlying assumption is that good managers are ones who hold the overall view of what the department should be doing and have the knowledge and responsibility for seeing that success is obtained. This is a very heroic way of viewing the manager's role. This heroism is a product of the way organizations mythologize about managers as well as the tendency in American culture to romanticize certain heroes. In describing this heroic image, we will be highlighting, perhaps exaggerating, some of its parts for illustrative purposes, but we repeatedly see the basic themes in the daily actions and language of managers.

Our premise is that all managers carry around a view of what the "good leader" is like. This view is rarely overtly articulated (which may be one factor that gives it such potency in influencing behavior), but it is held internally as a model of what managers ought to be like. Managers may not always live up to their personal models, but their actions are constantly being influenced by their conceptions of the ideal. When we have asked managers what interactions make them feel validated as competent (one way to get at their models of the ideal manager), their responses contain most of the following characteristics.

1. *The good manager knows at all times what is going on in the department.* Thus if a boss or peer from another department asks, "What's the status of the Williamson project?" the manager is disturbed if he has to respond, "I

don't know, but I'll check it out for you." Conversely, the manager feels better about him/herself (and stands a little taller), if able to rattle off all the facts and figures.

2. *The good manager should have more technical expertise than any subordinate.* Thus if a subordinate in a meeting says in response to a superior's suggestions, "No, we shouldn't do it that way; there's a new process that is better because . . . " the manager feels inadequate (although the subordinate wouldn't feel nearly so inadequate if the boss were to give that response to the subordinate's suggestion).

3. *The good manager should be able to solve any problem that comes up (or at least solve it before the subordinate can).* Thus, if a subordinate asks, "How are we going to solve the conflict between Parker and Jennings?" the superior feels less competent if forced to respond, "I really don't know. What do you think?" (If the subordinate then comes up with a good answer, the manager's sense of competence is further threatened.)

4. *The good manager should be the primary (if not the only) person responsible for how the department is working.* Thus, if two subordinates leave a staff meeting complaining to each other that the meeting was boring and didn't deal with important issues, the boss feels worse than the two subordinates.

Even though most managers would admit that they don't have this constant control, we have observed that most managers carry this view of how they *should* act. This heroic image also fits the cultural heroes in our society: the military commander whose coolness under fire and consistently correct orders win the day, the business maverick who doggedly holds to one idea and pushes it through to economic success, and the western hero who single-handedly eliminates the town's problems; without them the battles would not have been won.

No one can fault a manager's desire to see that whatever is needed gets done. Responsibility and control are commendable, but their dominance over other characteristics was more appropriate in the past. In previous decades, it was possible for leaders at least to understand, and often to execute, all department tasks better than the subordinates could. After all, most managers worked their way up through the ranks and had usually performed the same functions now carried out by their subordinates. Furthermore, changes in knowledge, technology, and external environment occurred slowly enough so that most of the answers the supervisor had mastered while working at lower levels still applied. Compared to the manager, employees were relatively uneducated—often immigrants of a significantly lower (and quite different) social class—which guaranteed a significant expertise gap between boss and subordinates. Furthermore, tasks were much simpler; jobs were narrowly defined and could be accomplished by a single person with little assistance. Most work was physical or mechanical, and the boss could easily watch and judge performance.

Under such conditions—where the tasks were simple, change was slow, and subordinates were unskilled—the manager *could* have all the answers: what had to be done, how problems were to be solved, and the exact best way to go about it. The major issue was control: finding the right answer, gaining subordinate acquiescence to predetermined tasks, and monitoring the quality of work. In the far past, such control was exerted by direct supervision and often coercion; it has still lingered on since World War II, although the heroic fist has been covered with the softer glove of "participative management." This was appropriate during the post-war period because the leader still knew the tasks and could manage by "getting things done through others." In order to get the best performance from everyone, managers could take everything on their shoulders.

These organizational conditions, however, are becoming less and less frequent; fewer contemporary organizations fit this model. Tasks and priorities are constantly changing; new knowledge and technology are dramatically increasing, and the environment in which work is implemented is repeatedly shifting. The solution that worked yesterday is only slightly appropriate today and will be irrelevant tomorrow. Task complexity virtually insures that no one person can have all the necessary knowledge, which forces a heightened degree of interdependency among subordinates (and a much greater demand for coordination) if work is to be successfully accomplished, especially at an excellent level.

Organizations facing complexity and change must hire competent, educated people at the managerial level. Thus the subordinates of contemporary middle and upper-middle managers will almost all be college graduates, many with MBA's and other advanced or technical degrees. Try as the managers might, they will rarely be able to keep technically ahead of their new subordinates in all areas. Managers certainly have to keep abreast of recent developments, but in general terms, at best; the most specific knowledge of the task must be left to the highly trained subordinates who now often have their own areas of expertise. Task complexity is further increased by the fact that work itself has become highly interdependent. Information, cooperation, agreement, and assistance from many areas are needed. Since such input is frequently from others who are peers, issues of coordination and integration are more important and more difficult. Furthermore, having the leader provide the necessary coordination is less feasible, since much of the subordinate's work involves thinking, developing, inventing, and relating, which means that performance cannot be directly observed. No longer is there an hourly or daily product to count and measure; sometimes months pass before any tangible outcome appears. A manager can therefore no longer give orders and be certain that they are carried out properly by watching everything the subordinate does.

CONSEQUENCES OF USING AN INAPPROPRIATE MANAGEMENT STYLE

What happens when modern, complex organizations are managed with a traditional, heroic leadership style? What are the effects when a model of leadership stressing *managerial* responsibility, knowledge, coordination, and control is utilized in an organization where subordinates possess increasing proportions of needed expertise leading to complex and interdependent tasks?

First, information often does not flow freely and easily to the right places. Problems are noticed down the line in such an organization, but rarely identified, because subordinates do not feel responsible for identifying difficulties. Each area shields information in its dealings with other areas, which adversely affects coordination. When information finally does work its way up, it is likely to be distorted and filtered by its transit through many people, each with a different vested interest in reinterpreting the situation. Managers are responsible for the larger view, even though situational complexity combined with an inadequate managerial model makes it almost impossible for managers to stay fully informed.

If responsibility rests at the top, the unit's responsiveness to new demands and new opportunities is greatly slowed. In rapidly changing environments, departmental success will go to those who can adapt quickly. But under heroic management, nonroutine decisions dealing with unforeseen situations are likely to have to pass to the top through many layers of approval. (One overcontrolling organization we worked with required 19 signatures for each research-and-development expenditure.) Even in less extreme cases, if decision makers are distant from the actual situation, time is wasted and information is distorted as the problem is forwarded to managers who will never understand it as fully as subordinates with first-hand experience.

Recent research on innovative middle managers revealed that fluid organizational arrangements make an extraordinary difference in performance (Kanter, 1983). Such an arrangement requires subordinates who can be responsive and committed to seizing opportunities; they have to be free to take initiative and to respond to problems, unfettered by excessively rigid rules and procedures.

When decisions get pushed up to the heroic manager, major bottlenecks develop in the coordination process. If it is up to the leader, rather than to the subordinate, to see that all parts are working together smoothly, every dispute tends to get bumped upward to the superior. Issues of who has jurisdiction, who isn't coming through with the required work at the required time, which technique should be adopted, the sequence of decision making, and just about every other problem, large and small, land on the leader's desk. No wonder managers feel overwhelmed by the constant brush fires set off by conflicting subordinate demands.

Another problem faced by a heroic manager in contemporary changing organizations is the lowered quality of decisions. Not only are problems hidden until they become major, but important information is frequently withheld. Furthermore, the manager who holds a heroic stance tends to restrict possible solutions and approaches to those he or she feels competent using. Heroic leadership fails to make full use of the knowledge and competencies for which their subordinates were hired.

Heroism may be motivating for the superior but it has the opposite effect on subordinates. The traditional leadership style, valid when the superior was truly more knowledgeable than subordinates, underutilizes contemporary subordinates' technical abilities and problem-solving skills. Today, there are far more subordinates who want to be challenged by work; they place "challenging jobs" and "a chance to grow and develop" ahead of such rewards as pay, status, and job security (Yankelovich, 1974, 1981). Economic recessions may temporarily overshadow these growth needs, but they are present nonetheless. When subordinates are managed by someone who feels responsible for, and in charge of, everything, they feel deprived of important job challenges. In addition, they perceive that such management neither produces quality decisions nor adequate coordination.

By assuming sole responsibility for their departments, managers produce the very narrowness and self-interest they deplore in subordinates. When subordinates are relegated to their narrow specialties, they tend to promote their own practical interests, which then forces other subordinates into counteradvocacy. The manager is thereby thrust into the roles of arbitrator, judge, and referee. Not only do priorities become distorted, but decisions become loaded with win/lose dynamics. Even a King Solomon–like manager cannot always be right or appear always to be fair. So, try as the manager might, decisions inevitably lead to disgruntlement and plotting for the next battle. Organizational politics of the most petty and unsavory kind flourish when only the head feels overall responsibility for the unit. Traditional leaders, who bear such great responsibility for coordinating all activities, by their very existence decrease the responsibility felt by subordinates.

One of the paradoxical consequences of a heroic orientation is that it keeps the manager from sufficiently fulfilling the needed leadership role. Often the distinction is made between "managing" and "leading," with the former referring to administering the present organization and the latter connoting a view to the future. But in contemporary organizations both functions are necessary. It may be overstatement to compare managing solely within existing frameworks to rearranging deck chairs on the *Titanic*, but a manager who fails to determine future needs and to move subordinates toward readiness for fulfilling them is courting disaster. Because we think that excellence can be achieved only through simultaneously taking care of the present and planning for the future, the terms *manager* and *leader* are used interchangeably in this book.

Heroic managers, whose days are occupied with putting out brush fires, handling the exceptions, resolving disputes, and coming up with all the answers, do not have the time to develop an adequate vision of what the department should become. Without an exciting view of the future, another major source of motivation for subordinates is lost. People want to believe in something. Leaders who do have a vision about what is needed and can show subordinates how personal needs for growth and challenge can be met by pursuing this new direction, can tap hidden reserves of commitment and energy, enabling them to strive beyond the ordinary (Berlew, 1974).

Finally, leaving the entire responsibility to the boss hinders the growth and learning of subordinates. If subordinates aren't encouraged to understand the wide organizational perspective, included in key meetings and issues, and given some overall responsibility, they miss opportunities to expand their managerial capacities. Their own prospects within the company are dim, since they will seldom assume the big picture on their own or even know how to do it if invited. No boss wants to promote or give opportunities to persons who appear to be too narrow—even if their narrowness was compelled by the boss's decision to maintain overall unit responsibility in a heroic way.

Although a traditional, heroic management style well suited a simpler setting (and may still be best in departments whose tasks are simple and where change is slow), heroic management fights a losing battle for performance in complex, changing organizations with competent subordinates. Failure to achieve excellence does not rest with lazy or incompetent subordinates. Management failures inevitably come from holding onto an approach to management that does not fit contemporary organizations.

The most paradoxical and frustrating trap for the heroic manager is that greater effort exacerbates the problem. While increasingly Herculean efforts are demanded of the leader, the abilities of subordinates are further ignored, causing frustration and weakening of motivation throughout the department. Heroism sets up a self-defeating cycle: The more the manager accepts the responsibility for departmental success, the greater the likelihood that subordinates will yield it, forcing the manager to take more, and so on. The manager is driven to get more involved—to be as central to the department as a nerve center or orchestra conductor—desperately trying to control all the diverse parts of the organization, but still unable to produce excellence.

MIDDLE MANAGERS' VIEWS ON BEING MANAGED

As a way of beginning to map a way out of this managerial trap, let us look at the experiences middle managers had when they were subordinates. In training programs and courses we have conducted for middle managers, we have used an exercise that illuminates issues of leadership style and motivation. We first ask the managers about their present jobs—to what extent their abilities and competencies are used on their present job and to what degree they feel challenged and stretched by their work.

About 25% of the managers reported that they used less than a third of their ability! "I could do that job in the dark," "It was all routine to me," "I had a wide range of skills the company needed but I wasn't allowed to use," were common answers. Well over half of the managers said they were using between 30 and 60% of their skills. The rest of the managers, usually fewer than one in five, said they were really challenged and that the organization was using most of their skills; no more than one in twenty said they were using all the resources they had. Note that we are *not* talking about the number of hours managers worked. Work time did not clearly differentiate these groups, only how well the time was spent.

We then asked managers in the top 10 to 20% what had caused them to be more challenged, to have such a high percentage of their abilities used. In an overwhelming number of cases, two themes emerged.

First, *the job itself was highly challenging.* The job frequently reflected a new product, new service, or new thrust of the organization. Since it had never been done before, there were few precedents, and the person had to discover new solutions to fit a unique situation. In most cases, the problems were "soft" and ambiguous in that often the exact scope of the difficulty was unclear. In other situations, people reported that they had multiple tasks requiring simultaneous accomplishment. Frequently, the problems required assistance or approval from others in the organization over whom the manager had no formal power. In all these cases, the tasks themselves forced the manager to work near the boundaries of personal competence, rather than to repeat known activities done many times before.

Second, in almost all cases, our respondents reported that *they had rarely seen their boss!* "I didn't have a boss." "He was too busy with other projects and was never around." "I was left totally on my own." "I only checked in when I wanted to or when I needed something I couldn't do myself." "He pointed me in a general direction, but then I had to work it out myself." The highly challenged managers worked without any close supervision.

The remaining managers, whose talents were not being used, universally reported that their jobs lacked challenge. The tasks may have been previously challenging but had been long since mastered, so that the excitement and "stretch" quality had passed.

We then inquired among this 80 to 90% who were underutilized about their bosses—were they "good" or "bad" bosses? What characteristics did they have? The bad bosses were described as might be expected: They supervised too closely, were punitive and blaming, autocratic and capricious in decision making, petty, had to have things done their way, and the like. The so-called good bosses, however, sounded like model traditional managers. They were typically described as bosses who spent a lot of time "managing" the subordinate. When pressed for clearer definitions, the managers answered that the boss did most of the planning and allocation of tasks, solved most of the major departmental challenges, and assumed responsibility for providing the coordination among peers—that is, the boss fulfilled the traditional managerial functions. When there was the potential of job challenge from ambiguous tasks or tasks that required working with people outside the department, these allegedly good bosses, in an effort to fulfill their role, were likely to assume the responsibility for structuring the task and providing the necessary linkages with the outside people.

Across all the examples that the managers gave, subordinate satisfaction (and perceived productivity) tended to be in direct proportion to how *little* their boss intruded. But there were some exceptions. In a few cases, people found themselves highly frustrated and less productive despite high task challenge and no boss contact. They said, "I needed my boss to give me the information I had to have to solve problems." "I needed her expertise so that I didn't have to reinvent the wheel each time." "I needed him to go to bat for me upstairs." In these instances, the subordinate had passed the point of challenge and was feeling overwhelmed.

LEADERSHIP REVISITED

What are the implications for managers? Is less leadership better leadership? Such may be the case when leadership is defined in the traditional sense, as the manager who comes up with the answers and is in control of how subordinates carry out their work. But before we settle too quickly on the virtues of anarchy, let's examine the other requirements of employees and organizations.

In addition to needing challenging tasks and the autonomy to carry them out, subordinates also at times need support, coaching, and assistance. Part of that assistance involves helping them to integrate their efforts with others. Although competent subordinates will usually want plenty of room to work things out for themselves, there will be times when they want information, advice, a sounding board, encouragement, support with higher ups, or aid in obtaining agreements with peers. Even rules, procedures, and the like are welcomed when appropriately developed, because they provide agreed methods for coordinating work and resolving disputes. Total freedom could be paralyzing when people and units are interdependent. Likewise, organizations need coordination of effort. Individual initiative is exhilarating, but if everybody is marching to a different drummer and seeking different goals, the band does not win awards.

Thus, the traditional emphasis on control and coordination has validity. Efforts will not automatically be integrated, nor will goals inevitably be accepted and met, just because talented people are turned loose. Even eminently reasonable people can differ about what is important, about whose vision or project should have priority and greater resources. Thus, in pointing out the problem with traditional management, we are not suggesting that all the leadership development of the last decades be thrown out. Excellence requires budget and control systems, formalized ways to appraise, reward, and promote, long-range planning and forecasting systems, and division of labor and job descriptions. The dilemma for the manager, then, is not whether control needs to be exercised, but how to see that it is exercised without weakening the motivation of those with energy and enthusiasm.

The manager who uses a conventional leadership model cannot resolve this dilemma. The heroic response from the leader who is responsible for "managing, motivating, controlling, and coordinating subordinates" cuts into the needs of the subordinates for job challenge and freedom. Managers sense this dilemma and often vacillate on control. When subordinate dissatisfaction increases, the reins are loosened. But when coordination or performance problems develop, the reins are again pulled up short. These managers continue to worry about subordinate motivation, not recognizing the fact that their leadership style takes away the primary source of motivation for employees in contemporary organizations: the challenge of the job. Employees, especially the educated, talented subordinates of most middle managers, arrive with motivation; the way that they are managed sometimes causes behavior that is interpreted as a lack of motivation. Managers demand so much from themselves that they do not demand enough from their subordinates. They do not make full use of the talents of their expensive employees.

Somehow this problem must be resolved; a new form of leadership is essential in contemporary organizations. However, this change cannot be the passive approach of "handing the store over to subordinates." New leadership must be active and strong, yet without traditional heroics. It must tap the energies and potential of talented subordinates whose skills and knowledge are vital for dealing with complexity and change.

This new form of leadership has to move beyond "participative management." Even though that approach has attempted to struggle with many of the same problems we have identified, it has not been completely successful. As it has been practiced, "participation" has not thrown off the heroic orientation. Managers may consult with subordinates, but they still retain firm control over the actual decisions. Opinions may be solicited and even taken seriously, but it is always clear that the boss is in charge and can take away the participation at any time. Second, a great deal of participation has tended to focus on the least important issues within a department. Instead of allowing full involvement on tough issues such as budget allocations, appraisal of performance, job assignments, and strategy planning, participation tends to concentrate on routine matters. Finally, managers are inclined to use participation as a way of gaining acceptance for their own ideas and solutions rather than as a way of making full use of subordinates' abilities in the attainment of departmental goals.

Before turning to this new leadership model, it is important to examine, in greater detail, how the heroic manager operates. Chapter 2 will describe the situations in which that style is still appropriate, as well as explain exactly how it causes problems in complex organizations. Chapter 3 will delineate the postheroic leadership model we have evolved with managers eager to go beyond the adequate performances their heroic methods had accomplished. This model, which we call Manager-as-Developer, has three main components, each explained in more detail in separate chapters. Chapter 4 looks at how to formulate and use an overarching goal to provide common direction and inspire extra effort. Chapter 5 shows how to manage individual subordinates for continuous development and how to deal with those who are talented but difficult. Ways to build a team that genuinely shares with you responsibility for managing your unit are presented in chapter 6. Chapters 7 and 8 show how to go about moving toward the new model of leadership, with many examples of how managers like you have done it. Special attention is paid to the problems of preparing your boss and peers for changes in the way you manage your subordinates; few organizational changes of any kind can be implemented without proper linkages to those who might be affected by them, even indirectly. Although our focus is on managing down, effective changes cannot happen in a departmental vacuum. Finally, Chapter 9 offers advice about the paradoxes inherent in using any leadership style.

Our plan, then, is to help you explore the limits of the old heroic models, the possibilities for achieving excellence with our new model, the ways of managing the key elements of the model, and how to introduce it in your own organization. Let us begin by imagining, as you turn the page to chapter 2, the galloping hoofbeats and hearty "Hi-O Silver" of that famous management hero, the Lone Ranger. We have found that he's still alive and well in the hearts of managers everywhere.

CHAPTER 2
THE MANAGER
AS TECHNICIAN OR
CONDUCTOR

HEROIC MODELS
OF LEADERSHIP

INTRODUCTION

When American managers talk about their vision of managing —the idealized models of their imagination—the same few cultural heroes glorified in film and fiction are frequently mentioned. Heroic managers secretly view themselves as direct descendants of the frontiersman, that quiet but tough adventurer who was constantly setting out for new territory, long an ideal in American literature, film, mythology, and consciousness. The Lone Ranger, an imposing masked figure, rides up on a white horse to overcome great odds in solving the problem of the day. This model of the vanquishing leader—a bit mysterious, generous but aloof—is a very common theme. Think of the setting: Helpless, disorganized townsfolk are being threatened by some bad guys. The Lone Ranger, helped by just his trusty and loyal sidekick, arrives in the nick of time with the right blend of courage and cunning, faces down the bad guys by being just a little quicker, smarter, and tougher, leaves a silver bullet as a symbol of his having solved the problem, and at the end rides stoically off into the sunset.

The grateful townspeople wonder who that masked man is —and wish he could stay—but are left to go about their mundane tasks no wiser or better prepared to deal with the next big problem. When again faced with a major crisis, they'll just have to hope for a return of the thundering hoofbeats and another last-minute rescue by the daring hero. The hero, meanwhile, has to remain ever alert and vigilant, for the world is filled with evildoers and helpless townsfolk, and one can never be too careful. There's never even time for pursuing the pleasures of the company of the opposite sex; someone has to be responsible for seeing that no harm comes to the hardworking and innocent.

This heroic theme also runs through John Wayne movies; he is inevitably a tough guy, individualistic, who alone takes on the bad guys with only a few well-chosen words and lots of action. Our military heroes in fact and in fiction are often portrayed in this mode. The showdown, in which everything depends on the hero's nerves of steel, complete command of the situation, quickness, and guts, dominates the fantasies of managers who grew up on cowboys and Indians, war movies, and male heroes. Even many women who have made it into middle management tend to think in these heroic terms, although their specific imaginings may resemble Wonder Woman: beautiful, strong, surrounded by admirers but still the cleverest, toughest, miracle worker around.

It hardly matters that these images, largely based on the development of the Western frontier, may not be historically accurate. Rather than individuals working alone, the settling of the West demanded mutual assistance—community barn raising, fire fighting, and reciprocal protection. Probably greater collaboration was the rule in those small towns and communities than in the impersonal environs of many present-day cities. But myths do not have to be accurate to be powerful; myths reflect a culture's needs at a certain point in time.

Listen to a student at a top business school talking about his image of managers.

> In thinking about it, my ideal of a leader is a person who would really be looked up to by those around him as a model for their lives and for help and guidance. Many people might even have kind of an awe or reverence for him. He would be much more concerned with being respected than liked. Close personal relationships would be somewhat incidental. The person would clearly be seen as in control of the organization and know everything that is going on and how to handle it. He would be viewed as infallible and unaffected by things going on around him, not very emotional, and rarely, if ever, displaying emotions to others. He'd usually be perceived as the brightest person in the organization, able to solve things quickly and with a high degree of sophistication. The leader would be essential to the functioning of the organization; without him it would quickly fall apart. He's responsible for orchestrating the workings of the entire system.

Although few managers consciously or deliberately imagine themselves to be exactly like these heroes, the models are powerful and pervasive. It is hard for leaders to face the constant strains of managerial life without falling back on such organizing metaphors. Recent attacks on the tough guy, macho, or hero image, which have arisen in the aftermath of the Vietnam war, the women's movement, and other social changes, have mostly served to increase guilt about heroism rather than provide an alternative model. The image of "the androgynous manager," although gaining more attention (Sargent, 1981), is still too new and different to serve as an alternative guide for most (especially male) managers. No widespread models yet exist for managers who might be tender *and* tough, team-minded *and* independent, development- *and* performance-oriented.

Heroism Leads to Overcontrol

Part of the fascination with these heroes is their great control —of themselves and others. Our frontier heroes faced many unpredictable dangers, which they then somehow tamed or mastered by anticipating their opponents' moves and being faster and smarter. They kept the bad guys in line by controlling their moves and their own emotions.

Middle and upper-middle managers are almost invariably preoccupied with control, partly because they usually have less control than is personally comfortable or organizationally necessary to guarantee results. As we have mentioned, being in the middle of a large organization means that managers are subject to pressure from all sides. And the more they feel unable to control the force exerted by superiors and peers the more they will try to master their subordinates. That they thereby only increase subordinate resistance is overlooked; even worse, further resistance just leads to redoubled managerial efforts at downward control.

Even managers who have sufficient power or control do not readily drop their obsession with it, since the heroic model is so deeply ingrained in the culture. After all, the bad guys could bust out of jail any minute now, couldn't they? Does

John Wayne ever let down his guard? The temptation to stay in control is great, especially in organizations where, as one frustrated manager put it, "Our way of doing things around here is 'shoot first, then draw'."

Of course, heroic images are not constantly on the minds of contemporary managers, who often talk about "team play," "participation," or "Theory Y," and it has become less fashionable to describe oneself as "quick on the draw." Day-to-day work can go on without heroics, just as the townspeople could get along for most of the year without the Lone Ranger.

Nevertheless, when things get tense at work, a crisis arises, or tough decisions are called for, many managers instinctively revert to heroic images and action. Feeling responsible, they take over and go into high gear to collect data, marshal resources, and get the problem solved. They believe that they have to know all the answers and can't be caught without a solution. Managers can all talk about the thrill of leaving the silver bullet—overcoming tough odds and difficult opponents to save the day—although they are often sheepish when doing so and make modest noises about "only being able to do it with the help of others."

The Seduction of Heroism

Here's one of the ways we came to see just how potent the lure of heroism is, even to managers who talk a good game of participation. In our leadership workshops, we often begin with an exercise that simulates a top-management team (The Young Manufacturing Case).* Bob Young is faced with a problem: Increasingly, customers have been complaining about defective gaskets, a crucial component in the company's key product. Concerned about this dangerous situation, Bob has called a special meeting of the operations committee. The four

*This exercise is a modification of a case, Young Manufacturing, developed by Donald D. Bowen, published in *Experiences in Management and Organizational Behavior* by D. T. Hall et al, New York. Wiley, 1982.

other members of the committee have strong feelings—positive and negative—about one another and about Bob Young, which lead them to be reluctant to talk openly about the actual source of the problem—a change in suppliers and inspection procedures.

We set up this simulation by asking the workshop participants to plan how they, as Bob Young, could run the meeting so that "the problem gets solved while building a stronger team." Different persons then take turns being Bob Young.

In more than 40 attempts we have rarely observed a "Bob Young" who didn't, within minutes after starting the meeting and realizing that his or her subordinates seemed to be covering and sniping at one another, revert to an heroic attempt to solve the problem *personally*. In the most frequent maneuver, Bob Young takes over the meeting and starts playing a detective-like version of the Lone Ranger, questioning each person in turn about what he knew, what she had done, what he saw as the problem, and so on. As soon as Bob Young begins to play a solo-rescue mission (conveying by tone, posture, and questions the message "*I* am going to get to the bottom of this"), those playing the four subordinates instinctively get even cagier and more snide with one another. They either try to push the blame off on each other or cover up so they will not be exposed in front of the boss. As a result, the problem is usually not solved.

Even those few Bob Youngs who are so good at playing Lone Ranger that they manage to extract all the facts about the history of the quality problem are not able to build any team cooperation in carrying out the solution. Once Bob understands the sequence of events that led to defective parts slipping through, he is stuck with trying to invent a solution that has to be implemented by subordinates who are further polarized and embarrassed as well.

The fascinating thing is that even when we stop after each role-play and discuss all this, pointing out the heroic behavior that gets in the way and agreeing on what not to do, the subsequent Bob Young almost inevitably slides into some other version of heroism within a few interactions! In a tough situation, heroic attempts to take the complete responsibility for coming up with the answer seem irresistible.

Conventional Leadership Models

Behind these interactions are two key assumptions. First, it is the manager, not the members, who in the last analysis is responsible for seeing that the problem gets solved, getting the right data out, coming up with the solution, or making the decision. Second, it is the manager who is responsible for running the meeting and seeing that the subordinates work together in carrying out the solution. The heroic model is in part a function of the leader's feeling of responsibility for doing a good job.

Unfortunately, this sense of centrality and responsibility, even while it can insure adequate performance, can *prevent* excellence from being obtained. The difficulty arises because this model of management, too commonly practiced and too commonly taught, increases the manager's feeling of responsibility while it sets up mechanisms that block the upward flow of communication and the commitment of subordinates.

When a leader views others either as helpless—like the townsfolk—or evil—like the bad guys—and jumps in to take control, the very behavior that confirms this heroic view is elicited from others. When the manager assumes sole responsibility for the larger view, subordinates retreat to a defense of their narrow parochial interests. When subordinates are constantly rescued, treated as weak and unable to cope, they lose motivation and become increasingly passive. These subordinate responses in turn "prove" to the boss that more "help" is necessary. Similarly, those treated as untrustworthy, inept, or malicious, soon begin to behave that way, since they are seldom included, informed, or given latitude.

To understand this self-defeating cycle, let us review the classic definitions of management. "Getting work done through others" is the standard definition of the manager's role. This goal is accomplished through the traditional functions of staffing, planning, delegating, coordinating, and controlling. The leader is in charge of assigning, monitoring, and coordinating work. Such an orientation, as illustrated by recent observations of what managers do, leads the manager to become the information hub and nerve center of the unit (Mintzberg, 1973). The best managers are seen as the most wired-in and central, tuned-in to everything. This stage-center image of the manager feeds heroic fantasies.

Despite the fact that most leaders say that they support some form of participative management, the movement toward more subordinate involvement is only partial. Any participation that occurs is still within the manager's self-image: having one's hands always on the helm, knowing precisely where the vessel is going and what is happening on the ship.

Though most managers would admit that they don't believe they have this constant control, they think they ought to. Even our younger management students carry these idealized images of responsibility, control, and omnipotence in their heads (making the less self-confident among them scared to death of getting into management).

Thus far, we have spoken of the heroic model as a unitary concept, but in observing managers in action as well as role-playing Bob Young, we see the model taking two distinct forms: The Manager-as-Master-Technician and the Manager-as-Conductor. These models grew out of specific organizational needs in the past century and were appropriate to that time, but they are still commonly used, even in many of the most technologically advanced companies—unfortunately, often in ways that have a major negative impact. Both models share the assumption that the leader is expected to be the heroic problem solver and to keep hands firmly on the reins, although the Manager-as-Technician and Manager-as-Conductor ride to the rescue with answers, wisdom, and supreme effort in different ways. As we describe each model, note carefully what is expected of the manager and what managers, in each model, expect of themselves.

MANAGER-AS-MASTER-TECHNICIAN

The manager-as-master-technician approach has a long heritage. The tradition includes the master craftsman who knew all aspects of the trade and passed it on to apprentices and the 19th-century textile manager who understood all jobs in the factory so well that when a problem arose, he could be counted on to solve it. Such an approach to management still prevails in a number of industries. For example, in many entrepreneurial high-technology firms, the chief designer manages by knowing what has to be done, telling subordinates how to do it, and then stepping in to handle difficulties. These managers lead by using their technical knowledge to run operations.

One reason this approach is still so common is that most persons are considered for and ultimately promoted into management because of their past performance in the technical aspects of the job. Success in sales leads to a job as sales manager, the engineer who has been highly productive in technical design is promoted to department head, and the bank officer with a history of successful loan decisions moves up to manage other loan officers. Those people who have done well in the tasks of selling products, serving accounts, or developing new programs and who show managerial potential by "getting along well with people" become managers of others who are to do these tasks.

It is difficult for the individual (as well as the organization) to disagree with success. Many people reason that if technical expertise got them into management, why not manage subordinates through acting as technical expert? In addition, knowledge is a powerful source of influence, much less likely to create resistance than insisting on compliance due to higher rank. Using expertise may take the form of giving directions about what is to be done and how it is to be accomplished, serving as resident expert to answer subordinates' questions and solve problems, or even jumping in and doing the work. The image is of knowing all aspects of the technical work, knowing what to do in every situation, and having the answers to all problems. Saying "I don't know" is a sign of personal and managerial failure.

In this style of leadership, the relationship between the leader and subordinates tends to be personal and particularistic, governed less by rules and procedures and more by the particular relationship between the manager and each subordinate. Control is exerted by informal interaction, more than by use of formal administrative systems. Because this style places great demands on the technical competence of leaders, those who are successful with it in complex task situations tend to be exceptional, which in turn reinforces the idea that great leaders are born, not made. Leaders are expected, especially in times of crisis, to have all the answers and to be willing to roll up their sleeves, take on the villains (or villainous problems), and in a blaze of glory, restore peace to the old homestead. Truly, this leader is "a person you can lean on," which can produce great respect and commitment.

The particularistic manner of the Manager-as-Technician who has genuine expertise is often perceived as charismatic. The brilliant engineer, daring entrepreneur, and imaginative marketeer can in their personal styles reflect what their department and organization stand for. One of our clients was head of the computer services for a large government agency. As brilliant as he was irascible, Warner had no tolerance for governmental rules and regulations. He and his staff did whatever was necessary to get the job done. Although his department was highly effective in solving technical problems, his style left a trail of strained relationships with other department heads. His ability to cut through red tape won him great admiration and allegiance from his subordinates, who thought of him as a wizard. On the other hand, other departments were reluctant to use his department's services, which left his group more isolated than was desirable from the agency's point of view.

To get a richer sense of what the Manager-as-Technician is like, listen to this description of a manager we'll call Bill Patton, written by the research-and-development manager who reports to him. Bill is general manager of a manufacturing division of a medium-size firm.

As a manager, Bill tries to keep complete control of all divisional activities. Production schedules, process modifications, and product development are closely watched by Bill, and no changes can be made without his approval. This becomes demoralizing to the staff, who at times seem to avoid decision making because they realize their boss will have the last say. One instance of this was when Mike, the production manager, was to develop some cost figures on a certain stage of manufacturing. When Bill got the facts several days later, he did not find them to his liking and sent Mike back to redo the study. After another trial and subsequent refusal by the boss, Mike asked him to tell him the results he wanted so that Mike could collect the "right" data. The other engineering and technical managers often face this same problem. After all, Bill knows that he has all the right answers.

One manager who feels the pressure of Bill's expertise is Morry, the plant engineer. Bill once held this position, and he considers himself a good mechanical engineer. Morry agrees that Bill is a good engineer, but only the second-best in the division. Bill is always working with Morry, monitoring his work, and frequently demanding that something be redesigned to reflect the way he would have done it. Often, to Morry's dismay, Bill's ideas are somewhat out of date. He is still designing as he did 10 years ago when it was his full-time job. He has not been able to stay on top of his field, but still insists on putting in his ideas.

In general, Bill's relationship with his subordinates is on a one-to-one basis. He generally meets with one or occasionally two subordinates in front of his blackboard and ends up being the one at the board lobbying for his ideas. This type of relationship cements his control over the subordinate. Also, it removes much of the need for managers to interact with each other, since Bill controls the cross-flow of information. Should he happen upon a group of managers in a bull session, he joins in, takes control, and again, limits communication.

In staff meetings, the solutions are only as good as Bill's questioning. They are also influenced by what he is good at. People problems are not his forte; when production problems are people related, Bill does not respond well. For instance, someone mentioned that a quality problem was directly related to the lack of training of a semiskilled worker. Rather than simply initiate a training program to alleviate the problem, Bill charged the process-control group to devise a mechanical system that removed the responsibility from the worker. The system was installed and the semiskilled operator now has no influence on the operation and is employed only as a monitor. The system works at the expense of the usefulness of the operator.

In his desire to control all aspects under his authority, Bill limits the interactions of his subordinates with other divisions of the company. He attends all interdivisional meetings personally and seldom delegates such duties to subordinates. Subsequently, all information concerning the other divisions, sales, or upper management is processed through Bill before it gets to the division.

Although subordinates resent his style, it is that very style that makes it impossible for them to voice their concerns. Bill has to win every argument, so pointing out to him the problem with his behavior only invokes a war of words until the subordinate is worn down. Bill's heroic style has no tolerance for weakness, in himself or others, so if subordinates were to complain that his leadership style demonstrates this, Bill would interpret this as a sign of their inadequacies. As a result, one of Bill's key subordinates, whom he is grooming for advancement, is looking for a new job in another division. Bill will be shocked and will feel betrayed when he learns that the subordinate is leaving.

As suggested by this example, the focus on technical rather than managerial aspects of the job leads most managers using this style to make little use of group meetings. Instead, most work is one-on-one between the superior and each subordinate. The few staff meetings tend to be more for transmission of information than for joint problem solving. The leader is either passing information down or seeking it upward. One dyed-in-the-wool technician plant manager, prodded by his boss to build a team, decided that he would do this by getting his staff together once a month for dinner. He literally couldn't think of anything to add to his weekly individual meetings with subordinates, during which he found out what they were doing and answered all unresolved issues.

The superior's interaction with subordinates in group meetings or in one-on-one sessions typically consists almost exclusively of seeing that problems are being solved and that work is being done. Each subordinate comes in with a progress report that is carefully checked over. When any difficulties are discovered, the Manager-as-Technician's style is to focus on the problem and question the subordinate for information. Again the manager's orientation is to find the facts in order to determine the best solution. Since it's the manager who makes the decision, the subordinates' roles are confined to providing information, with an occasional attempt to persuade the leader of the desirability of a particular position.

A representative example of how a Manager-as-Technician handles a subordinate who comes in with a problem illustrates the communication difficulties.

SUBORDINATE. We're having trouble delivering disposable widgets to Techcorp.

MANAGER T. But they're our most important customer. Have you talked to Dan in production?

SUBORDINATE. Yes, but he says that yields are off because of poor material.

MANAGER T. He always uses that excuse. Have you checked the materials report?

SUBORDINATE. Yes, I've got it right here. I thought we ought to check . . .

MANAGER T. [Interrupting] Look at that: The material quality is within 1.5% of our usual standard. That can't be the problem. Anyway, yields can be increased by reprocessing material on overtime shifts.

SUBORDINATE. That's right. We could use overtime.

MANAGER T. OK, here's what to do: Get Alice to go over and tell Dan to increase the percentage of alloy by 7% and decrease the time in the second-batch processing. In fact, never mind— I'll call Dan myself and explain that, along with how he can shift extra materials over to

widget making. Then he won't have any excuse.

In this familiar scenario, the manager tunes into the technical aspects of the problem. When he asks a question, it is
aimed at finding out what is wrong. He then quickly moves in
toward a solution he has developed through rapid diagnosis.
He owns the problem; he works like a detective to get the
necessary clues, and then he solves it.

In this leadership style, it is not infrequent that the manager
continues to fulfill task activities as well as managing others.
For example, partners in accounting, consulting, and law firms
spend much of their time working on client engagements as
well as supervising junior members. Even those who are department heads often have their own accounts—or long for
the days when they did. An engineering supervisor may still
have projects to do as well as the responsibility for a group of
other engineers. The head of underwriting may still handle a
portfolio of insurance applications. Even in some enormous
companies, such as Digital Equipment and Polaroid (until Dr.
Land resigned), the chief executive officer–founder still occasionally drops into the lab and runs tests or makes suggestions.
Under some conditions, fulfilling these task activities may be
appropriate, but too often they are taken on only because the
manager feels good when doing them.

It would be too easy to assume, with this description of the
leader as the technical expert, that we are only describing a
person who supervises closely, takes away all autonomy, and
treats subordinates as flunkies, which can indeed be true when
the leader designates exactly how work is to be carried out.
But the other extreme can also exist with a Manager-as-Technician, who may provide autonomy not only in terms of implementation methods but even as to what work is undertaken
(for example, when subordinates can choose among projects or
clients). Even in that case, however, the manager leads by providing answers to subordinates whenever they run into technical difficulties and by directing activities through his or her
expertise.

When the Manager-as-Technician Style Works

The Manager-as-Technician leadership style is effective when the manager truly has much greater knowledge than the subordinates, and it can be the desirable approach when the wise old hand is dealing with new, untrained subordinates. Allowing others to flounder when the leader has the answer may produce more frustration than learning. Time is wasted when the true expert does not provide needed input. However, this style requires that managers continue to be technically on top of the work, or like Bill Patton, the answers they provide will soon become outdated. Thus, such leadership is appropriate either when the field is developing slowly (so that the methods the superior learned while at the subordinate's level still apply) or when the manager has been able to keep up with the state of the art.

Furthermore, the Manager-as-Technician style works when the managerial and interpersonal requirements are relatively minimal. For example, if subordinates' work allows them to be relatively autonomous from each other or if the span of control is not too wide, coordination requirements may be minimal. Many subordinates who are professionals can work well with little supervision, since their tasks are relatively autonomous and require little interaction with peers. What they need most from their boss may truly be the supervisor's technical expertise rather than the managerial functions of coordination and control.

The Technician style is also effective when there are emergency problems in the organization that are within the manager's area of technical expertise. A senior vice president of an insurance company recently spent a series of evenings and weekends debugging and modifying a computer program originally installed years before when she had worked as a programmer. Her intervention didn't help teach anything to the current programmers, their supervisor, or the head of data processing, but a crucial problem got solved which would otherwise have been very costly. Another high level executive of a $100 million textile company is never so happy as when he is on emergency duty, solving the latest crisis. Not too long ago, a key supplier suddenly stopped making a crucial yarn. The executive went into action, first meeting with manufacturers of an alternative material, then calling the European subsidiary of the yarn manufacturer in Italy at 3 AM to find out if they would still be spinning, and flying there to negotiate waivers of the geographical trade restrictions of the parent company. Neither his purchasing manager nor legal vice president was included until later, but he prevented a complete shutdown of the plant which might have bankrupted the company. In genuine emergencies requiring their expertise, Manager-Technicians shine. When they are gifted technically, their leadership can be highly charismatic and inspirational.

Finally, there are times when subordinates, although knowledgeable, still can't be included in the problem-solving process, and the leader may have to be the sole driving force toward the correct answers. Subordinates may be uncommitted, or highly dependent, or so divided that a quality answer can't emerge. The danger, of course, is that continued use of the Manager-as-Technician style may not work to change these conditions.

Problems with the Manager-as-Technician Style

However, even in situations where this leadership approach fits, it can be inappropriately used. The superior may stress a certain technique, not because it is objectively best, but because it reflects what he once learned and still favors. For example, many colliery managers in Great Britain's National Coal Board, having worked their way up from the pits and expected to be tough and in charge, are encountering difficulties with new technologies. Some of their subordinates and central staff specialists know things they do not, yet these managers cling to being in control and to doing things as they were taught.

Furthermore, managers who lead only through genuine expertise can undermine subordinate confidence because they indeed always do know better and do not hesitate to jump in and prove it. Or they can supervise too closely, which reduces subordinates' growth by removing the challenge of learning how to resolve problems. We saw this in a medical research lab headed by a renowned scientist who determined what direction the lab's research would take and allocated subprojects accordingly. In that case, the control was so unilateral that several very bright junior scientists left for other places where they could pick projects that fit their interests. In another organization, bright subordinates got bored and left, since the Technician solved all the challenging problems.

The technical focus can also get in the way of providing adequate management. Leaders with a technical bent tend to ignore or bypass formal planning, coordination, and control mechanisms. They get satisfaction from rushing into chaos and shaping things up, not from anticipating problems, organizing others, and using or developing procedures to deal with difficulties. This situation was apparent in a professional organization where the three upper managers were technical leaders in their field, yet subordinate frustration was high. One subordinate complained, "We are constantly suffering from crisis management because they never adequately schedule jobs to even out the peaks and valleys of our work load."

Technicians often see organizational procedures, systems, and paperwork as nuisances to be worked around rather than as tools to be used for managing. Even when the organization has provided them with complex systems, they try to avoid the "unnecessary paperwork" and fill out forms without believing in their efficacy. Their style is usually too highly personalized and individualistic to allow for much organizational work. A kind of crisis management arises, which continually calls for the Technician to rush in with answers, "confirming" the need for just such a style!

The Manager-as-Technician finds it hard to avoid another shortcoming common to this style: a focus on technological problems, to the detriment of human factors. Technicians do not respond well to human problems, which require flexibility, improvisation, listening, and patience. They prefer to stick to problems that don't talk back—determining a bid price, doing a financial analysis, designing a new scheduling system for loading the milling machines—and often do not notice when a subordinate could use coaching, wants support, or needs a push. Work is assigned to subordinates in terms of who is available and what tasks have to get done, rather than in order to maximize motivation by matching jobs with a subordinate's interests. Technician-Managers may love technical problem solving but hate the messiness of people problems.

Managerial Choices for Personal Satisfaction

One reason this style of leadership may be overused arises from what the superior seeks in terms of job satisfaction. Some managers focus on the technical aspects of the job, not because such emphasis is required and appropriate, but because it is the source of their professional rewards. These people love their field, be it engineering, accounting, computers, research, sales, banking, law, or finance, because of the satisfaction from successful task accomplishment. After all, that is why they entered that profession in the first place. They find difficulty receiving comparable rewards from the process of management, which they realize is often more ambiguous and less amenable to orderly solutions. Problems in managing people are felt as irritants that interfere with what they really want to do rather than as challenges that, when resolved, can yield pleasure in their own right. They think of "work" as what they do when people leave them alone (that is, solving challenging technical problems) and resent the time they have to spend with the difficult people who cause what are termed irrelevant distractions. As one department head put it, "I really don't have patience with the emotional needs of my staff. I know I should go around and talk with them once in a while, but I'm not very good at chatting and there's always so much work to do. I can't wait to end the aimless conversations so I can get back to the tasks!"

Managing in this style, not because it is appropriate for the setting but because it is the source of leader satisfaction (or the only way the person knows how to manage), can limit organizational effectiveness as well as subordinate development. If the criterion for being a successful manager is having all the answers, the manager may restrict organizational activities to areas where he or she feels personally competent (as Bill Patton did). In this case, the department is only as good as the leader, which puts a great and costly burden on that person's shoulders. The supervisor would experience much greater freedom in action (and more chances to feel personally competent) if success as a manager were not defined as "having the answer," but being able to manage "so that all feel responsible for finding the answer." In that context, there would be challenge in making full use of subordinate creativity. Attention might also be paid to the needs of subordinates, their opinions and feelings, their disputes with one another, their desire for occasional emotional support or nurturance, and all the nontechnical sentiments that real people bring to work settings. But such functions would have to be seen as an important part of the manager's job, not as irrelevant nuisances.

MANAGER-AS-CONDUCTOR

Many leaders have experienced the frustrations and limitations of managing as a Technician. They know they can't provide all the answers, be on top of every problem, and constantly check up on every subordinate, and they realize that doing so can be discouraging to those who resent close supervision. These managers realize that cooperation is needed from subordinates and that forcing compliance produces sluggishness and resistance. The emphasis since World War II on participative management, Theory Y, and involvement of subordinates has led such managers to move beyond a Technician style.

But this new direction can be disquieting; if the heroic orientation is still present, then the question remains of how to reconcile the heroic tendency with the pressures to listen to subordinates, involve them in the decision-making process, delegate tasks, and be concerned for their feelings. When there is still the belief that the "leader ought to have the answers," how can a boss perform in a way that doesn't give subordinates the feeling their opinions aren't listened to? When the manager believes it is important to "be in control and know what's happening," how can she accomplish that goal in a way that isn't stultifying? The resolution to this dilemma is often the Manager-as-Conductor.

The Manager-as-Conductor has given up trying to manage by doing the task, instead seeing that the task is accomplished by managing the people. Since Conductors understand that their responsibilities have to be accomplished through others, they are aware of how highly dependent they are on their subordinates. They are inevitably concerned with controlling subordinates to be certain that what they do is right, so conductors place themselves as the central decision makers, nerve-centers, and coordinators of activities. Being able to see the entire picture, they determine how a department's tasks are to be divided, who is to be assigned the subfunctions, and how work is to be integrated. Then it is the manager's task to coordinate these parts to insure that all members do their tasks and that everything comes together. The Conductor may be no less focused on having the right answer than the Technician, but knows it is crucial that subordinates feel committed to agreeing with that right answer and to carrying it out.

Conducting is accomplished in two major ways. The first major component is the interpersonal style the Manager-Conductor uses with subordinates. Conductors tend to divide subordinates into two camps—willful and clever or resistant and inept. In either case, the subordinates need the Conductor's guidance and maneuvering to keep them on the right track. After all, "You can't turn your back on some people," and "You can't help getting a few turkeys," although sometimes you find "a few you can count on." Conductors accept the conventional notion that management is "getting work done through others," but they believe they must work very hard to stay in charge and on top of others to prevent chaos, inertia, incompetence, or rebellion.

This image of the leader's role, compared with the Technician model, more explicitly involves the followers, but still casts the leader as the central, heroic figure who orchestrates all the individual parts of the organization into one harmonious whole. The spotlight is on the leader, who has a grand plan and keeps everyone working at his or her piece of it. The leader still needs technical knowledge, but only as a tool for keeping respect and knowing how to get everyone to do what is needed.

The second major characteristic of the Conductor's leadership style involves administrative systems for staffing and work flow. The Conductor is more likely than the Technician to use such organizational procedures as Critical Path Analysis, accountability statements, management information systems (MIS), management by objectives (MBO), and performance reviews, and to use them to control subordinates' behavior. These administrative procedures allow the Conductor to track what is going on without having to interfere personally in everything subordinates are doing. The systems help achieve planning and coordination and reduce hands-on management. Many functions can be made routine, including funneling of information to the manager, who thereby extends his or her observation powers into the organization.

At the same time, the use of management systems permits more impersonal forms of control. Conductors have learned that overt displays of power and control are costly and should be avoided unless absolutely necessary. They know that the appearance of their hands manipulating the strings is less desirable than firm guidelines, which are impersonal, routine, and therefore less susceptible to resentment and challenge. Of course, they still hold the strings, but Conductors have to pull on them less often since the "strings" exert their own influence. This leadership style does not necessarily imply Machiavellian intent; someone who feels responsible for seeing that everything happens as it is supposed to sensibly tries to avoid arousing resistance. It is hard enough to get full cooperation.

Furthermore, such systems often benefit the subordinates as well. If more long-range planning is allowed, subordinates can predict their job tasks for a relatively extended period, which provides more day-to-day autonomy for subordinates. Initial checking of subordinate performance can be done through examination of the MIS reports, rather than by personal inquiry and direct observation. Nevertheless, whether personal or behind-the-scenes pulling of strings occurs, the conductor works to see that each player plays the right part. As one manager commented, "It is the Conductor who knows the score."

We have labeled this kind of leader Manager-as-Conductor because of the similarity this leadership bears to that central, visible role of coordinating all the parts of the orchestra. Musical conductors follow complex, separate strands of music and weave them into one whole, coordinated performance. Through careful preparation, knowledge of what is needed, and exact control, the conductor sees that every player is doing his or her share as needed and is in proper harmony. To see how this style works in practice, let's go back to our widget example and the subordinate with a problem.

SUBORDINATE.	We're having trouble delivering disposable widgets to Techcorp.
MANAGER C.	What are the causes of the problem and who is involved?
SUBORDINATE.	Well, let's see. Dan claims that he's getting lousy material so that yield is down. The quality-control people are refusing to bend standard, even though Techcorp would probably accept less precision than specifications call for. The purchasing agent from Techcorp is hounding us to speed up delivery, and he won't listen to any excuses. Ellen, our purchasing agent, claims that the material is fine but that it was exposed to excess moisture by Dan's receiving clerks.
MANAGER C.	OK. This has to be solved right away.

SUBORDINATE.   What do you suggest? Should I check the material?

MANAGER C.   That certainly would help. Have we done any favors lately for Dan? A little charm applied to Ellen might get her to loosen up.

SUBORDINATE.   I'll get right on it. Should I work on Ellen first?

MANAGER C.   Better yet, I'll get Dan, the quality-control people, Techcorp's representative, and Ellen together and see if I can get them to bend a bit. Do we have other orders that can be delayed? Any likely cancellations to free up production capacity? Before I go into that meeting, I want to know what leeway I have for maneuvering. You check with Techcorp's purchasing people and find out what's driving them; I'll talk to Bill, Ellen, and old Ted over in quality control before the meeting. Let me know what you find out.

As with the Manager-as-Technician, the Conductor is quick to push toward an answer. But this approach is more oriented to pulling together disparate strands than to focusing in on one particular solution. Nevertheless, the Conductor is still very much out in front of the orchestra, using force, charm, and political skill to coordinate action. The results may well be an excellent resolution of the problem, but the subordinate may not be any more competent now than before this interaction, except for whatever is gained through observing an expert in action.

There are two major differences between the Manager-as-Technician and the Manager-as-Conductor. The person using the latter style is less likely to do any of the technical tasks personally and more likely to spend time thinking through how to work with each subordinate in order to maximize motivation and gain compliance. Where the Manager-as-Technician goes right after the problem and may be so focused on getting a solution that little attention is paid to the people involved, the Manager-as-Conductor takes on the burden of figuring out how to influence subordinates to do what is necessary. Although the Conductor is trying to work through others, the assumptions are still the same: that the manager knows what has to be done and that without the manager's efforts, good work would not be accomplished.

An effective Conductor is impressive to watch, since this style requires so much energy, careful planning, and sustained effort. One outstanding regional sales manager for a Fortune 500 company, for example, puts in extremely long work days. On one typical day, he spends many hours rehearsing a presentation to management with his subordinates, since polished presentations are one way a person makes a reputation at his company. When he sees for the first time some of the work produced by his subordinates and doesn't like it, he does not inform them directly, which could be badly demoralizing, but works in an exquisitely careful fashion with a trusted subordinate in order to figure out how to get the material changed without crushing the people responsible for it. Meticulous planning, great effort, multiple relationships, and dextrous juggling of many elusive elements are clearly present.

His subordinates and others who observe him have divided responses. Those who identify with him are impressed by his cleverness and subtlety and eager to learn more about how to be like him. They envy his quickness, charisma, intensity, charm, thoroughness, and knowledge of "all the psychological tricks." Others, however, are chilled by what they see as manipulative and talk at length about how motivation suffers under such a boss. His way of staying on top of everything leads to their holding back since, "he will change things to get his own way anyhow." They do enough to get by, but take far less initiative than they otherwise might. These reactions vividly demonstrate the attraction to managers and danger to subordinates of the heroic Conductor style.

When dealing with subordinates, the Manager-Conductor is always thinking about what to say and what not to say in order to gain compliance. Even when the Conductor has a preferred outcome on an issue, subordinates may be asked for advice or input to give at least the semblance of participation. Involvement serves to produce good human relations and to gain acceptance, not necessarily to make full use of human resources to achieve a higher quality solution (Miles and Ritchie, 1971). If the subordinate gives the "wrong" answer, the Conductor goes to great lengths to persuade him of the better way without having to order anything directly. If necessary, the manager will encourage someone else to offer evidence countering the subordinate's logic, but is less likely to disagree openly (as would the Manger-as-Technician). Conductors do not like to display their authority directly; they prefer to appear reasonable and influenceable as long as possible, hoping to maintain good will and cooperation. They know that using a heavy hand in the 1980s usually creates resistance.

The Manager-as-Conductor is more likely than the Technician to hold and value regular staff meetings, although the meetings are carefully controlled and still revolve around the manager. Such meetings are seen as opportunities to get (and influence) everybody's views so that the entire unit is working in concert. The Conductor usually enters the meeting with a notion of the desired answer. After all, Conductors know it's important to do their homework. Since such managers are highly conscious of the responsibility resting on their shoulders, they determine beforehand the blind alleys and promising pathways.

The leader does not necessarily come out explicitly in favor of a particular solution; rather, the Conductor style calls for some indirect but active maneuvering to lead members to arrive at the Conductor's solution on their own. The manager takes care to encourage at the right time anyone who has the "correct" position on the issue, and to counter anyone who does not see the issue in "proper" perspective. In fact, on important issues, the Manager-as-Conductor might talk to all members ahead of time to discover their positions and do whatever one-on-one influencing seems necessary. No boss likes surprises, but Conductors take extra care to have their ducks lined up ahead of time.

The Conductor, like the Technician, holds a rather tight rein on the meetings, but focuses less exclusively on task issues and more on personal guidance of discussion toward members' arriving at the "right" decision. The leader generally states the dimensions of the problem, asks for opinions, questions members' premises, makes sure all people get heard (or at least all those perceived to be on target and "right-thinking"), and draws the threads of the discussion toward the preferred solution. Thus, the manager "conducts" the meeting, deciding when all the relevant information has surfaced and when it is time to move on to considering solutions. This focus on leading the discussion does not mean that the Conductor ignores the task dimension. If the conversation takes an "undesirable" turn, the manager is likely to intercede to get it back on track.

In a talk to aspiring managers, one Conductor, an insurance company vice-president, revealed that he would "far prefer to be the one asking the questions that get discussed than the one answering them. If I can determine the questions, I can be sure to get the answers I want."

Whereas the Manager-Technician is likely to make the decision autonomously, the Manager-Conductor stresses the value —and appearance—of arriving at a group decision. Of course, the manager does have veto power if the group's preference seems wrong, and in any case the manager's inclinations carry much more weight than the opinion of any other member ("After all, in the last analysis, I am the one held accountable for what happens"). Still, this kind of manager does spend time trying to get all members to accept the desired solution.

In this respect, Conductors are much more concerned with getting tasks accomplished than with bringing people along or preparing them for future assignments. They are instrumental and pragmatic. One extraordinarily good Conductor describes his method in a few sharp strokes (after he had made it to company president).

I look at whom I've got and what they can do, assess their strengths, and then try to organize around their weaknesses. I am not interested in, and haven't got the patience for, developing people or teaching them how to improve themselves. I just carve things up to take advantage of what they can do and to overcome what they aren't good at.

Departments managed by Conductors who do it well are described as well-organized, well-planned units, with a minimum of surprises and internally caused emergencies. People know what their jobs are (as laid out in position descriptions and job assignments) and what the operating rules are. They are less likely to feel themselves victims of the boss's capricious whims (more of a danger with the Technician's style). Unless the Conductor is unusually visionary, however, this less personal and more indirect style decreases the chances of being inspirational to subordinates. The Conductor is more likely to be seen as a "manager" rather than a "leader"—that is, as an effective administrator carrying out what has to be done, not a "mover–shaker" who forges new directions.

When the Manager-as-Conductor Style Works

Although Conductors feel just as responsible as Technicians do for the success of their units, rather than focusing on hands-on assistance, they concentrate on setting up and coordinating the people and processes to get the job done. This form of management should be superior in more complex situations, where coordination among subordinates is a prerequisite for maximum performance. Furthermore, since the Conductor style is quite common and highly valued by many organizations, it is likely to be effective with subordinates, who naturally expect their boss to be on top of things and a jump ahead of them. Competitive subordinates might find the Conductor style challenging, and if well done, worthy of respect. While the Technician might be admired for having all the answers, the Conductor would be admired for being managerially clever and tuned in. Having wide contacts and using them to stay current with organizational politics, trends, and hot issues, requires considerable talent and initiative. Knowledge is a form of power, and knowledge of what is going on in the organization may be a more valuable power source than specific answers to technical issues, especially in large and diffuse organizations.

The management techniques utilized in this leadership style are also necessary for coordinating and controlling members' behavior when there are many subordinates and their work is interdependent. The leader can't be at all places at all times, and procedures serve in lieu of the boss's physical presence. Furthermore, to the extent that such rules and procedures assist in getting work done, they can increase motivation among subordinates. There is probably little that is more frustrating than total freedom and therefore total ambiguity. In general, the Conductor style and skills can be very effective where specialties and departments require coordination or where political skills are highly necessary though coordination is not. Conductor leadership is also appropriate when making full use of member resources is not worth the effort. Examples of conditions well suited to Conductor management are listed below.

The members are not very skilled or competent, so not much can be expected beyond accomplishment of their assigned job.

The task is relatively simple and/or the amount of task interdependence among members is moderate but not high.

The leader is willing to settle for adequate performance; excellence is not desired.

The members are so political and/or personally (rather than organizationally) oriented that the leader must do extra strategizing and maneuvering just to hold the group together.

Problems with the Manager-as-Conductor Model

Despite the advantages we have noted, the Conductor approach presents several practical difficulties. One problem arises from the very characteristic that makes the style so effective—its greater coordination of subordinates. Remember that the organizations where the Conductor is prevalent are those where subordinates' tasks are sufficiently interdependent so that effective coordination is crucial for departmental success. But how Conductors fulfill this coordination function works to minimize subordinate concern about the overall integration of the various parts of the unit. When subordinates know that all communication and important decisions flow through the manager, they can most freely pursue the narrow interests of their own subunits. They don't have to worry about balancing diverse specialized concerns to achieve overall departmental interests; that's the leader's problem.

A second problem with the Conductor approach again relates to the issue of subordinate task interdependence. When one individual's performance is dependent on another's, disagreements will inevitably arise. When these disputes can't be easily and mutually resolved, the natural tendency of subordinates who are coordinated by a conducting boss is to go to the boss. Not only is the leader put into the awkward position of having to come up with the all-wise solution; each subordinate is encouraged to push only his or her viewpoint, which can lead to subordinates' withholding or distorting of information and reluctance to accept compromise or a creative solution that satisfies both parties.

Because this leadership style places all responsibility for pulling things together in the hands of the manager and does little to encourage subordinates to take a wider viewpoint and to develop problem-solving approaches that require working out solutions with peers, it actively suppresses subordinate development. Subordinates are not led to increase their abilities and skills and are not forced to take wider perspectives. This limiting of the subordinates' performance in turn hinders their advancement in the organization. It is hard to promote a person who "only pushes his own area" and "who can't work well with others." Thus, an unintended consequence of a Conductor form of leadership is to cause the individual players to behave in ways that make them look unready for greater responsibility. This situation can rebound on the manager. Often a manager's own advancement is hindered because an adequate replacement hasn't been developed among the natural heirs—the subordinates.

Another difficulty with the Conductor style comes from its emphasis on control. Even when such managers try to influence discretely and indirectly, it is difficult for subordinates not to feel overcontrolled. The result is likely to be that subordinates invest considerable energy in regaining control for themselves. This, in turn, forces Conductors to work harder and harder to maintain control, and the cycle continues. Staying on top, rather than accomplishing the unit's work, can thus easily become the boss's objective; the Conductor style ends up causing increased manipulation and strategic maneuvering. We have seen many such leaders running numerous staff meetings that resemble elaborate chess games with moves and countermoves. Because Conductors feel simply that the burden is theirs—and get reinforced in this belief by the resistance and ploys of their subordinates—they find they have to invoke more and more intricate moves. Soon the leader totally loses sight of the possibility of a direct approach. As in the Bob Young role-play described earlier, if the subordinates seem to be reluctant to discuss something, the Conductor feels obliged to play musical detective, searching for the missing score by privately constructing possible scenarios, then grilling subordinates with closed-ended questions designed to lead to admission of the predetermined problem.

When a manager, either as Technician or Conductor, starts to cross-examine subordinates, it's a good sign of having personally shouldered all problems. For example, when a group of subordinates keeps skirting an issue, despite its apparent urgency, it never occurs to the overmaneuvering Conductor to ask an open-ended question such as "What's going on here?" and then wait for an answer. Even less likely is a direct observation like, "Some of you are shifting in your seats and avoiding my eyes when we talk about this subject. Everyone seems to be embarrassed; so what's going on here?" Instead, heroic leaders try to puzzle out what's happening, construct possible explanations in their heads, then proceed to question people in a closed-ended way designed to prove the truth of the hypothesized explanations. This process is useful for fitting people into a prearranged structure, but it isn't very adaptive, and it reduces the likelihood of getting full information from below. Conductors place the burden for all solutions on themselves rather than on subordinates, which often leads to an overresponsible boss with underresponsible subordinates. In this way Conductors often outsmart themselves.

Similarly, because Conductors use systems and procedures a control device rather than as tools to help subordinates perform, the results often fall short of full potential. As anyone knows who has been around organizations awhile, there is no system that can't be beaten if those subject to it do not accept its intended use. One form of beating control systems is to do just the minimum necessary to get by. Working to rules, and the many variations of this form of passive resistance, makes almost any system impotent—and may encourage the Conductor to build even more elaborate controls. Again, the manager works harder and accepts more of the responsibility, which, in turn, produces in subordinates the exact lack of overall commitment that the manager's machinations were designed to overcome.

Summary of the Problems with Heroic Styles

Although the Conductor model of leadership allows for greater coordination among subordinates dealing with interdependent tasks and suits some work situations, such as where the boss has much more expertise, it still has limitations for many contemporary organizations. In organizations (or situations within units) characterized by complex tasks, highly interdependent subordinates' work, a constantly changing environment, and competent subordinates, both the Technician and Conductor models are likely to prevent excellence, even though each may produce adequate performance. Since both styles emphasize the manager having the answers and being in control, they overuse the task abilities of the leader, and underutilize the competencies of subordinates. Heroic overconcentration of responsibility reduces the organization's chances to tap subordinate talent fully. Figure 2-1 summarizes the workplace conditions that favor different management models.

Furthermore, since coordination of effort is both prevalent and crucial in complex organizations, it is difficult for Conductors (and virtually impossible for the Technicians) to provide single-handedly the necessary integration and coordination. They are forced to run faster and faster to keep up, which reinforces their already too great sense of responsibility. When the Conductor attempts to fulfill these needs through formal rules and procedures, the high degree of change in task, technology, and environment quickly causes any rules or regulations to become outdated.

Even worse, each of these leadership approaches tends to lessen subordinate motivation. Insofar as the leader defines that role as coming up with the answers, part of the job challenge that competent subordinates seek from their work is removed. Furthermore, if the manager is responsible for resolving problems of coordination and integration, subordi-

	Technician	Conductor	Postheroic
1. Subordinates work independently	X		
2. Subordinates do simple tasks	X		
3. Environment is stable	X	X	
4. Subordinates have low technical knowledge compared to boss	X	X	
5. Subordinate commitment not needed for success	X	X	
6. Subordinates do complex tasks		X	X
7. Subordinates require considerable coordination		X	X
8. Environment is changing			X
9. Subordinates have high technical knowledge			X
10. Subordinate commitment necessary for excellence			X

Figure 2-1 When each management model is appropriate.

nates' views become increasingly parochial, which neatly confirms that worry about the big picture belongs solely to the manager. Inevitably, frustration increases as competent subordinates remain blocked until their harried boss can get around to untangling the latest snarl. This series of self-fulfilling prophecies is diagrammed in Figure 2-2.

By now it should be clear how heroic ways of managing are themselves part of the cause of the problems that in Chapter 1

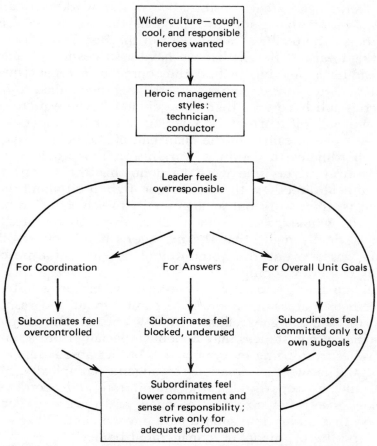

Figure 2-2 The self-fulfilling consequences of heroic management styles.

we reported managers complained about: low subordinate initiative and commitment, less than excellent quality, defensiveness, and so on. Is there a way out of this ironic mess that managers have put themselves in?

One temptation for managers who are struggling with the issue of how to let go of heroic methods is to refrain from supervising. Since many managers we studied report that they personally have often done their best work when their own boss left them alone, they conclude that their subordinates might value the same hands-off treatment.

In fact, to the great consternation of our workshop participants, we have been able to reproduce the positive effects of "less boss is better boss" when we run the Bob Young exercise described earlier. Recall that we have a succession of managers leading a meeting to find the source of a recent quality problem. After four or five managers have succumbed to heroic tactics and have seen their subordinates become more difficult, we pull the current Bob Young out of the meeting "to answer a phone call from the chairman of the board." We ask the subordinates to continue working on the problem while Bob is away. Everytime we have done this, the subordinates start to deal directly with one another, fight a bit about whose fault it is, then work out arrangements to solve the problem. Since the whole process seldom takes even 10 minutes, the point is vividly made that the manager's heroic efforts often themselves prevent the commitment to successful problem solving from developing.

But "no boss" is hardly a long-term, viable answer to the problem of increasing subordinate commitment and responsibility for achieving excellence. A few outstanding people in particular circumstances may benefit (especially from a temporary relief from being overmanaged), but an absent supervisor is not the answer in situations of ongoing complexity. Work must still be properly allocated, monitored, and coordinated, employees selected, sized up, coached, and rewarded, yet not in ways that undermine subordinate engagement. What would such a postheroic model of management be like?

CHAPTER 3
THE POSTHEROIC LEADER

THE MANAGER-AS-DEVELOPER

INTRODUCTION

How can managers act in ways that will achieve excellence rather than block it? How can leaders act so that heroic overresponsibility doesn't prevent full use of subordinates' abilities, doesn't dampen their commitment to high performance, and doesn't cause them to avoid taking initiative when problems arise?

The answer is not for the manager to renounce responsibility and abandon all control. Although we have occasionally observed conscientious subordinates who respond well to being left alone, there are too many important managerial tasks to guarantee that a no-boss-is-the-best-boss approach will work.

It is also futile to seek a magical midpoint between the extremes of too much and too little leader responsibility and control. Rather, an entirely new definition of leadership is required if a department is to be led into new and unanticipated areas. This new definition is a fundamental reorientation away from the heroic model as well as a minor alteration in focus. Shared responsibility and control take the place of the individual hero carrying the burdens alone. For those who have staggered around trying to do it all—and have ended up forcing more burden onto their own shoulders by causing the very problems with subordinates that they wanted to avoid—the postheroic view of managing is a profound shift. At the same time, no part of the new model is all that unfamiliar to any contemporary manager. Everyone knows about tapping subordinate talents, exciting them about the mission, and building effective teams, just as astronomers in the time of Copernicus knew about earth, sun, and stars whirling in the heavens. Yet the "simple" reversal of putting the sun, rather than the earth, at the center of relationships caused a revolution in philosophy as well as science.

To achieve excellence in earthly organizations, a manager must first believe in the concept and then act in the creation of a team of key subordinates who are jointly responsible with the manager for the department's success. *At the same time that the manager works to develop management responsibility in subordinates, he or she must help develop the subordinates' abilities to share management of the unit's performance.* Only when all directly reporting subordinates are committed to joint responsibility for overall excellence—when pieces of the task are no longer conditionally delegated, but become parts of decisions—will control cease to be the sole province of the boss. At the same time, only when subordinates become skilled in the managerial tasks required for total departmental success can the sharing of responsibility lead to excellence. Since neither willingness to accept overall responsibility nor ability to do so are automatic and instant, we have called this model the Manager-as-Developer. Skills have to be learned, common goals accepted, expectations changed, and norms modified. Over time a team can be built.

This management model was created by examining leaders who achieve excellence and the images they seem to hold of managing. Rather than depending on heroic rides to the rescue—with the answers and the total responsibility—they have sought the far greater power and potential for excellence available in the commitment and abilities of their whole group. These managers have in mind a developmental, collaborative, galvanizing, but subordinate-centered image.

Unfortunately, a good, easily recognized image of this kind of leader does not seem to exist. Flashes of description occasionally appear when leaders refer to times when "we were all in it together and we knew we could conquer the world." Certain inspirational moments display the quality of shared responsibility; the leader does not command yet is willingly joined in a pursuit where all are at risk. The stakes are large, but the belief in the team's ability to come through is pervasive. Yet there is no central metaphor for leaders in those situations. Perhaps the image is most like a very demanding but supportive and inspirational coach, who works hard to bring the team along, insists on high standards and rigorous effort, but passes on all the knowledge that will help the athletes grow. This coach often works alongside the team, but delegates increasing responsibility for the game plan and especially for on-the-spot adjustments. All of this inspires great collective effort. From the sidelines during the game itself, the coach takes great pleasure in the centrality and achievements of the athletes.

But this coaching analogy imperfectly transfers to managing: Managers often take part in the big events while coaches can't, managers must deal more with peers, superiors, and organizational politics than do most coaches, and managers are usually closer to their direct subordinates in age and recent experience. Basically, the manager is a more involved participant in the action than a coach can ever be.

Nevertheless, leaders who achieve excellence are less likely to be guided by images of the central, overresponsible, and overcontrolling hero—an image that ultimately dilutes the effectiveness of Technicians and Conductors when they have expert subordinates doing complex and interdependent work in changing circumstances. This new model calls for no less effort, energy, investment, or imagination than does the Lone Ranger style. Since active engagement is necessary to undertake and sustain increased subordinate learning and overall responsibility, we think of the Developer as postheroic rather than nonheroic. Indeed, for some managers who are used to rushing in with the answers (whether correct or not), it takes heroic efforts not to be so heroic! Developer-managers learn to have impact without exerting total control, to be helpful without having all the answers, to get involved without demanding centrality, to be powerful without needing to dominate, and to act responsible without squeezing others out.

CENTRAL ORIENTATION OF THE MANAGER-AS-DEVELOPER

What does it take to fulfill this tall order in management? First and foremost, is a change in orientation. We have found a significant impact on subordinates and on the departments when managers can drop their heroic mind-sets of total personal responsibility. A whole new array of options open up when the leader's orientation becomes: "How can each problem be solved in a way that further develops my subordinates' commitment and capabilities?"

This new orientation may lead the manager to throw some problems back to subordinates ("I think you have a good handle on the difficulty, so why don't you do a first cut and come back in two days"). The manager may ask questions that help subordinates focus in on the key issues, while at still other times, the leader can best aid development by exploring the situation jointly with a subordinate. There may also be times when it is most "developmental" for the manager to provide the answer. After all, when the manager truly knows the best solution, holding back can produce more frustration than learning. Whichever alternative is chosen, the underlying developmental orientation of the leader remains consistent.

What these responses have in common is achieving the dual goal of getting the job done while engaging subordinates in a way that helps them stretch. This orientation does not sacrifice task accomplishment for development (or vice versa). The leader is not saying, "I will develop today and put off solving the problem until tomorrow." Both goals are kept firmly in the forefront. This postheroic orientation also requires that subordinate development is not restricted to off-site training functions. It occurs on the job—in real-time with real issues. Finally, fuller use is made of the already existing abilities of the subordinate while potential ones are developed.

Let's look closely at how a Manager-as-Developer would use this orientation to deal with a problem. We can utilize the Bob Young case where the company is faced with defective gaskets, and see how a skilled manager used the Developer model in this situation. Remember, this is just the sort of issue that is likely to elicit the heroic response; the organization is under severe time pressure to solve a crucial problem that subordinates are colluding to bury. This "Bob" opened the meeting with his four subordinates of the operations committee as follows.

As you know, we are having major problems meeting our deliveries on time. Furthermore, customers are reporting that quality is not up to standard. I have heard this from several of our very important customers and I am quite bothered, as I am sure you are. You know that we are in a highly competitive market and they can go elsewhere. We have always prided ourselves on our ability to produce gaskets that have no defects, that our customers can use without worry. Our financial future is in jeopardy unless we quickly find out what is going wrong and correct it. You are the people who best know the situation; you know what caused it, and you know what the best solution looks like. Therefore, I want us in this meeting to work together and come up with the best answer.

This introduction signaled the importance of the problem, reminded subordinates of the company's identification with quality, and gave an initial indication of how Bob wanted this situation to be tackled.

Yet subordinates know that words are cheap. What did Bob really mean? Was he out to find someone to blame? Were heads going to roll? Did he really have an idea of how the problem should be solved and merely used a "pseudoparticipation" style to get them to buy into his solution? In addition, Bob Young's statement indicated a change in the rules of the game. In trying to develop a management team whose members feel responsible for the operations of the plant and not just for individual areas, Bob Young was demanding that members change their ways of operating. No matter what objections they might have had to Bob's previous style, the subordinates had learned to live with (and around) it. Thus, they tested the waters very carefully before they jumped in and accepted at face value his statement about their enlarged responsibility.

First, they tried to revert to the previous way of operating by throwing the responsibility back to him.

I don't know, Bob. You know the operations inside and out. What do you think the best solution is?

Bob replied,

This is the kind of issue we need to tackle together, because then we'll be sure not only of getting this problem solved, but we'll be able to prevent similar dilemmas in the future.

This exchange was followed with long silence; subordinates hoped they could outlast Bob and force him to take over. When it was clear that he wouldn't move in, there was another attempt to resurrect the old way of operating (where information that might appear detrimental to any one of the four subordinates was kept from Bob while they worked out their problems on the side). The head of production (Don Blue) glanced over to the quality control manager (Roy Gray) and turned back to Bob:

> Bob, you are busy getting us major contracts. We don't have to take up valuable meeting time going around and around on this issue. Roy Gray and I will meet and come up with the solution, and I'll let you know tomorrow.

This suggestion gives the appearance of subordinates assuming responsibility, but it was actually an attempt to hide any dirty linen from Bob Young. Also, the response did nothing to build the operations committee into a mature team that could handle the major operating problems.

As a Developer, this Bob Young recognized the presence of two problems: a technical one—quality products were not being delivered on time—and a managerial one—for some reason the operations group had been unable over the past several weeks to resolve the task problem. The defective-gaskets problem wasn't news to any of them. Thus, Bob realized that if he delegated responsibility for solving the technical problem to two of his subordinates (or if Bob, being heroic, came up with an answer himself), it wouldn't solve the team/managerial problem even if a good technical solution was produced. Rather than wading in to solve the problem personally, Bob decided that he had to hold his subordinates' feet to the fire while they solved the problem. He had to be sure they knew he expected them to work jointly on the solution. Bob thus responded to Don Blue's suggestion by saying:

> Don, I'm sure you and Roy could come up with something, but I also want all of us to improve our collective ability to solve problems. To do that we need to work on it together, since everyone's involved.

After a long silence, Bob turned to Fran, the most junior member of the group, and asked for possible causes of the problem. Bob wanted to be certain that Don's seniority and dominant style would not keep Fran from contributing. After Fran made a few comments, suggesting that the old-timers' resistance to new methods was an issue, the others leaped in to start blaming one another. A hail of "you didn'ts" and "you should have's" filled the room. Bob showed no signs of being upset about this arguing, and after several minutes, when the accusations had died down, he said,

> Let's see if we can keep our eyes on what happened and how to fix it. Pointing fingers only makes everyone defensive, which doesn't help control quality. What advantages did the old system have, and what were the goals in changing the system? Once we have these answers, we can determine the kind of changes we should make in purchasing practice so we get the advantages without the problems.

Although the mutual accusations did not reappear after this attempt to refocus the discussion into a problem-solving mode, Don Blue made one last attempt to settle the issue without team responsibility being generated for working through the problem. Perhaps still fearing he might be exposed to blame for the problem, he seized on a proposal for action and tried to ramrod it through the group with intensity and a flood of words. Bob made sure he understood what was being proposed, then said:

> What do the rest of you think about Don's idea? How would it affect each of your areas? What would be its impact on manufacturing as a whole?

This last directing of the discussion back into the group worked; other members pointed out problems with Don's solution and then collectively dug in to get at the basic issues. They acknowledged that they should stop playing at "It's not my fault," and instead they set up a series of procedures for solving the immediate consequences of the procurement change. They also agreed that a more thorough discussion of inventory policy was needed and set a time the next day to work out the specifics.

This Bob Young had worked very hard to increase the team's willingness to share the responsibility for managing the plant. He recognized that one general statement would not be sufficient. His active and strong efforts were needed to get the group to tackle the problem, and he refused the heroic role of personally finding enough information to resolve the issue. He wanted the team to own not only the problem, but the solution as well. He pushed them hard—all was not sweetness and light—but in a different way than a Technician or Conductor would have elected. Instead of trying to get them to disclose the information that would give him determination of the solution or manipulating them to come up with his solution, he continuously worked at how to get the problem solved while increasing the team's commitment and capacity to solve such problems. He kept standards high by using their tradition of quality as the measure against which they could all judge what was being proposed. And by sticking to his determination to increase shared responsibility, he helped develop the team's ability to work together on future problems.

BENEFITS OF THE DEVELOPER APPROACH

The Developer approach to management has several distinct biases toward excellence. First, the chance is increased that tasks will be accomplished at a high level of quality. Task excellence is more likely when members seize new opportunities as they develop; uncover problems and difficulties early, before they become major crises; share their knowledge and expertise; and feel committed to carrying out decisions.

These four determinants of excellence are especially important in contemporary organizations. High rates of change are accompanied by increased opportunities for innovation. When members feel responsible for departmental excellence, their responses to new conditions are quicker and more appropriate. The leader is not alone in having contact with critical persons outside the department; members often interface with clients, suppliers, and other units within the organization.

Rapid change also brings with it greater likelihood that old solutions, practices, and procedures will soon become outdated. Often, members are aware of developing problems before the leader. If the working climate encourages such difficulties to be raised quickly, not hidden, problems can be tackled as they are beginning to smolder rather than when they have grown into major conflagrations.

When tasks are complex, it is likely that different people know different parts of the problem. When subordinates are competent, they are likely to bring diverse knowledge and expertise. If the problem is multifaceted and members have different but complementary abilities, groups can make superior decisions.

Finally, high member commitment to departmental excellence increases the likelihood that solutions will be fully implemented. Part of the quality of a solution rests with how well it is carried out. Workable solutions take into account political factors in the organization, the skills and styles of those having to implement the decision, and unique aspects of each situation. Thus even a leader's technically correct answer may be inferior in practice to collaborative solutions of members who know the specific conditions that must be met to put the solution into practice. Actual implementation, in turn, has a greater chance for success if multiple resources stand behind it. A task is too often assumed to be the sole province of the individual to whom it is formally assigned; the heroic style prevents an individual from asking for help. A team that is committed to excellence will also recognize what assistance is needed.

When the perspective of subordinates is broadened beyond a narrow concern for the specialized area of each and includes responsibility for the unit as a whole, chances are increased that the four components of task quality will be achieved. Quality will naturally increase as member competencies to solve future difficulties grow from success in solving present problems.

The Developer approach has the second benefit that increased feelings of responsibility by subordinates are not limited to task issues but extend to managerial ones as well. The various forms of participative management have done a better job of involving subordinates in specific task problems than they have in making subordinates feel responsibility for the successful management of the unit. Meetings that don't run well and peers who aren't carrying their load are problems that are too often seen as the responsibility of the leader. But as members of the operations committee found in the Bob Young exercise, excellence is more likely to occur when subordinates share in the management of keeping each other honest.

A third benefit of the Developer approach is increased subordinate motivation. If subordinates seek jobs that use and develop their abilities and want tasks that challenge and stretch, they will find the increased responsibility of this management model highly satisfying. If they want to advance into managerial positions, they will be attracted to a job that involves learning how to work with others and sharing in the management of the unit. The opportunities for personal learning and development help build useful career skills. Expanded responsibilities will attract subordinates who want to feel a measure of personal influence and power. Full participation in departmental decision making means fewer frustrating bottlenecks at the level of the boss. Shared responsibility increases job challenge, personal learning, influence, and opportunity—all key motivational elements of subordinates in the kinds of organizational units we have been discussing.

The Manager-as-Developer phrase is useful shorthand for the leadership orientation we are describing, which depends on an important set of attitudes.

If excellence is to be achieved, I need to make full use of my subordinates' abilities. I can't demotivate them by taking all the responsibility on myself. They often have access to new information because of their job contacts and expertise, and they certainly know about many problems before I do. If they also feel responsible for our success and bring up problems they've spotted, we can find earlier solutions. They often have knowledge and skills I don't have; if all of these resources can be pooled, the quality of our decisions has to increase.

Furthermore, the kind of work we do requires their commitment, not just their presence. I can get their extra effort by helping them be more competent in handling these challenging responsibilities. I have to be concerned about them—their learning, talent, and careers—so that they want to perform.

But achieving excellence will not come just from using each individual's capacities better; I need to use their collective skills as a group. I have to get them to join me in figuring out what has to be done and how to do it. They too can help to make sure that we are all working toward the same end.

I can't manage by constantly looking over their shoulders. Also excellence won't come by means of even more sophisticated control and surveillance mechanisms. I need to get them to feel the same responsibility I feel for seeing that things are carried out well. They will control themselves. If they feel greater departmental responsibility, they will influence each other toward attaining departmental goals far beyond what I could demand.

Beyond the Model as a Mind-Set; Components of the Model in Action

We have stressed the importance of a new conceptual orientation. Even though we have seen its power in managers we have observed (see Chapters 7 and 8), the model, by itself, is not usually sufficient. It can be dangerous to have subordinates feel responsible for departmental success when each member defines the core mission in different ways. Performance falls short of excellence if members do not have the managerial skills and technical knowledge to carry out this added task. And it can be frustrating for subordinates to feel greater responsibility if they have no vehicle for exercising it. In action, the Developer model consists of three components that must be nurtured to ensure that excellence is achieved.

COMPONENT 1—BUILDING A SHARED-RESPONSIBILITY TEAM

The kinds of organizational settings we have been discussing are faced with complex problems whose solutions require complicated coordination before they can be achieved and then implemented. Only rarely do members have self-contained tasks; in most cases, others possess critical information and expertise. Assistance from others is often required to implement decisions and programs. Difficulties with adequate coordination are compounded by a never-ending stream of externally induced changes. Policies, procedures, and regulations must be frequently modified in response to changes in tasks, technologies, and clients' needs. Thus, previously arranged modes of cooperation and past practices rapidly become obsolete.

Departments that strive for excellence have to develop methods to handle this high degree of interdependence and increasing rate of change. Successful departments must be quickly responsive to new conditions and be able to untangle swiftly the snarls that inevitably develop when strong, capable individuals have to integrate their efforts.

Inevitably, bright, ambitious people working together will have differing views on many issues, because of their individual talents and their positions; differing assignments, functions, and responsibilities contribute to differing perspectives on issues. Although such diversity is healthy, it can lead to disputes that must be settled in ways that balance individual and subunit goals with departmental needs.

Finally, problems of coordination and responsiveness increase as members themselves strive for excellence. People may be willing to put up with frustration and bureaucratic delays when they are not personally invested in their work or when they seek merely to perform at a minimum level of

competence. But as they become more committed to quality
work, their tolerance decreases for what they see as unnecessary delays and inadequate solutions on the part of their peers.

These problems of bringing together all the necessary information and producing all the needed coordination are growing
each year at increasing speed. As a result, leaders who feel totally responsible for resolving these issues take on an impossible burden. Seeing that work is fairly allocated, tasks are
properly coordinated, problems raised and resolved, and work
performed at quality standards turns the manager into the
white rabbit of *Alice in Wonderland*, always hurrying but forever being late. There is just too much for one person to know
and do.

The solution, then, is not for the leader to work harder and
run faster, but instead to build a team that shares in the responsibility of managing the department. A departmental
team is not a group whose function is to advise and counsel
the leader; it is a joint responsibility group that shares in making the core decisions and in influencing each other to insure
high-level performance. Since the subordinates are the ones
who have to be coordinated and thus have a vested interest in
their peers performing well, adequate coordination and control is more likely to occur if members can influence each other. There are more points of contact: all-controlling-all allows
more influence than one-controlling-all. Members of the team
must function not only as heads of their own specialized areas
but as part of the overall management function for the department. Subordinates must wear both hats—fighting for the interests of their subunit but equally on the line for the
department's overall interest.

An example of these dynamics can be seen in a staff discussion about Blue Cross benefits. Hourly employees objected to
the existing plan and had suggested changes; it was clear that
the company's response would be seen as a measure of its concern for dissatisfied workers. The production manager, personnel head, and marketing manager all readily agreed with the
general manager that they "had no choice and had to be responsive." The finance manager, however, insisted on raising

the issue of costs. Frustrated by his fellow managers' apparent fear of worker reactions, the finance manager finally turned to the marketing manager and said, "Do you realize this new plan will add 1.5 cents per unit to our product cost? Are you ready to tell that to your customers?"

"You really know how to hurt a guy," was the reply, and an animated discussion followed. The finance manager eventually acknowledged the need to respond to worker concerns and agreed to the health plan changes, but he succeeded in seeing that financial issues were not overlooked in the stampede to a decision. Bringing a team to where subunit viewpoints are fully considered, yet the total context receives every member's concern, is difficult but essential.

Having to deal with the dual loyalties of the members teaches important managerial skills: balancing competing interests; seeing issues in a wider context; working collaboratively; sustaining good working relationships with others who do not agree on all issues and who are prepared to fight for their views; and making sacrifices for the greater good without being a pushover. These skills are useful even for subordinates who do not directly supervise anyone else.

Building such a team, whose members are involved in the key decisions and genuinely share responsibility for the working of all the parts, should lead to greater subordinate commitment and motivation as well as better performance. Responsibility best develops when people can exert influence. Under this leadership approach, both the areas in which subordinates can be influential and the extent of their influence are increased. After all, being responsible for making the decision is more involving for a subordinate than trying to influence the leader who is making the decision. Joint responsibility increases individual challenge and expands the areas for potential learning and growth. Development occurs not just in technical areas but in managerial skills as well.

A cohesive, mature team increases the range of skills and knowledge available to the department. In a rapidly changing larger environment, constantly requiring new knowledge and skills, the leaders can no longer be expected always to have all the necessary experience. If a team can be built whose members feel free to share knowledge, a much wider range of skills becomes accessible.

A more diverse range of managerial behavior also becomes available. As others have pointed out (for example, Adizes, 1978), often contradictory demands are placed on a leader. Sometimes the manager needs to be risk-taking and entrepreneurial, other times more prudent. Sometimes the manager should hold fast to a position, sometimes should be more conciliatory. Rather than expecting one person to be able to perform perfectly at all times, it is more realistic to expect that a richer variety of leadership skills will exist among the total membership of the management team. Drawing upon members' skills can supplement the leader's flat sides.

As discussed in the previous section, a shared-responsibility team is more likely to produce quality performance. Considerable research has shown that groups tend to make better decisions than individuals when the problem is complex and different people have different information. If the leader can build a mature team whose members work collaboratively to solve the major complex issues facing the department, solutions should be of higher quality than when the leader makes all the important decisions autonomously.

Another advantage of such a team is that the amount of control in the unit is increased since its sources are multiplied. Managers therefore seldom have to deal with the natural limits to their personal control capacities, to how many projects and subordinates they can personally oversee. For example, in the Bob Young exercise, the few times when a heroic manager was able, through careful questioning, to come up with a good solution, there was still no indication that subordinates would carry it out with much enthusiasm. The heroic Bob Young would still have to chase around trying to gain compliance. On the other hand, members who feel ownership of a solution also feel that it is their right and responsibility to influence others who are implementing the solution. Member adoption of this managerial perspective serves as an excellent control mechanism to see that tasks are completed well and on time. Groups can exert greater pressure than one individual can, even when that individual is the boss. Most people are even less willing to face their peers with an unfinished or inadequate performance than they are the boss.

Developer managing makes fuller use of the resources of the members and increases their competencies. It forces subordinates to take account of a wider array of issues, and it requires more sophisticated abilities—the same managerial ones that the leader uses. Thus, this is a system that starts to build on itself. Members more rapidly learn management skills when working collectively to make the decisions with which they all have to live.

Unfortunately, too few management teams come anywhere close to realizing the potential benefits from teamwork. Complaints about groups and their inefficiencies are rife in virtually every organization in the United States. Working with executive teams in a wide variety of organizations, we have concluded that it is possible to achieve performance and learning benefits only if managers are willing to give up their heroic styles and work in a more developmental way. In Chapter 6 we show how to transform a collection of individuals who push their individual interests and hide or avoid the real issues into a mature, productive team. This process is neither easy nor instantaneous, but it can be done.

COMPONENT 2—CONTINUOUS DEVELOPMENT OF INDIVIDUAL SKILLS

A shared-responsibility team can work well only when all members have the skills to master these additional responsibilities. As one concerned manager put it, "All this stuff about real teamwork and sharing of the overall problems is well and good, but you wouldn't be so positive if you saw some of the turkeys who work for me." Ideally, everyone who reports to a would-be Developer should already be fully competent, but the usual situation finds most subordinates with reasonable technical competence, some with managerial skills, but few who are strong in interpersonal and group areas.

A team cannot mature if some of its members can't be trusted to take responsibility. Although even the most developed group will include variations in member competence, each person has to have a minimal level of managerial ability to accompany the requisite technical knowledge. For members to engage in consensual decision making and mutual influence, they must have managerial and interpersonal skills. And if members are to comment on problems that involve their colleagues, they must have enough technical knowledge of these areas to help form judicious decisions.

Expanded technical knowledge can be gained through work assignments and discussions in team meetings, where members can learn from each other—particularly when everybody feels free to share the problems and issues of subareas. But the managerial and interpersonal skills pose the greatest obstacle in this system. Lack of technical knowledge is seldom the reason that a person above the rank of supervisor fails to perform. Performance difficulties usually arise from the "softer" and more touchy issues of how to motivate others, handle conflict and disagreements, make and meet commitments, conduct meetings, and use influence. The most frequently mentioned reason (except for economic staff reduction) in numerous surveys conducted by recruiting firms for why managerial-rank personnel lose their jobs is that the person in some way "didn't get along well." not because particular knowledge was lacking.

It is in these cooperative, managerial areas that Developers need to pay greatest attention to subordinate growth and learning. These skills are the most vital toward subordinates' becoming fully contributing participants in the management of the unit. Too often managers tend to share responsibility with those few subordinates they regard as already fully developed, and leave the remainder of the team unengaged until everything else is out of the way, risk is low, and time is ample —a state that never arrives. Such a manager might alternatively choose to ship the difficult ones off to a management-training program, where they can be "shaped up." But improvement by means of the latter option is problematic and firmly out of the manager's control. This is not to say that no development ever occurs, but it tends to be restricted to technical areas or takes place away from the job. A survey of 28 companies identified 14 common types of developmental activities.

Developmental Activity*	Percentage of Companies Reporting Its Use
Project teams	96
University executive programs	92
Task force	92
Permanent lateral moves to a different geographical location	88
Temporary lateral move to a different division	88
Consulting or troubleshooting assignment inside the organization	79
University degree or certificate programs	71
Outplacement	71
Career counseling	71
Technical ladder positions	67
Consulting or troubleshooting for an outside organization	67
Temporary lateral move to a different geographical location	67
Employee-exchange program with a university or government agency	58
Sabbatical	33

*Information adapted from Barbara Abdelnour and Douglas T. Hall, "Career Development of Established Employees," *Career Development Bulletin*, 2, 1 (1980), 5–8.

Although all these activities are perfectly good ways to foster development, in themselves they are insufficient to produce department excellence. Learning that occurs away from regular work may be difficult to transfer to ongoing tasks, and increasing a subordinate's technical ability may not necessarily improve the person's interpersonal skills. Instead, the Manager-as-Developer must use daily interaction with the subordinate as the setting for growth. Day-to-day interactions—of various members of the team—contain the greatest potential for teaching and learning crucial interactive managerial skills.

Development as a Continuous Process

Learning that occurs on the job, in ongoing interactions, is likely to be the most relevant to department members. Tasks can be assigned that broaden the subordinate's knowledge and skills, coaching can occur that builds competencies (as well as increases the probability of successful task accomplishment), and feedback can be given on an ongoing basis. In addition, the subordinate learns from how bosses go about developing—how they ask questions, support and confront, make suggestions. Acquiring technical, managerial, and interpersonal knowledge becomes even more salient when the subordinate is learning to help manage the whole department. The subordinate is not being groomed for nebulous future responsibilities, but for crucial present ones. Thus continuous development is a critically important aspect of the postheroic model.

This approach offers several important benefits for the manager and subordinate. First, the material being worked on is fresh and first-hand. The clumsy subordinate, for example, may not need an (expensive) external workshop on influence skills if the manager gets together with the subordinate immediately after the meeting and says, "Chris, I think you gave up your position too quickly—as I've seen you do before. If you had instead tried recasting your points to show the person you were arguing with how she would benefit, your view might have been understood without your appearing bullheaded." This kind of interaction, close to the event and reinforced over time, increases the chance that new learning will take hold.

The second benefit of this developmental orientation is that it can turn a behavioral problem into an opportunity for growth. Most managers resist giving negative feedback for fear that it will alienate and discourage subordinates, which indeed occurs if the underlying message is, "Aha, I knew you didn't have the ability to do it." But if the underlying message is more like, "There is more you can do and I have confidence that you can do it," then problems can be raised directly.

The third benefit of an ongoing developmental orientation is its extremely motivating and energizing effect on the subordinate. Since we are talking about the kind of subordinates who are turned on by challenge and opportunity, the Developer, in keeping the growth of individuals central and in the service of task accomplishment, keeps motivation high. Thus even difficult, nasty tasks may become occasions for learning needed managerial skills. The chance to grow by being helped to learn from even negative experiences is a powerful attraction to ambitious subordinates—they can tolerate almost anything, including the intense dedication needed to achieve excellence, if their efforts are perceived as leading somewhere. Young professionals like lawyers, medical interns, and new business graduates will knock themselves out for several years, because they accept their hard labor as necessary training before they can handle even larger responsibilities in the future. But rather than requiring extra present effort as dues for future rewards, the Developer links today's learning with carrying out today's important technical and managerial responsibilities.

The discussion thus far should not be taken to suggest that all subordinates can be developed. Some do not have the interest, motivation, or ability. But, before any subordinate is written off or relegated to a dead-end job, the manager should strive to know his or her full potential. As we show in Chapter 5, a "developmental stance" toward both the performer and underperformer has the dual advantage of making fuller use of abilities while quickly revealing those cases where a subordinate can't or won't perform adequately. Furthermore, since this orientation is not punitive, an incompatibility between what the department needs and what the subordinate can deliver generally leads to a mutual agreement to separate rather than a disputed termination.

To illustrate how subordinate development can occur through day-to-day tasks, let's return to the widget problem with a Manager-as-Developer.

SUBORDINATE. We're having trouble delivering disposable widgets to Techcorp.

MANAGER D. Oh-oh, that doesn't sound good. What's going on? Can I be of any assistance?

SUBORDINATE. Well, I thought I'd let you know about it and run through the actions I've taken already. I think I know what to do, but I don't want to miss any bases.

MANAGER D. Fine. Go ahead.

SUBORDINATE. I got a call from Dan saying we couldn't make schedule. When I asked why, he gave me a song-and-dance about poor materials. Since I know he likes to use that as an excuse, I called Ellen in purchasing, who told me the stuff was exposed to excess moisture while Dan was storing it. He, of course, denies it.

MANAGER D. So what did you do?

SUBORDINATE. I haven't done anything about that part of it yet. I don't think we should get directly into a confrontation with Dan, do you?

MANAGER D. That depends on what our options are. In general, it's not a good idea to make anyone lose face, but let's see if there are any other choices. We've got to find a way to meet our commitments or we'll lose our edge as the most reliable manufacturing unit in the business. What else have you done?

SUBORDINATE. I checked with Techcorp's purchasing agent about why the pressure. Turns out that their people made some promises to one of their customers without checking on actual availability. She's going to see whether she can get the customer to allow some slippage.

MANAGER D.   Will they accept a looser tolerance on the widgets? If they would, would that help us?

SUBORDINATE.   She's going to check that too. Then we'd have to fight with our quality-control people. If I need you, would you talk to Ted's boss to pave the way?

MANAGER D.   You expect trouble from Ted?

SUBORDINATE.   He's done it before.

MANAGER D.   How would you approach him?

SUBORDINATE.   I've always tried to play it straight and tell him what our needs are. But he's a stubborn old coot.

MANAGER D.   What do you suppose his interests are?

SUBORDINATE.   I don't know; I've never thought about that— I suppose he's very proud of our quality and doesn't want his reputation to be hurt.

MANAGER D.   Besides, he's been at that job a long time and is likely to be there forever.

SUBORDINATE.   Yes, and I suppose he needs to feel valued and recognized. If I involve him in deciding how much tolerance the product can take, he'd respond better, and we'll come up with something reasonable.

MANAGER D.   That sounds on target. Do you suppose it would help to reinforce with him the organization's theme of dependable and reliable service?

SUBORDINATE.   I think so, especially if I put it in that light. In fact, I've got another idea. I'll call him and get him together with the Techcorp buyer. That would be exciting for him, I'll bet.

MANAGER D.   Sounds good. When you put yourself in the shoes of someone who gives you a hard time, it's amazing how different things look. What else?

SUBORDINATE.   It just hit me; there may be some ways to reschedule some other production so we can

concentrate on widgets. I know how to proceed now. I'll touch base this afternoon.
Thanks.

MANAGER D.   [Smiles]

In this exchange, the Developer is constantly working to help
the subordinate reach an excellent solution while acquiring
important managerial skills. Working out problems around an
issue that involves many parties, which in turn requires the
ability to diagnose other people's needs and develop an appropriate strategy for gaining cooperation, is a valuable lesson for
this subordinate. The Developer uses the conversation to reinforce the unit's reliability goal and, with that as a base, expands on what the subordinate must take into account when
trying to solve a potentially difficult organizational problem.

Balancing Organizational and Individual Needs

The Developer perspective not only allows focus on the crucial managerial skills that help subordinates prepare for advancement; it helps the manager balance the organization's
needs with the individual's interests. The potential for tension
always exists between individual and organizational needs; heroic styles are almost inevitably overconcerned with short-
term task accomplishments at the expense of member interests. "Get the job done and we'll worry about your personal
development when we have time" is an all-too-familiar refrain.
Although the Developer must also be working toward outstanding task accomplishment, the skills the individual will
need for advancement are linked with responsibility for total
unit task accomplishment.

Of course, some subordinates are interested only in learning
further technical skills or working on technical problems, even
after they understand how this view may limit their career opportunities. When being solely technical is what the person
wants, he or she should be supported with appropriate assign-

ments. In those few organizations that have effective parallel career ladders for professionals and scientists, development activities can be kept within a narrow technical band and still be quite satisfactory to the individuals who elect such a course.

Nevertheless, for the type of work setting we have been describing, the interest of most subordinates in learning to be more effective managers coincides with the organization's needs to give managerial talent a chance to unfold. Working in a department that strives for excellence by sharing overall responsibility and teaches managerial skills through daily interaction is an excellent way to enhance one's career opportunities; the accomplishment of tasks at an excellent level of performance in turn enhances the department's objectives. Thus continuous development leads to outstanding performance.

This approach to managing also encourages the best use of the maximum number of people. If all reporting subordinates (except perhaps the "closet technicians" who just want to be left alone) are to share in unit responsibility, the Developer has to find ways to work well with each one. This imperative applies even to those individuals who are, from the manager's point of view, a pain. Since the Developer must develop the kind of relationship with each person that will encourage full cooperation and a willingness to learn, success will come only with open communication and mutual influence. Both conditions are necessary, if the boss is to know subordinates well enough to support and stretch them in ways that allow for continued learning and impact. In Chapter 5, we discuss how openness and mutuality can be created, even with difficult subordinates.

COMPONENT 3—DETERMINING AND BUILDING A COMMON DEPARTMENT VISION

Even though the creation of a shared-responsibility team and developmental relationships may move a department far beyond the heroic model in building member commitment, it may still not be sufficient to produce the level of excellence the department is capable of. As rewarding as increased job challenge and managerial responsibility may be, something more is needed to lead people to give their best effort consistently, particularly in the case of routine functions—not all aspects of all jobs can be made to challenge and stretch. What is needed, then, is the third component of the Manager-as-Developer model: a larger purpose that gives meaning to work, whether routine or nonroutine. Unexciting but necessary tasks can still have importance if they are in the service of larger, clearly important goals.

A central, agreed-on vision can also improve the coordination of effort. Even if the key management team assumes some of the responsibility for coordination of individual efforts, problems of integration may yet persist. After all, reasonable people differ. Coordination problems can be especially acute if there is no agreement on the department's central purpose. Decisions about priorities and allocation of scarce resources and agreement on new products and services may be difficult or even impossible to achieve.

For example, we observed this dilemma in a loosely organized professional association that struggled for years because there was no agreement on a common goal. Four or five different goals each had their proponents in separate subgroups. Since members had a great deal of influence over operational and even policy decisions, reaching quality solutions was very difficult. Meetings tended to be highly politicized, with frequent personal attacks on members' competency and character as factions fought for ascendancy. However, no group was able to gain dominance, so a stalemate ensued. Although much of the warring has since stopped, the organization functions at an only moderate level of performance, far from its potential. Armed truces seldom produce excellence.

For all the above reasons, there has to be this third focus of the Manager-as-Developer: The leader must articulate and gain member commitment to an exciting departmental *overarching goal*. Although all departments have a purpose, and some even have perfunctory mission statements, more is needed: an overarching goal that is a meaningful description of the purpose that captures the unique thrust of this specific unit.

Such a goal fulfills several functions. First, it unites and inspires members with a vision that justifies extra effort. People do not want to work for money alone; financial security alone cannot inspire people to give their best consistently. If subordinates are to move beyond a minimum level of performance and above the mundane, there has to be a purpose—a reason that makes the extra effort worthwhile.

Evidence indicates that no successful superordinate goal can be exclusively financial (Peters, 1979). That is, aiming for "the best return on investment" or "the greatest financial growth" by itself won't excite organizational members to work to potential. They may work hard to gain the associated monetary rewards, but they won't consistently give the level of effort and commitment needed to produce excellence. It isn't that economic success is unimportant, just that it is necessary but not sufficient. The real value of financial measures in a productive organization is to mark the achievement of other goals —such as overcoming a challenge or being a cutting-edge operation.

In some ways it is easier to frame exciting goals for whole organizations—"progress is our most important product" or "we cure diseases by new medicines." But such statements are often abstract and vague for members not at the top. Regardless of whether the organization as a whole has a clear, inspiring mission, excellent departments need to have their own exciting goals. An engineering department that designs machine tools might focus on its aim "to fight inflation by designing equipment that reduces manufacturing costs." Or, a computer-software design group might define itself by the motto: "We know our clients' needs so well that our programs produce far more benefits than any of our clients anticipate."

Common themes in these examples are innovation and quality in important human areas. At some very personal level, goals of this kind speak to the individual's concern about doing something of value. Thus, the reason such goals can move people beyond the merely adequate is that they provide a purpose, a raison d'être for one's activities. The individual is not just working for a paycheck, to support a family, or to escape from the stigma of being unemployed. Instead, there is the potential for the work to speak to a core need within each person—the need to be a part of an organization that makes a difference.

The second important function of an agreed-on overarching goal is to serve as a standard by which to make decisions. If the goal is specific enough, it can be a guideline for choosing among options. For example, the sales departments of two separate companies operating in the same field might have very different overarching goals. One department might say,"We are the best in providing low-cost, yet quality, goods to help our clients compete in the marketplace." The other department might define itself as "the best in the business at anticipating changes in consumer desires," a statement that reflects the firm's lead in product development. In order to be consistent with these quite different goals, each of these sales departments must make strikingly different decisions about the way they are organized, who is hired, the training to be provided, the nature of intracompany relationships, and the types of reward systems offered.

The third function of an overarching goal is to make clear the direction the department should strive toward: It defines the future. Part of the responsibility of leadership is to move beyond status quo in a number of important areas—quality of performance, products or services, work methods, or organizational structure. By specifying the area in which the department seeks to be excellent, the goal points toward tomorrow and can carry members beyond today's irritations.

INTERACTIONS AMONG THE THREE COMPONENTS

The impact of the three parts of this leadership model is further increased because each one builds on the others. For example, the leader may help the group function better by taking individuals aside after meetings and showing them how they can be more productive in the team. Likewise, as the group develops in trust and maturity, members will be willing to examine openly how they are working together. That examination, in turn, is a further source of individual learning as members comment on each other's behavior. Part of how a leader can get members to adopt new behavior is in the service of a larger goal. Groups are more willing to disagree over the means if there is consensus that all are striving to achieve the same goal. And members pulling together further strengthens that vision. (We will turn shortly to a detailed description of a Developer at work to illustrate how the three components—overarching goal, shared-responsibility team, and individual development—build on each other.)

Development from the Beginning

The unusual thing about the Manager-as-Developer model is that it is both a description of an end state—where subordinates have formed a team that achieves excellence by sharing responsibility for achieving an exciting goal—and a description of how to achieve that state. With the Developer orientation, it is possible to use the concept of the team from the beginning and begin to share responsibility immediately. The importance of the decisions increases as the individuals and team mature. The leader can immediately start to improve working relationships with individual subordinates and even begin to explore a viable overarching goal. Indeed, a good way to figure out how to move a group of recalcitrant or inept individuals into a shared-responsibility team is to share that responsibility with them! Engaging subordinates in determining what the problems are and how these are to be resolved increases their understanding of what is needed, as well as their commitment to joining in to solve the difficulties.

When the individual subordinates are technically competent and working at complex interdependent tasks, development activities can move quickly. However, when these basic conditions are not in place, they must be addressed, which some-

times means that the leader must act autonomously to build
technical competencies, find new people, or reorganize tasks.
But at other times, a developmental approach can be used in
tackling these deficiencies.

For a leader who is just starting along the path of managing
as a Developer, it does not make sense to renounce control totally when some subordinates are resistant, dependent, abra-
sive, uncooperative, or unable to work together. However, the
fear a manager has that giving up heroic control and responsibility will inevitably lead to chaos is exactly what prevents traditional managers from changing. By polarizing leadership
possibilities into two extremes, such managers find it impossible to move at all. Thinking developmentally can free the
manager from this paralysis. Seeing change as a step at a time
moves the issue beyond "giving up control" to "expanding
control." As noted earlier, an increase in shared responsibility
increases the total amount of control available. Subordinates
can indeed help deal with problems of motivation, commitment, or collaboration.

Another way to keep problems from blocking change is to
see those very difficulties as opportunities for change. Problems are problems for the Technician or Conductor (to be personally solved or maneuvered around). But for the Developer,
the daily crises can be useful excuses to introduce change. Just
as the Developer Bob Young used a severe quality problem to
build his team, and the widget manager used a typical production problem to teach problem-solving skills, managers who
start interacting daily in developmental ways on ongoing issues
can rapidly create tangible progress. People are often most
willing to consider new alternatives in times of dilemma (occasions that signify that the "old way isn't working"). In Chapters
7 and 8 considerable attention is given to how you can determine an appropriate sequence of steps for introducing this
new, postheroic style of leadership, even under not so idyllic
conditions.

Development is a continuous, never-ending process. Development never arrives at an end place, where all is in order
and the machinery moves so smoothly that maintenance is no

longer needed. Once a unit reaches high gear, it is possible to manage with less friction and uphill pushing, but development will always be needed. Even the most advanced departments face changes in external conditions, shifts in priorities and assignments, turnover in personnel, expansion and contraction in size of the unit, and just normal running down.

An Example of a Successful Developer

A first-hand account by a manager who fully utilizes the Developer model in her department can make this approach and its implementations more concrete. Deborah Linke is chief of the repayment staff of one of the offices in the Federal Bureau of Reclamation. At the end of a year-long assignment in Washington, to upgrade her technical and managerial skills, she had attended our leadership workshop. She was returning to the same group she had left a year before. The job of her staff was to "negotiate, write, and administer all contracts in the geographic area to recover the federal investment in water-resource development," which involved multimillion-dollar dealings with industries, municipalities, and agricultural interests needing water. Her staff's job was complex because they were dealing with multiple constituencies and each of the various water uses was governed by several different set of laws and regulations. Her description of how she built an excellent department serves as a detailed, step-by-step analysis of the developer model.

When I first returned to my job after the workshop, I held a two-hour staff meeting with my three key subordinates in the office (there were three others scattered through the region in local field offices but the former was my core group). I talked about how I felt I had changed in the nearly 12 months I had been away. Some of the areas that were different were a greater openness to feedback (both a greater willingness to give it and to hear it from others) and a much greater appreciation of and tolerance toward conflict (in the past, I had tended to be conflict-avoidant and smooth it over). I shared with them my leadership questionnaire results by handing out copies of the scores.* We talked as a group about areas that I could improve on. Out of this discussion came an informal contract that they would call me on behavior that wasn't changing. This discussion went very well. Naturally, I was apprehensive beforehand about doing this, but it opened a lot of doors—both ways—and made change much less threatening. It all had a very positive tone.

The discussion of my questionnaire results led naturally into exploring how I could modify my leadership style. I talked a little bit about the "Effective Styles of Leadership" conference and the concept of Manager-as-Developer. I said that I wanted to make our staff meetings much more important and a place where all of us could share in managing the office. I stated my much greater commitment to their professional development. My intention was to give them a sense of my managerial style so they would know how best to use it.

The concept of an Overarching Goal was introduced, and each of them was given some of the written material on goals from the workshop. They were asked to think about it before our next meeting. I concluded by saying that one of the things that I felt I really had learned in my year at Washington was to appreciate the political process and how it affects our work. More than in the past, I wanted to involve them in political issues as a way to pass on my knowledge.

After this initial session, I decided to wait three or four weeks until our next meeting. My concern was to not overwhelm the staff with working on goals, developing a team, and so forth, until they had a chance to get used to my being back as their supervisor and, more specifically, a matter of their getting used to this new management style which was different, markedly different in many respects, from what I had used previously. Also, because I had been away so long, I felt a critical need to get on top of the issues of where we were on a number of projects.

That time was used, however, to follow up on one of the comments I had made during that initial meeting about appreciating the work they had done in the last year. I realized that words are cheap, so to demonstrate my commitment to them, I sat down and did the volumes of paperwork that were necessary to get a performance award for the entire team for how they had carried through in my absence (there was no replacement for me for that year; they collectively took over my functions). That award

---

*To prepare for our Effective Styles of Leadership workshop, we asked all participants a month before the session to have their subordinates fill out questionnaires on leadership style, which were then sent to us. (The "Leadership Style Questionnaire" is reproduced in the Appendix.) We tabulated the results and summarized the responses to the open-ended questions; half-way through the workshop we gave each participant this summary.

had to be shepherded through Personnel but I saw that they got the award and the visibility for the good job that they had done. I also used that period to do a careful assessment of our workload. This involved examining not only what we were already doing but also what we should be doing. On the basis of this analysis, I was eventually able to get my central office professional staff increased from the initial three to our present group of five.

At our second staff meeting, we started to work on drafting an Overarching Goal for our office. Even though I had jotted down a possible goal while at the Leadership Conference, I decided not to share this with my staff at this time, recognizing that what I thought might be appropriate might not be their first choice and that introducing my idea might unduly influence them. What was crucial was that the goal be our goal and not just my goal. I must say that the hardest part was letting the group do the work! In developing the goal, the first thing we did was brainstorm a list of things that we found exciting about our work. I acted as recorder for the team and wrote down all the words they came up with. At the end of the meeting, each of us took a copy of this list as the basis for our discussion at the next meeting.

At this next meeting we picked out the two or three concepts that we felt as a team were most exciting and that we wanted to expand on for our goal. (What was also nice was discovering that many of the same points I had originally found important, they did also.) After much discussion, our final goal was:

"We work with our clients with imagination and an attitude of 'there is a problem, let's solve it.' When we have a good answer, we give it visibility."

The two key words in our discussion were "imagination" and "visibility." I was pleasantly surprised that these two values were extremely important to my subordinates and that they really took great pride in being on the cutting edge and being where they could be seen—no easy feat for government employees. We had our goal lettered up nicely and everybody got a copy—and interestingly, all of them have it prominently displayed and have referred to it as our activities have progressed. One validation for this new leadership approach is that the goal we collectively developed was a significant improvement over what I had written myself during the conference. My original goal was more stilted, put in "governmentese," and less exciting.

Determining our Overarching Goal was just the first step in building a team where they, and not just I, have influence. Another action was to have each of the subordinates take turns on a rotating basis in chairing our weekly staff meeting. The leader for that week goes through the agenda and sets the priorities; I will buy into those priorities if that is what the group feels is most important. (Sometimes when we are dealing with very delicate issues, I chair the meetings since I still have the best group skills, but those occasions are rare.) The major task issues in the office are decided by this team.

I have also built a climate in the group where people feel free to raise problems (and not just have a "show-and-tell" of what is going well). In fact, frequently the format is for people to go around and talk about the difficulties encountered and the progress they have made since the previous meeting. Others feel free to make suggestions both in terms of ideas about alternative actions that might have been taken ("this step is something you might have tried") as well as suggestions for ways to handle the problems coming up next week ("you might want to do thus and so"). These suggestions usually resolve any problems. But when a person's performance doesn't improve, the group gets increasingly confrontative, so I worry much less about having to be the one who keeps standards high.

We try to do a lot of coaching at these meetings particularly focusing on the political/nontechnical areas through encouraging consideration of issues from a political perspective. As I mentioned, I think that is probably my strongest suit and one that is very difficult, but important, to impart to others. When I am the only one who is privy to information and can share that, I spend time explaining what has happened in and outside the Department which may affect decisions or policy.

The team is increasingly working on those complex problems that would have been very difficult for any one of us to resolve alone (but which, in my previous style, I would have tried to handle myself). For example, recently a key employee (and a member of this team) brought up a problem she was having. This person has been working on a project for three years and was getting increasingly bored with the work. After this much time, she was no longer finding it interesting or exciting (although it was still an important project). To compound the difficulty, the project was major enough so that it looked like it might drag on for another two or three years. The group discussed how this might best be handled and explored various ways the work could be reassigned to alleviate the boredom. On the basis of the discussion, I drew up a suggested work-reassignment list which represented a rather major shift in that person's responsibilities and entailed some of the group members taking on additional tasks. The group at the next meeting went over the list, made some modifications and then accepted the changes. Such a major reshuffling of tasks is usually a sore point, but because it was something they helped design, the change was implemented with very little upheaval.

In terms of dealing one-on-one with my subordinates, I was fortunate in not having any major problems (such as personality clashes or feeling that any of my people were "trouble-makers" or incompetent) with those whom I directly supervised. The difficulties I did have were with a couple of the people out in the field; people I worked with and had to influence but over whom I had no direct supervisory authority or control. I spent a lot of time thinking about them and what the difficulties were. I discovered that part of the problem was mine. Rather than noticing their strengths, I was focusing on their weaknesses. I decided to try a strategy I learned at the leadership workshop; the next time I got upset or angry at their behavior, I would first look at whether this wasn't a case of their using one of their strengths, but in a way (or a situation) that wasn't appropriate. (Rather than taking the attitude, which I had done in the past, of thinking that the problem behavior was due to their being irresponsible or incompetent.) In most cases, I found that the problem was an inappropriate use of what could otherwise be seen as a strength. That let me deal with their behavior directly by pointing out (in an authentic way, not for the purpose of flattering them) their positive strengths and how these were being inappropriately used. Not only was this message heard (and actually led to their changing) but it also made our relationship more open. This has been important to me, because in the past I have felt blocked. In the Government, one doesn't easily have the option of getting rid of people or transferring them to another division.

Even though I didn't have any real relational problems with my staff, that is not to say that relationships couldn't be improved. It turned out that the change in my management style did lead to even greater openness of communication between us, with each side feeling freer to raise issues that were getting in the way. Not only have I done less pussy-footing with them, but they have also been willing to be more confrontative with me. For example, recently one of my employees told me, "That's certainly a negative way of looking at that—why don't you stop it—it's not doing any of us any good." I could hear and accept that now without getting defensive because I felt the subordinate was saying it with the intention of us working better and this being a better department.

I should add that this informal feedback does not replace the formal systems that are in place. I still do quarterly performance appraisals for each employee; that involves not only feedback to them, but also a chance for feedback from them on how I'm doing with my performance contract.

The improved relationship that now exists with each of my subordinates not only meant that problems could be raised and resolved when they were still minor, but getting our annoyances out of the way, lets me focus attention on developmental activities with my staff. Soon after my return, I sat down with each of them to work out an individual development plan with specific goals. I spent a lot of time listening to what their dreams and aspirations were, where they wanted to be in five to ten years and I tried to build the development plan (and my coaching) around those dreams.

I also worked hard to enrich their jobs. I have used such things as new assignments, trips to Washington, and having them represent the department at some of the meetings in other parts of the Agency or with external groups. The last was not easy for me to do but I found that they handled those meetings as well as I would have, if not better in some cases. For those meetings where I had to be present, a different subordinate would join me each time and afterwards we would talk about how they saw the meetings and how they would have handled it if they had been running it.

This method of expanding opportunities and providing visibility has been used not only with those who directly report to me but to others who are not my direct subordinates yet whose cooperation we need to carry out our departmental tasks. This approach, plus recognition of jobs well done, has led to bringing out even more of the positive behaviors we need. Government doesn't offer many opportunities for perks so I have been looking at such things as chances to give talks (especially presentations to other management groups), attending special meetings, travel opportunities and chances to design training for others as rewards and encouragements for further improved performance.

In terms of my relationships with my boss and peers, these have been good. Immediately after my return, I sat down with my boss to talk about how I had changed and what my goals for the office were. I didn't want these changes to be perceived in the wrong way. My boss's style is very different from mine, especially with this new Developer style that I am using. Although he likes people, he is much more interested in the technical problems. This difference has not caused any resistance in him. He respects me for my ability to manage my shop and in how I relate to my subordinates.

With my peers I find this management style to be very helpful. It is possible to "coach" and even "develop" my peers without being condescending. I can say, "Oh, by the way, I noticed that Mary hasn't been getting any field assignments. One of the things that I learned in my stint in Washington is that this could be construed as discrimination and I don't know if you were aware of that." Such off-hand comments are non-threatening, and are getting me a great deal of payoff from my peers and preventing some of the jealousy that might otherwise occur.

Most of these changes were accomplished in the first three to four months after I came back. But for this progress to be truly effective and meaningful, I found that it had to be followed through in the long haul—it is easy to get sloppy in the press of everyday business. We have done several things to sustain these changes. One is to make sure there is open communication among all of us. For my part I have taken the Leadership Questionnaire out several times and gone back to the group to get further feedback on those areas that my subordinates perceived I needed to work on. I have also worked extra hard with feedback one-on-one to each of them to be sure that they know that they are doing productive work of high quality. In our team meetings, I am better about letting conflicts develop and anger be expressed. When we see problems, we plop them out on the table to be directly dealt with. Also, at the end of each session, the leader for that meeting asks the group how they feel the meeting worked, what didn't work, how the team is functioning, and what needs improving. It is now accepted, by the new members as well, that "this is the way we do business." One of the new arrivals came from a department which was quite repressive and is astounded at how open we are in talking about problems and about issues that come up in the office.

I also found that our Overarching Goal helped sustain this new leadership approach. As I said, all of the members posted their copy of the goal on the wall of their office and I have mentioned the goal many times with such comments as, "This is an imaginative solution, like our goal suggests," or, "We are getting a lot of visibility for that, which is what we want to be doing," or, "We could be getting more visibility, meet our goal and be more excited if we did this. . . ." Typically we use the goal to formulate how we go about doing our business. Even though many of the contracting decisions are set and cannot be influenced that much, the goal can be used in planning how we go about attacking a problem. We use it as a yardstick as well as a criterion to assess decisions on individual projects and in our group meetings. I also have found that the goal is a good way to integrate our new personnel into the office. When a new employee is hired, I give that person a copy of our goal and say why it is important. The goal thus serves as a standard around which we manage the office.

It has been about a year since we first developed the goal. Even though it has gotten increasingly clear over time with use, I want it to be a contemporary vision and not be outdated. So last month, I mentioned to the team that it was time to look at that goal and see if it needed changing. That examination will take place later this month so that we all have some time to think about it.

Has this new leadership style been effective? I think so. One measure is that our office went from last out of seven offices (in terms of responsiveness to changing policy) to being on the top. We have gained a great deal of respect throughout the Agency and are listened to in the head office.

There have been many changes in procedures and policies which require a great deal of adaptability on our part. I find this way of managing, of having a common goal and urging subordinates to take initiative and responsibility in reaching that goal, has led us to be more adaptable. In fact, we are used as an example to the other offices. We have even been asked to develop a training program for others in those areas in which we have been out in front (in our marketing and pricing policies). I will not be doing that training myself; it will be done by my subordinates. That entails some risk because most of them have not done any training before, but I am not worried. Based on last year's experience, I have every confidence that by next quarter we will have a top-notch training program that is presented from a unique perspective and given in a very professional manner.

Important Elements in Deborah Linke's Use of the Developer Model

Deborah's situation was uniquely receptive to the introduction of the Manager-as-Developer approach. Since she had been away for a year, her subordinates were used to assuming responsibility for the department. Furthermore, she already had a good relationship with them, and her boss was supportive of her using a style different from his. But her situation was also quite typical of a high percentage of the managers we have encountered. Her subordinates worked at complex, interdependent tasks, wanted more recognition, welcomed challenge, and had the interests of the department at heart. She also had many of the same reactions that other managers report. Although eager to improve performance, she was anxious about the risks of being open with subordinates about her desires, weaknesses, and needs to learn. Even though no other manager would proceed exactly as she did, it is worth identifying the important elements of her use of the model. That analysis should help crystallize the overall model before we proceed to the remaining chapters, which focus in more detail on the components and generic implementation strategies of the developer model.

An important thing Deborah Linke did was to lead her subordinates in developing a common vision, a unifying standard for all work. Having that agreed-on goal allowed more delegation of work; it is easier to let go when all agree on the general direction.

She built a cohesive group that could assume more of the departmental responsibility, sharing both decision making on task issues and the function of "managing" the members. She linked "team development" with "goal development" by having the group construct the goal. Goal construction was simplified, because the department's function was clearly mandated, and the goal had to focus more on "how" they were to go about fulfilling the unit's tasks rather than on "what" should be done.

Deborah Linke saw that developing subordinates could only occur if the communication and influence channels between her and each of her subordinates were as clear as possible, going up as well as going down. She was willing to entertain the possibility that she had a part in difficult relationships. Her willingness to share the questionnaire results and ask for further feedback set the standard that "development" applied to her as well as to others.

Another way to analyze her actions is that she was pushing both responsibility and influence down to her subordinates. She gave them greater responsibilities in their individual assignments and in the tasks handled by the team. But since responsibility without influence produces stress, she increased their influence by letting them speak for the department on many occasions and by giving them more say in how the department was run. In effect, she increased the total amount of power in the office (as evidenced by the facts that they were better able to get their jobs done and their ideas and procedures were carefully listened to throughout their government agency).

The greater delegation of responsibility and influence occurred without the leader's having to forgo control. In fact, probably greater "control" on members existed than previously, but the control derived from multiple sources— from the agreed-on goal, from others on the team, and from within, as each individual personally wanted to do a good job.

Giving people responsibility usually increases the extent to which they will act responsibly. It's not a matter of blindly trusting people and having faith that everything will work out all right. There will always be times when people do not come through or fail to act appropriately. But Deborah Linke built in an important control mechanism (both one-on-one and in the group meetings); she legitimized everyone's right to raise and resolve openly any interpersonal and task problems that arose. This management situation was not devoid of problems. The degree of expressed conflict went up (which the leader and her subordinates had to learn to accept). However, the disagreements centered on the best way to accomplish tasks, not jockeying for turf or private personality issues.

Perhaps most important of all, Deborah Linke was able to remove the quasi-adversarial relationship that so frequently exists between the leader and (some) subordinates. This kind of relationship frequently develops when the manager is not so sure that certain subordinates are on the team and the subordinates are not so sure that the boss is on their side. Note that she started by doing extra work to get them special recognition from the bureaucracy, which undoubtedly eased the way for the rest of what she did. Then by developing an open, mutual-influence relationship with each subordinate so that problems could be raised and resolved, by building a team that worked together and dealt cleanly with each other, and by forming a common definition of what they were to strive for, all members could come together in collaborative effort. When people feel no need to be guarded and suspicious with each other, considerable energy for task attainment is released, and a strong joint commitment to foster excellence is possible.

In the next three chapters, we will take a closer look at the three components necessary to create excellence in your own organization. First is the creation of an overarching goal that is exciting and challenging. Creating such a goal is crucial but difficult. How can it be done? How can you do it?

CHAPTER 4
OVERARCHING GOALS

*If we are to renew, it's because we have a vision of
something worth saving or worth doing.*
JOHN GARDNER

*To tackle something mammoth and then to accomplish
something of real consequence—that's the only thing
that matters. Fame, money, position—none of that stuff
comes near.*
ROBERT IRWIN, quoted by Lawrence Wechsler

INTRODUCTION

One of the key components for the Manager-as-Developer in
reaching excellence is the establishment of an overarching
goal for the unit, which serves to give coherence, excitement,
and meaning to the department's work. An overarching goal
can motivate, provide direction, and serve as a focus for
change in the department. To lead a unit to excel, rather than
just to manage existing arrangements well, the Developer has
to create an explicit goal to serve as a guiding star, to shape
actions so that all parts of the organization reinforce one another and the goal. Without identifiable purpose, greatness
cannot emerge.

The concept of the overarching goal is directly analogous to
the concept of a superordinate goal or mission for the total organization (Pascale and Athos, 1982). Peters and Waterman
(1982) found in their study of excellent companies that each
had a chief executive officer who had articulated a goal that
used only a few words to summarize what was unique and special about the company, what all employees could focus on
and use as a guideline, what the company stood for. IBM, for
example, has as its superordinate goal "customer service."
Hewlett Packard's is "innovative people at all levels." Sears
stands for "value at a decent price." AT&T has been guided
by the idea of "universal service." Bechtel, a huge construction company, prides itself on "a fine feel for the doable." GE
is known for its "progress is our most important product"

theme. Although each of these goals or themes could be, and in many other companies are, treated as empty, meaningless slogans, the chief executives identified by Peters and Waterman not only believe and constantly talk about these goals, but work to reinforce them by their personal actions, reward systems, hiring practices, organizational structure, and other aspects of managing. Having adopted a goal that uniquely distinguishes the organization, the chief executive works to align all parts of the organization in support of the goal.

When well formulated and backed up with appropriate executive action and organizational support mechanisms, these superordinate goals help managers at all levels of the organization make better decisions and function in ways that advance the organization. But the organization's goal needs to be translated, or specifically formulated, for each department or unit. Exactly what is the goal that General Electric's CAT scanner service department should follow to be consistent with the idea of progress as a product? What is the goal of the finance department within IBM's office products division that supports "customer service?" How does the contract estimating department at Bechtel run itself to have "a fine feel for the doable?" Even when the organization as a whole has a clearly articulated and well-supported superordinate goal—an all-too-rare occurrence in American companies—each unit must also have an overarching goal that does specifically for the unit's members what the corporate goal does for the company at large. Even if the organization has nothing more explicit than its generalized purposes, a unit can be greatly aided by adopting a goal.

In our leadership training programs we have worked with more than 200 highly competent managers from some of America's premier organizations. They manage units that are important to their companies and to consumers, yet very few of them had ever translated their department's functions into a clear and exciting overarching goal. They were missing a significant opportunity for inspiring excellence, especially since we were able in a short time to help almost all of them develop a goal.

The unit's goal must be consistent with overall corporate goals, but it is more than a mere restatement of a company purpose. Instead, it must be distinctive and suited to the specific unit's purposes and competences. In organizations that have no superordinate goal beyond a vague mission statement that no one looks at, the unit's goal can still be distinctive and challenging, so long as it does not violate the implicit goals of top management. In either case, the first step toward excellent unit performance is the identification of a challenging, unifying, unique, and creditable overarching goal.

An overarching goal has several important effects. It builds a common frame of reference that allows people with different backgrounds and varying orientations to pull collectively toward the same ends. It is an important force for change; it describes what could be, what the department should strive for. Finally, it is highly motivational. It places individual tasks within a larger framework, thereby giving work greater significance. This motivational power is enhanced when the goal is stated as a challenge, a difficulty that is to be overcome.

Too often, the only time anything resembling an overarching goal appears is in a disaster or around the development of a new task or product. Only under conditions such as a plant closing or start-up, a unionization drive, or possible loss of a major consumer do people rally around a common issue, giving greater effort than ever before. Similarly, the struggle to meet deadlines in coming out with a state-of-the-art machine or service often galvanizes member effort. (One excellent example is the description in *The Soul of a New Machine* [Kidder, 1981] of how a group of engineers at Data General worked night and day to design a badly needed computer.) But such occasions occur irregularly; when they do occur, they are often out of the manager's control (although some leaders may manufacture crises to produce this outcome, even though this ruse is often transparent to subordinates). The challenge comes with trying to build that same common focus and collective effort in nonemergency, regular work conditions. We believe that most departments can set such an overarching goal. To determine an exciting and challenging goal, one must find out how this specific department achieves its mission in ways that are different from comparable departments faced with the same general purpose.

For example, 10 production departments in 10 different organizations may manufacture video terminals. Yet each can have a unique thrust. The production department in organization A defines its goal as "customized work to meet idiosyncratic customer demands." Organization B's production department prides itself on doing "state-of-the-art video terminal manufacturing." Organization C stresses reliability, the lowest failure rate. Organization D strives for responsiveness by shipping all customer orders within four working days. Organization E focuses on high-volume, low-cost styles; F on producing a design that can be easily serviced; G on simplifying design to speed installation; H on high-margin standard types, and so on. Each department can be successful, despite the differences, if its goal serves to unite the department while meeting market needs and being consistent with the thrust of the rest of the organization.

In some ways the overarching goal is the departmental parallel to a corporate strategic posture, in which a firm examines the environment and its opportunities, assesses its own capabilities, and then determines a market niche that will allow it to be successful. Just as the chief executive officer must lead the effort to formulate a strategy that can be encapsuled in an exciting, challenging, superordinate goal statement, the middle manager needs to work toward the formulation and dissemination of a departmental overarching goal.

CHARACTERISTICS OF AN OVERARCHING GOAL

An effective overarching goal has four essential characteristics:

1. *The goal reflects the core purpose of the department.* The human relations movement over the past few decades has sometimes caused managers to forget the centrality and

motivating potential of work. The very important need for appropriate relationships can sometimes be confused with, or even displace, the department's tasks as an objective. For example, if the goal is to focus member effort around task attainment, the goal must reflect that task; a departmental goal of "fielding the best volleyball team in the company" or "being the department where people have the most fun" may build esprit de corps, but it does not guarantee high work performance.

2. *The goal is feasible.* Feasibility has several measures. First, as suggested earlier, the goal must be consistent with the general purposes of the organization as a whole. Thus, it has to be compatible with the organization's superordinate goal. For example, if the organization aims to provide low-cost products on a mass basis, the research and development department can't define its goals as developing state-of-the-art, customized technology. Second, the departmental goal has to be compatible with what the other departments can deliver. The sales department can't work toward immediate turnaround time if the production department's technology requires continuous-process batches with a 10-day cycle. The goal also has to be feasible in terms of what subordinates within the department are capable of producing. The goal can't be "providing end-user training to all clients" if the salesmen aren't themselves highly skilled and knowledgeable or at least capable of acquiring needed skills. Finally, the goal has to be feasible in terms of the departmental manager's personal capacities. Bold, risky marketing approaches are not appropriate if the marketing manager's style doesn't include risk taking.

3. *The goal is challenging.* One of the most fundamental motivations for any employee, especially one who is basically competent and doing complex tasks, is challenge. Tasks that are stretching—difficult but achievable—will pull the best from most subordinates. Challenge creates the willingness to invest in work, high commitment, and pursuit of excellence (Kanter, 1977). The overarching goal must include a challenge—a way toward a future state of excel-

lence: the department that is best, first, most, fastest, or some other superlative that fits with the core task.

4. *The goal has larger significance.* Work is a central aspect of most people's life, a way the person defines identity and self-worth. Thus, people will extend themselves for work that they can see is important. Though not all tasks can have earth-shattering significance, most work can be put in terms that highlight its meaning to others. Whether the unit produces outputs for external customers or for other units within the organization, an overarching goal that stresses benefits to other people or their objectives can put even routine work into a larger perspective.

Core purpose, feasibility, challenge, and larger significance help transcend the merely adequate performance that occurs when goals are only short-term financial targets or nebulous platitudes.

One example of a useful, although unusual, overarching goal, occurred in the maintenance and engineering department of a medium-size company. The leader saw his department as "the glue that holds the organization together." Normally, this opinion might be a bit presumptuous, but it was somewhat valid in this situation since the company was faced with stringent economic belt-tightening in order to survive. There would be no money in the foreseeable future for new equipment or major renovations. Engineering had to help other departments make do with what plant and equipment they had, so the department's ability to respond quickly to requests for repairs and refurbishing did much to boost morale in the struggling organization. Members of the department increasingly saw themselves as vital to the organization's survival rather than as the ones who had to do the dirty work. The manager found he needed far less time seeing that people actually put in their hours and more time jointly solving problems raised by subordinates who were eager to perform. When combined with challenge, a goal that underlines the larger organizational significance of everyday tasks can be highly motivating.

A Case of the Development of an
Overarching Goal

The setting was a suburban office of a major bank that was experiencing low morale and lower productivity than had been forecast. One of the difficulties was that this office had been used as an informal "training center" for young managers. New hires who needed experience as loan officers or assistant branch managers were assigned here for training; when they reached a certain level of competence they were promoted out. Such a practice was demoralizing to the less mobile tellers and other assistants, who saw no personal reward in "training their boss" and instead felt exploited by the process.

After some checking with her boss and other people at corporate headquarters, a new branch manager concluded that it would be impossible to change this rotation procedure; her branch and several others were used as the backbone of executive development in this bank. During this exploratory period, she also got to know her subordinates, particularly those who were "solid citizens" and had been carrying the place while numerous superiors had rotated in and out. She found that many of them were quite capable and could do much more than they were presently doing, but they had never seen themselves as "going anywhere" in that bank.

The branch manager searched for what could be a unique thrust for this branch, one that would integrate an individual's needs with the bank's rotation objectives and in the process better serve the branch's customers. She formulated as a goal the desire to be "the branch in the organization that best develops managerial talent while still offering quality customer service." From this decision, a series of actions flowed. First, she declared that if the task is development, opportunities for growth would be open to all. She inaugurated a career development program for each of her employees. She and the other managers sat down with each of their subordinates to find out what aspirations they had. For those who did want to advance, she negotiated with the central training department of the bank for spaces in some of their programs. She negotiated with the personnel department to inform her regularly of job openings, which might interest some of her subordinates, and not just those assigned to the branch for "development." Next, she built rewards into the appraisal system for those who did help others learn, so that even those who did not personally aspire to advance would get some benefit from the new thrust. In order to provide adequate backup in service functions, she instituted cross-training so that people in one area could fulfill functions in another. Not only did this arrangement provide a reserve of assistance when one area was experiencing peak work and development demands, but interdepartmental cooperation increased as each area more fully understood the policies and procedures in other areas. The branch manager also used this practice with her own immediate subordinates; she frequently had the assistant branch manager run staff meetings, other subordinates represent the office at some of the central bank meetings downtown, and members of her staff carry out some of her other designated tasks.

These efforts resulted in major gains. By stressing and restressing these goals in words and actions, the branch manager gave the office a distinctive character. Members felt increased pride in their place and morale improved. Some of the old-timers acquired new aspirations, developed their skills, and moved into higher positions. Even those who remained at the branch office felt good about the advancement of others because they saw their role not as fulfilling thankless tasks but as crucial for individual and organizational success. The spirit of the place carried over to how customers were treated. Service also benefited from the cross-training, since there was now less shuffling of customers around to other employees.

Note how the formulation of an overarching goal also served as a guide to many aspects of operating the department. The goal functioned as both a reference point and a stimulus. It was not just an endlessly repeated slogan; a number of concrete actions reinforced the goal and built commitment to it. Though each of the changes the manager made—creating new opportunities, fitting them to individual aspirations, altering rewards, cross-training, delegating responsibilities—was in itself a useful device, collectively they were more potent because of the common theme. In addition, the theme's articulation suggested actions she otherwise might not have considered. The manager-as-developer has to sell the overarching goal, but any goal is likely to be believed, and therefore be impactful on excellence, only when it is backed with supporting actions.

THE IMPORTANCE OF AN OVERARCHING GOAL

The lack of an overarching goal represents a major loss of potential power on the part of the manager. In the absence of a challenging goal that sets high aspirations, the manager tends to fall into a maintenance role that at best produces a more efficient version of an existing situation. Developing toward potential is a necessary ingredient of excellence and also encourages a manager to assume a leadership role.

Thus, one major purpose of such a goal is as a *vehicle of change*. If the manager can articulate and gain member commitment to a vision of the future, the goal then serves as an important stimulus for change toward excellence. As occurred in Deborah Linke's department, subordinates' acceptance of the goal means that they too push for change. This mandate for change spreads to include not only what is to be done but how the unit is to operate.

For example, if a personnel department that is used to just making sure that all forms are properly filled in now redefines its role as "creating the conditions that will increase corporate-wide managerial competence to meet the new goals the executive committee is setting," pressure inevitably develops for all sorts of improvement within the personnel department itself. Forms and procedures are reexamined: Are they only for the convenience of personnel, or do they really help the managers supervise better? Training has to be insituted that meets the managers' needs. Wage and salary policy, as well as the performance appraisal system and career development pathways, have to be improved so that subordinates get accurate and timely feedback and appropriate rewards for their performance. Finally, the skills and abilities of personnel department employees may need to be retrained so that they can deliver on these new tasks.

Use of a challenging goal *alters the nature of the Developer's relationships with subordinates.* The impetus for change becomes the need to meet the goal, not pressure from the leader. Depersonalization of justification for the change can make it easier for subordinates; they do not feel they have to subjugate themselves to a superior's grandiose, personal power play or ego trip in order to stay employed. Once the goal is articulated, it assumes a life of its own; influence seems more objective and impersonal. The demand is for commitment to the goal rather than to a person, which in turn means less coercion and a greater likelihood that joint problem solving will occur. Energy can go into finding the best solutions to achieve the goal, not into one person's "winning." Subordinates can be fully involved in deciding what barriers prevent goal attainment, what steps are needed, and how to implement action. A far more potent form of control is created than the traditional, close supervision that breeds resentment.

The acceptance of an overarching goal *provides a common vision,* a similar frame of reference for all. If members buy into the same goal, the likelihood is increased that they will act in compatible ways despite strong individual differences. Compatibility is an increasingly important issue as heterogeneity in background, experiences, knowledge, and values grows— contemporary organizations need to recruit diverse talents to deal with a changing, complex environment. The conventional practice of limiting access to management to those homogeneous in background, race, sex, and schooling severely limits organizational capacity to adapt to complexity. But with increased differences among members, a way must be found to achieve a common orientation if coordinated behavior is to occur, particularly important for shared responsibility. The advantage of using the overarching goal to achieve the commonality, rather than common social background, is that the goal is directly task related. People with diverse viewpoints can strive to achieve the same ends.

This objectification of the goal also allows for *better resolution of those conflicts that are inevitable* whenever people work together. Honest disagreements take the place of power plays. Differences can be productively explored rather than used to foster further divisiveness. Too many managers fear conflict so much that they prematurely stifle it. They worry that everything will fall apart if they allow conflicts to surface. Yet conflict is inherent in the nature of organizations; dividing tasks requires that each person have slightly differing goals to do his or her job well. Struggling over issues helps promote more creative resolution of issues.

Problems arise—impasse or fragmentation—when subordinates pursue their subgoals *only.* Acceptance of a clear, overarching goal can allow the manager to *promote* conflict, to encourage the expression of differences and full engagement among the subordinates, because the goal serves as an integrator. Reference to the common goal can help even a manager who is nervous about his or her personal ability to manage conflict; the goal is an objective standard to refer to when fur is flying.

In short, the existence of a common vision pushes subordinates and the superior to see the larger picture, the overall purpose for bringing subunits together. This understanding is crucial if subordinates are to share responsibility for the managing of the whole department.

An overarching goal helps *keep the leader and members focused on the larger issues.* Managers can easily be swamped by the day-to-day minutiae of procedures, rules, deadlines, and other annoyances and lose sight of the department's reasons for existence, but continued reference to the goal guards against tunnel vision.

Further, the overarching goal is important for its *motivational properties.* When the departmental task is defined in terms of a challenge that has a larger meaning, involvement goes up. As we have mentioned, most people need to believe in something that is larger than their day-to-day, often mundane, tasks. They are more likely to become committed to making things happen right if they believe in the significance of the unit's goal.

In fact, many people, even quite independent professionals, want a clear overarching goal almost apart from its specific advantages. They want to know that the organization has a clear direction; if they strongly disagree with it they will leave, but so long as it doesn't strongly violate their beliefs, they are more comfortable with clarity. For example, soon after an accounting firm chose a new managing director, one of the senior partners commented, "I have some questions about our new activities, but at least with Thomas we have a direction; we know where we are going and we are actually moving."

If any goal is better than none, how much more potent is a goal that also inspires! The leader who can excite subordinates about a larger vision is able to tap a vast pool of dedication and motivation. In most contemporary organizations, where mobility is high and allegiance is more frequently granted to each person's professional group than to the company, it is probably misguided to expect intense commitment to the leader as a person. There is natural reluctance to overcommit to a boss who may soon be moving or who might be arbitrary. It is less threatening and less dependency-creating to become excited about a specific goal. Therefore, an important leadership skill is the ability to articulate a superordinate goal that is congruent with organization requirements and member needs.

This is not to say there is no room for personal style or energy. Charisma can be inspirational. But the most organizationally relevant aspect of charisma is the ability to formulate and sell a goal that taps into member needs for belonging to a unit that does challenging and meaningful work. Not "charm," but showing subordinates how they can meet their needs for significant accomplishment is the key to being charismatic.

Finally, the overall goal helps to *sustain attention to excellence*. Even though most people want to work well, putting out the extra effort to share responsibility can be burdensome. There frequently comes a point in any task when the motivation is strong to "just get it done." There is reluctance to put in the final extra effort. The report is adequate, but it really could use going over one more time; procedures seem to be working, but the routine isn't quite smooth enough; the action plan to implement the solution really should get one more review to make sure all conditions are covered.

In all these situations, it is likely that the initial excitement of the project has long since worn off, the challenge from problem solving has already been answered, and the learning has been achieved; new tasks look appealing and returns are definitely diminishing with this final push. Managers often feel their only recourse for keeping up quality is to ride herd on the troops, which irritates everyone. Instead, an overarching goal that stresses excellence can be used by the leader (and by other members) as the standard by which tasks are to be judged. Excellence is a much more useful standard than "Will

it get by?" or "Are we personally thrilled to continue working?" Pressure from the leader should be exercised in the pursuit of excellence, not because "work has to be done my way."

ESTABLISHING AN OVERARCHING GOAL

Establishing an operative overarching goal requires two dis-
tinctly different tasks of the leader: to *formulate* an appropriate overarching goal and to gain its *acceptance* by the
members. Each task requires different sets of skills. The first
task demands intuitive and analytic ability to sense what
would excite subordinates, even though they themselves might
not be able to; the second requires inspirational and selling
ability. Common to both sets of skills is an ability to think beyond the daily routine, to see a greater vision that ties day-to-
day activities to significant future goals.

Developing the Overarching Goal

A leader cannot discover a goal, as if it already existed and
waited to be unearthed. Instead, it is more appropriate to
think of a goal as being woven from many strands, including
core purpose, feasibility, challenge, and larger significance.
The process is dynamic, playing back and forth among ideas
about who needs the department's services, what is exciting to
members and to you, and what is feasible given the skills and
resources likely to be available.

The following sequence has proved to be useful in our work
with managers trying to develop an appropriate goal. First
identify what the department does for its clients, the total organization, and society. Look at your own interests, skills, and
areas of commitment, then at the department's internal resources. See what kind of match can be made between external service and internal capacities. Once you have formulated
the goal, sell it by talking first about what it does for the larger
good, then for the organization, for your clients, for you personally, and finally, for your subordinates. In general, identify

a goal component and then clarify how all interested constituents will benefit. Initially, a leader should think externally, identifying the department's clients (either inside or outside the organization) and their needs. We encourage managers to assume that their units are central to the organization and that what they produce—documents, information, services, or goods—is crucial to people outside the unit, who are also performing crucial functions. Often managers have not concentrated on what their department activities do for the rest of the organization or end users.

For example, one manager in our workshop headed a unit that repaired circuit boards in a computer company. She was so caught up in the technology of her unit's function that she had lost sight of its significance. Repairing parts sent back by customers appeared to have little glamour—a necessary task perhaps, but not one that seemed crucial to the organization, which prided itself on producing state-of-the-art computers. Given the problem of setting a goal for her department, she realized that although customers may initially buy the hardware on the basis of what it could deliver, continued customer satisfaction could be insured by speedy return of repaired parts. She thus formulated this goal statement: "We're the ones who sustain the reputation of Compucorp for quality and reliability."

The process of looking at departmental activities to discover their larger significance often means that a manager has to see through layers of grimy routine that over years have obscured the department's function. In some situations, the manager may have to reinterpret or expand a department's purpose to have greater relevance. A manager must undertake goal exploration with clear criteria for the goal's relevance, practicality, and capacity to excite.

Clearly, one must first look at the nature of the department's task. If the department markets sows' ears, dreams of silk purses are wholly irrelevant; but it can be satisfying to find just those sows that are in need of ears! Besides the task itself, the technology, technical expertise of the members, abundance of resources, and so forth all affect the determination of a goal. The loan department of a small bank might be very excited about moving into international lending, but their gratification may be short-lived if members experience failure in assessing risks or collecting on loans. Finding a match between what the unit can deliver and external market needs is necessary, but by itself not sufficient. A manager must consider what he or she can personally believe in and be excited or challenged by. As salespeople know, it is very difficult to sell a product that the seller is not personally committed to. Without genuine personal excitement, expressions of enthusiasm about the goal will seem hollow. Furthermore, a manager must take account of subordinates and what would excite them. What could they find challenging in the department's activities? An overarching goal with larger significance might work in one situation, but not in another, because it doesn't fit with members' skills and interests.

The answers to these issues are seldom obvious. It is usually necessary to experiment back and forth, balancing among external needs and different sources of personal excitement. A promising lead in one dimension may not be supportable in another. A goal that seems to fit all criteria may not reflect the core purpose of the department or might not be feasible, given external reality. But in our experience helping managers, we have found that successful goal identification mostly depends on time and effort. The experiences of one manager illustrates how the process of identifying a useful overarching goal might begin.

Mark was head of personnel in a small company that manufactured machinery for the oil industry. In mulling over what might be a possible overarching goal, he was unclear about what would make his group unique from personnel departments in other organizations of a comparable size. He had three assistants, all responsible for developing appropriate personnel procedures and forms and for training. How could the task be defined as challenging and exciting?

The company had recently gone through change and stress. It had been known as a leader in its field in terms of quality products (which had been a source of pride to both management and workers). In the past, the company had employed slightly under a thousand people, which allowed for a high degree of informal and personalized contact between superiors and subordinates. In fact, employees talked about the family atmosphere of the place and the high degree of concern shown by management. Employees displayed high loyalty, low turnover, willingness to put in overtime, and a general commitment to quality work.

Much of this work atmosphere had deteriorated recently. The oil crisis in the 1970s had produced a dramatic increase in demand for the company's products, and in the last 18 months, employment had doubled. Increased size led to new procedures, which led to a more formal, bureaucratized atmosphere. Employees complained that the friendly family feeling was gone and that the company was becoming "just like any other." Also, the new hires didn't have the same commitment and loyalty to the company of the older employees and tended to treat their jobs like "any other job."

Mark had received a lot of information about what his "clients" did and didn't want. Supervisors complained about unnecessary paperwork, about the personnel department not providing the sort of people who were "like our old employees," and about irrelevant training. Employees complained that it took too long to correct mistakes in benefits payments and that the personnel division was only interested in issuing rules and regulations.

Mark then started to think about what his department could do that would serve the needs of the consumers of his department's services. It didn't help just to think in terms of "better" services, because it wasn't clear just what that meant. Also, as a small department they were not able just to give "more"; instead, there had to be some way to prioritize services. After much thought, Mark had been able to formulate an exciting overarching goal for the personnel group: to provide the training and procedures that would enable managers to "manage humanely in a growing company." This goal might make it possible, Mark thought, to recapture the atmosphere of personal concern.

Mark believed that the goal reflected the key function of the personnel group and that it was feasible, given his skills and those of the three people reporting to him. It was certainly challenging, and it put their tasks into a larger framework that had great significance. The goal had fundamental implications for how the department operated. New personnel procedures would be judged not only on whether they got the job done; they had to prevent a bureaucratic atmosphere and foster a personalized one. New orientation programs would be needed to socialize recent hires into the past culture of the company. Training programs would have to be modified and new ones added that would help managers carry out leadership functions

in a more humane way. This formulation of the goal would shape what
was to be done *and* how the personnel group would go about it. Rather
than just imposing decisions, the group would need to solicit actively user
input in the development of new programs and procedures.

In this case, Mark worked in isolation to determine the goal;
he saw the convergence of client needs and his and his subordinates' interests and abilities. In most cases, however, it is
more productive to set up an interactive process between superior and subordinates to explore a range of possibilities before a decision is made. Usually a considerable amount of
talking it over, "chewing on it," looking at what is initially a
vaguely defined goal from different angles must occur before a
definition firmly captures the interest and energy of the leader
and the members. This informal approach also has the benefit
that such discussions build commitment among subordinates
while gathering data.

This initial discussion phase with subordinates enables the
leader to collect information. The actual determination of the
goal can be accomplished two ways: by the leader alone or, as
Deborah Linke did, by group consensus. The latter option increases the likelihood that the goal will meet members' needs;
the group struggling together often produces a more creative
outcome (as Deborah found), and through the process of arriving at a decision much of the next stage (gaining commitment)
is already achieved.

Nevertheless, quite often the determination of the overarching goal is a decision that ultimately the leader will have to
make. Like any creative act, determining an exciting, galvanizing overarching goal is something that often can best be
done by one person. Even though many variations are possible, a useful goal usually requires a creative blend of disparate
elements. It may not be possible for group consensus on such a
fundamental issue. After all, the selection of a specific goal
generally is more to some members' liking than to others',
depending on its fit with members' goals, aspirations, skills,
and current status.

Thus, unless a group is highly homogeneous and already

arrayed in just the right network of relationships, the chosen goal will increase the influence of some members at the expense of others. Those who would lose influence or who do not like the direction implied by the goal, have it in their best interest to block the group from reaching a decision. Any goal that all members would readily agree to, because it makes no one uncomfortable, is likely to be so general that it would have low potency for guiding departmental decisions. Goal statements that do not force choices may find easy acceptance, but their influence won't be worth the time it takes to say them.

It is also difficult for a group to achieve consensus because useful overarching goals have a stretch quality to them. They are intended to be challenging, which means that they postulate a higher standard of member performance than is current. Although the subordinates we have been discussing seek and are motivated by challenge, they often feel some ambivalence. The unknown raises fears of failure or at least gives pause to those who are comfortable now, even though they have longed for loftier goals. Sometimes those who have most pushed for changes are suddenly resistant when change is at hand; the security one felt from railing at the status quo is threatened. In the sense that social workers *need* the poor clients they are supposedly helping to overcome poverty, complainers often need the weak conditions about which they most complain. At any rate, research shows that the leader of a high performing department sets higher standards for members than members would set for themselves (Likert, 1961).

In the last analysis, it is the leader's responsibility to determine the overarching goal. If the goal can be developed and won by consensus, so much the better, but not all Developers may be as fortunate as Deborah and, might have to deal with the absence of a unanimously favorable reaction. But if there have been thorough and open discussions to assess members' interests and personal goals, and if preliminary versions of overarching goals have been shared with subordinates, a leader's selection of goal is likely to be acceptable and even inspiring to most members.

Gaining Member Commitment

Selecting an appropriate goal is only half the process. Equally important is what follows—gaining members' commitment, which is neither easily nor quickly done, especially if the goal was selected by the leader, not by the team. Subordinates will be justifiably skeptical and initially withhold acceptance. They will be asking themselves, "Is the boss really committed to this goal or is it a passing whim?" The last thing subordinates want is to give commitment and energy to a transitory goal.

Securing member acceptance must be viewed as a long-term effort that will require persistance and consistency. Without reinforcement, an initial lofty statement will sink largely unregarded. The goal must be recalled by repeated mentions on relevant occasions and backed by actions that give weight to the verbal statements. Subordinates need to see the overarching goal used as a basis for running the department and personally use it in helping to manage the department.

This stage of the goal process poses an interesting paradox. The aim is to gain member commitment to the overarching goal so that it will serve as a standard for their behavior. But one of the best avenues to such commitment is by using the goal as the basis for action, which demonstrates both your commitment and the goal's utility in building a more effective department. It's hard to build commitment without use, but difficult to get effective use without commitment! Perhaps the way out of this situation is first to acknowledge the dilemma, then to conceptualize implementation as a constantly alternating process, each part building on the other. But the leader must be willing to take the early risk of pushing the goal before support has been completely built.

Several methods can be used to further this process of commitment. As we mentioned, simply the persuasive articulating of the goal is important, with careful attention to the actual words used. The words don't have to be elegant but they must convey the core message. One of the best documented examples of a middle manager at work can be found in *The Soul of a New Machine*. Kidder (1981) shows how hard Tom West, the

manager of Data General's project team on the Eagle computer, works to define the team's goal in an exciting way. At first,
some of his key recruits refused to work on the machine, because they saw it merely as a variation of the existing 16-bit
model with which it had to be compatible—"a bag on the side
of the Eclipse," in the derogatory jargon of computer experts.
West characteristically responded with "his little grin," saying,
"It's more than that—we're really gonna build this fucker and
it's gonna be fast as greased lightning. We're gonna do it by
April." Though not exactly an elegant statement, West's goal
was challenging and formulated in an effective way that
directly tapped the key motivations of his subordinates.

Words do make a difference, and the way a goal is stated
and then reinforced in frequent references has great impact.
You do not have to be a gifted orator who can enthrall an au-
dience, but you must be able to talk about your unit's work
vividly and about its goal convincingly. Surprisingly, the ability
to convey enthusiam does not seem to be a natural managerial
skill—or has been stamped out by organizational routine.

In our work with managers we have been struck by the
blandness with which so many leaders convey their departmental goal. We have helped participants in our training programs improve their ability to gain subordinate commitment
by having each one role-play a meeting with a recent hire.
The boss's assignment is to convey the unit's overarching goal
in a way that inspires the new employee and wins commitment.

Each participant works with several others to think through
a possible goal statement for the real back-home department.
Then, one at a time, each manager talks to another participant, who plays the role of new employee. We instruct the
manager to "use this opportunity to be enthusiastic and con-
vincing about your (newly formulated) overarching goal." We
then videotape the manager's presentation.

After everybody has made a presentation, we play back the
tapes and observe. The results have a dismal similarity; the
manager's presentations of goal statements are almost universally unexciting. Managers have delivered their messages in a

flat, colorless way, or they have buried the core message in a
mound of trivia. After a few practice rounds, however, and after some coaching from fellow participants, most managers
find ways to generate enthusiasm about their goal.

Are the difficulties these managers experience due to the
emphasis on rationality held by professional organizations or to
the belief that enthusiasm is somehow immature? Perhaps
managerial sobriety is a carryover from Western heroic images, where taciturn understatement is the strongest emotion
allowed. Action, not fancy words, is the hallmark of our cultural heroes; the picture of John Wayne punching out a villain is
apparently worth a thousand sissified words. Whatever the
cause, managers who bemoan the lack of subordinate commitment are often those who have difficulty showing their own
enthusiasm to the department.

Peters and Waterman (1982) found that enthusiastic repetition of the goal, in many settings, was an important tool for
chief executive officers who wished to gain organizational
commitment to the superordinate goal. But even the best-de-
livered inspirational speeches have to be accompanied by actions that firmly plant the concept in the department's
operations. For example, the goal can be reinforced every
time an important decision is to be made by questioning how
the solutions being discussed are consistent with the goal. The
goal is thus seen as an action standard, not just pretty words.
Departmental policies and practices can be examined to insure
that they are consonant with the goal; espousing a goal of quality, for example, remains rhetorical if promotion policies are
based on friendship or seniority. In this case, aligning practices
with the department goal demands the introduction of a new,
more open procedure for promotions.

To get maximum leverage from new actions, situations
should be sought that would provide decisions that had symbolic value to demonstrate the centrality of the overarching
goal. This could mean looking for subordinate actions that reflect the goal and giving public supporting to them, dramatically shifting the reward system to reflect new priorities,
confronting a key resister who has consistently blocked prog-

ress, or finding some other way to signify in action that it is no longer business as usual.

The importance of the goal will be further demonstrated if it is visibly used to guide a decision under crisis conditions. When things are going well and resources are ample, it is relatively easy to espouse and enact a lofty goal. But the point will be more convincingly made when that goal is firmly maintained in problem times. For example, it is more difficult, but more persuasive, to hold fast to a goal of attention to customer service when a department is faced with a reduction in force. Yet if the first departmental cut eliminates the extended service hours that were to ease customer access, while the departmental travel budget remains intact, goal credibility is lost. Adverse conditions can provide the perfect challenge to move people out of their routines. The bank branch manager mentioned earlier used adversity in such a way to turn around low morale and productivity.

In addition to selling the goal and using it for crisis decision making, you can work to build norms and standards that are consistent with it. For instance, if the goal focuses on quality, then quality must guide personnel decisions, the way meetings are run, how the offices are furnished, what people wear, the thoroughness and formatting of reports, and everything else. When a large automobile manufacturer decided to stress quality, the head of an assembly plant rejected a shipment of interior trim from a feeder plant because the color didn't match the model's metal interior color. On closer inspection, feeder plant personnel discovered that the problem was "only" that plastic takes the identical dye differently from metal. To their astonishment, the assembly plant manager still refused to assemble the desperately needed automobiles until the problem was corrected. Although his was an expensive—and gutsy—decision, everyone in his organization and in his suppliers' organizations got the message that quality was indeed important.

The building of an environment that reflects and reinforces the overarching goal does not always require such dramatic moves, although drama is helpful to broadcast intentions widely. Organizational culture is also built in countless small ways, on a daily basis. The manager's interactions with others—interested in problems or disinterested, caring or not, thoughtful or not, honest or not, helpful or not—all help establish the department's norms about what is valued and how things are done. When these interactions are consistent with the overarching goal, the goal is reinforced, intermeshed with operations.

You can also work to implement and reinforce the overarching goal by linking it to individual work tasks as they are assigned. Subordinates will place more value on their work if they see its relationship with larger departmental and organizational goals. Yet too frequently managers assume that such relationships are obvious and don't bother to elucidate the connections, or worse, they fall into the trap of believing that subordinates should just carry out orders without having to know how their parts fit into the larger structure. Even the organization itself can be severely damaged by such a situation.

The computer operators in the data processing department of a large insurance firm were told to do an analysis of premium and claims payment at the end of each day. The task was unpleasant, because of frequent errors in the submitted data that required correction. Completing the run often held the operators past closing time. Periodically, the operators would delay finishing the computer run until the next morning, which brought admonitions from management and excuses from the computer operators. During one of these failures the exasperated manager said, "Don't you realize how crucial this run is?" An operator replied, "Not really. You only told us that it was important and to do the job."

The operators had never been told that the information not only reported the company's cash flow position, but was used the next morning as the basis for short-term investments. Not having that information, even periodically, had resulted in the company's losing millions of dollars of investment potential over the years.

Thus, the importance of the task can be forcefully underlined by the act of establishing linkages between individual tasks and the larger departmental purpose. You may discover weak linkages, which can be strengthened by utilizing an overarching goal in redefining and enlarging individual tasks. If the data processing department described above had had as a component of its overarching goal the development of user sophistication around data processing, the task of the computer operators would not have been perceived as merely responding to client requests. The task would have included service and instructional components, and both company and operators would have tangibly benefited. The effects of an overarching goal are not hype or public relations; the goal often leads to the modifying of work assignments or departmental procedures, which in turn lead to increased work challenge and task significance. The resulting altered work performance is a concrete demonstration of the centrality of the goal and increases the likelihood of goal acceptance.

In many of these initiating situations, it is the Developer alone who will make the connections between day-to-day actions and the overarching goal. But even when the goal is determined by you and not by group consensus, more direct subordinate involvement in deciding *how* the goal is to be implemented is relatively easy to obtain. In effect, the Developer can say, "Given that this is our goal, what do we need to do to make sure it is fully integrated into our department?" A great deal of latitude can be given to subordinates in determining implementation steps. As time passes and subordinates see that the goal has actual impact, they will begin to apply the goal on their own initiative (as was the case in Deborah Linke's unit).

Finally, it is important that you let subordinates in on your own feelings about the goal, its impact on your own effectiveness and career. Operating only in a selling mode, focusing only on what adherence to the goal will do for the subordinate, may act as a barrier to subordinate commitment. Subordinates will inevitably wonder about "what's in it for the boss," whether or not they ask, so it might as well be dealt with openly. You can talk about your own commitment to the department, what hopes you have for recognition when excellence is achieved, your aspirations within the organization, and even about your likely time horizons for staying in the department.

This kind of openness, though difficult for many managers, can not only help foster commitment to the overarching goal, but it will also accelerate the kind of reciprocal honesty that is needed for the shared-responsibility team. Although we do not advocate that managers go around spilling their guts about everything all the time, it is helpful to work toward the time when all important and relevant feelings can be mutually expressed and acknowledged.

To summarize, for the overarching goal to assume a central part in the department, all elements have to be congruent. You must not only talk convincingly about the goal, your own behavior must embody the goal. The goal has to be evoked not only in times of plenty but in times of want, and it has to be used for major decisions as well as minor. This degree of congruency is both the goal's power and the source of problems. All parts build on and reinforce each other, but definite limits are placed on superior and subordinate behavior. Although the limits set by a good overarching goal are legitimate, they nevertheless are constraints and can be perceived as confining.

POTENTIAL DIFFICULTIES WITH THE CONCEPT OF AN OVERARCHING GOAL

Can All Departments Have an Overarching Goal?

Although all departments have purpose and can have a mission statement, it is probably not possible for every department to have an exciting, inspirational, overarching goal. Remember that the criteria for such a goal include that it be challenging and have a larger significance. Some departments necessarily perform work that is so routine and so mundane that it could not possibly excite most people. Perhaps the industry has the cynical motive of taking advantage of particular conditions or customer gullibility. Or the top management may be interested only in activities that milk the corporation's assets, which render the productive work of departments meaningless, as was true in a company described by Cohen, Gadon, and Miaoulis (1976). For a leader to try to espouse an exciting and challenging overarching goal under any of these those conditions would be seen as a sham maneuver. Similarly, if top management has long accepted a manufacturing organization that turns out shoddy work, a service operation that consistently delivers less than it promises, or a sales group that can never deliver on time, subsequent development of a meaningful overarching goal is very difficult.

Nevertheless, we have almost never had a participant in our workshops who was unable to come up with at least a modestly challenging goal for his or her unit. Goal potential is probably more widespread than may be apparent at first.

Although we believe that most departments can have a useful overarching goal, many different variables determine how easy a goal is to develop. In some situations the goal is obvious and needs little leader persuasion to gain its acceptance. An example is the engineering modeling department of a large organization that works on America's space program. The ability of that department to respond quickly and accurately to scientists' requests for simulation tests is crucial to the success not only of that organization but to the entire space effort. On the other hand, for many other organizations, the relationship between individual work and larger significance is more obscure; greater leader effort is needed to make the connection.

We have seen many situations that would have been fertile grounds for the formulation and invocation of an overarching goal, but leadership was unable or unwilling to carry through such development. The production department of a major pharmaceutical company, for example, treated employees as extensions of the pill-forming equipment and never helped the employees see themselves as in the business of saving lives. The rehabilitation department of a major teaching hospital suffered from weak leadership and low status relative to other departments; no one helped its members think about the larger significance of the restorative work that built on the brilliant efforts of the higher status surgeons and radiologists. As a result, department members were depressed, low in energy, and unable to combine efforts or make a collective case for a reasonable share of the hospital's scarce resources.

These examples suggest failure of leadership imagination, not an inherent misfit between the department and an inspirational overarching goal. Of course, not all jobs or department work is easily placed in a wider context, but there is often more potential than managers realize. Even when top management pays little attention to wider purposes, a department head can often choose a challenging goal.

How Long Does It Take to Identify and Gain Commitment to a Workable Overarching Goal?

There is no fixed time for goal development, although a year is probably a closer estimate than a few months. The time needed depends in part on the extent to which an obvious connection exists between tasks and objective importance as well as the extent to which the goal is inherently exciting and challenging. The time varies as the level of leader commitment and effort to implement the goal. The strength of member resistance caused by the distance of the goal from member needs and the resultant necessary changes in orientation also affects the schedule of goal development. Peters and Waterman (1982) estimate that getting an entire large organization to accept a new superordinate goal takes five to ten years. Much less time, probably months, not years, is required, of course, to gain acceptance of one department's overarching goal. Fewer people are involved and the degree of change is likely to be less fundamental.

There is an important distinction between a goal's complete acceptance by most of the members in their day-to-day work and the impact of such a goal on the department. The former event may take a year's time, but the latter effect can occur almost immediately. If you fully believe in the goal, it will certainly affect your own behavior and that of others in your presence. Finally, we want to reiterate a previous point: One of the best ways to gain acceptance of the goal is to use it, which demonstrates both its value and your personal commitment to it.

How Easy Is It to Change an Overarching Goal Once It Is in Place? What Happens When Technology, Task, or External Conditions Necessitate a Shift?

Unfortunately, not much information exists on the circumstances of changing an established overarching goal. Our experience suggests that it is possible for the manager who created an overarching goal to modify it, but probably not fundamentally change it. Remember that a criterion for the goal is that it receive the manager's personal commitment. Because such commitment is difficult to build, it is equally difficult to abandon in a shift to a new objective. Although a goal certainly can be modified—changed somewhat in form and emphasis—even modified it remains the same basic goal. For example, if the overarching goal of a sales department had been to provide information and instruction to the customer so that the product could exactly fit their needs, it would subsequently be possible to modify the goal to emphasize semicustomized product development. But goal development would be seriously disrupted if the company decided to change it's focus to the provision of a limited range of low-cost products.

Support for this notion is found in work by Pfeffer (1983), who argues that for organizations within a turbulent, changing business environment there is a better match between the organization's goals and the environmental requirements when there are also relatively frequent changes of leadership. Perhaps even when the leader has recognized the need for change and has overcome his or her own resistance against giving up something accomplished with great effort, subordinates may be reluctant to credit such a change in course. When the goal has to be changed fundamentally, it is probably expedient for the previous leader to move on and a new leader to come in.

Leadership transfer may not be a severe penalty for change. Even in rapidly changing situations, most change is evolutionary rather than revolutionary, and in most organizations successful managers are expected to move. Indeed, the problem in many companies is not too slow a change in management but too rapid a change, as managers are rotated in and out in 18-month cycles—just long enough to stir things up but not to work out significant, stabilized operations. The personnel in more innovative companies in Kanter's (1983) research had high career mobility, but generally two to three years between moves.

How Compatible Are the Skills Needed by the Leader to Develop an Overarching Goal and the Skills Then to Gain Subordinates' Commitment to the Goal?

The question of complementary leadership skills for both steps of goal development is critical to the success of an overarching goal. Unfortunately, the set of skills needed to formulate a goal (that of being able to sense what would excite others) and the set needed to gain commitment (that of being persuasive) are often seen as contradictory. The former effort requires reflective behavior, taking in more than is given out and being highly responsive to others. The latter behavior, on the other hand, is frequently perceived as being more closed to outside influence and more certain of self-"rightness," so that the views and needs of others are ignored—at its extreme, the image of the hail-fellow-well-met salesperson whose enthusiasm overwhelms all opposition.

If both sets of skills are important, but by nature incompatible, how reasonable is it to expect that more than a few managers can successfully be ambidextrous with them? If the number is few, isn't doubt cast on the validity of this approach to managing complex organizations?

We agree that not many leaders are highly proficient in both skill areas, although the salesperson image may be more stereotype than reality. The highly successful salesperson probably succeeds by determining the customers' needs and then demonstrating the product's relevance. But even if few fully developed managers exist who fit the profile of our Developer model, we have observed that each set of skills can be learned. There are a multitude of training programs that develop listening skills.

Furthermore, we have found that in a relatively short time managers are able to learn how to redefine departmental purposes and missions in ways that produce exciting and challenging overarching goals. In our training exercise, when we ask managers to state the overarching goal to a new subordinate and few can generate enthusiasm on the first try—only a little coaching leads to great improvement. The problem seems to have been that managers had never conceived of the need for such goal statements, not that they were incapable of formulating them with some practice.

Goal formulation skills are more easily seen as teachable and learnable. What about the more persuasive, inspirational set of skills—can managers really learn charisma? We believe that almost any manager can learn the functional equivalent of charisma—inspiring high commitment—even if the manager does not become a magnetic personality. We are not saying that we can infuse all or even most managers with great oratorical powers, crowd-excitement talents, or personal charisma. But these extreme gifts are not necessary for the people we are talking about. Remember, we are focusing on middle and upper-middle managers who need to excite their departments —we are not talking about leaders who need to electrify a nation. The aim of the manager is not personally to be the source of excitement (that is, by producing adoration and commitment to oneself), but to attribute excitement to the departmental task. To the extent that the leader has done the job of defining an exciting goal, the goal will hold the power to excite. The goal should be based on untapped needs of the subordinates and should show how they can be larger than themselves by buying into it. If well formulated, the goal itself will carry a great deal of the excitement.

But the goal, no matter how well defined, still needs a con-
veyer who can represent the excitement in the message. We
have found in working with managers that they can learn how
to be truly enthusiastic about their goal and to convey their
enthusiasm. Even those who initially appear quite bland—
those whom the organization has made routine and bureaucratic—can learn to express effectively their personal commitment to the goal. With some coaching and practice, the
manager becomes able to show involvement and commitment,
without enormous effort and without recourse to a stereotypi-
cal rah-rah style. Each manager finds that he or she can generate excitement and commitment to an overarching goal in a
personally comfortable style, consistent with his or her usual
communication style. Some are fervent, some quietly intense,
some witty and charming, while others are straightforward or
blunt. Each can be effective.

As mentioned earlier, it's far easier to sell a product you
personally believe in. For a departmental overarching goal to
be accepted by subordinates as a central standard, you must
be able to sell it through words and actions. You need to be
able, at public occasions, during staff meetings, while meeting
one-to-one, to convey the importance of the goal and your
personal commitment to it. Enthusiasm, repetition, and brute
attention can outperform flashy delivery and slickness.

If the Concept of an Overarching Goal Is So Valuable and Possible for Most Departments, Why Isn't Its Use Widespread?

Only part of the reason for the underapplication of the concept of an overarching goal is that it is new. It is important to
realize that this concept goes counter to the thrust of most
management theory of the last 30 years. Past emphasis was on
logical rationality, planning out all contingencies, and reducing
the challenge in work (Pascale and Athos, 1981). The notion of
a manager having the responsibility to inspire fell more into
the domain of political leaders than organizational managers.

Furthermore, business was on the defensive throughout the 1960s and 1970s. Pollution concerns, the Vietnam war effort, discrimination policies, planned obsolescence, and other pressures created a business climate in which gung-ho enthusiasm seemed out of place, if not frankly misguided. And the heroic model didn't allow for much fancy talk.

But the answer must also be that developing skills to articulate well and to inspire subordinates is a difficult endeavor, not only because of the divergent efforts involved but also because of the demands it makes on the person. The Developer has to be able to "walk the talk"—that is, to be able to express the goal in all of his or her actions. If the overarching vision involves quality work, then the leader can't personally perform at a mediocre level. A manager can't stress performance and hire only friends, emphasize the importance of development and be defensive when receiving personal feedback. A department head can't say that people should take on challenging tasks and then reserve for personal use the pleasurable assignments.

Our basic observation about why so few departments have developed meaningful overarching goals is that many managers balk at taking on the added personal responsibility that living up to a goal requires. Yet we have seen the same longings in managers that we have noted in their subordinates: for challenge, something to believe in, significance. The creation of an overarching goal and the commitment to excellence make it possible for middle managers to take the initiative, to make their own work as meaningful as they would like.

INTRODUCTION

The manager is rare who does not claim a belief in developing subordinates. Many managers try to develop by giving subordinates challenging assignments or by sending them away for training. Technicians and Conductors also want productive subordinates, but their tactics are likely to be sink or swim: They throw their subordinates into turbulent waters and watch to see which ones manage to survive. The assumption is that the best, more-or-less "developed," subordinates surface, like cream rising to the top. The subordinates who do not function well in this testing are, at best, considered barely salvageable. Other managers would claim that development is a luxury they can't afford—there isn't enough time, or the dangers of subordinate failure are too great. Ironically, a certain amount of development takes place in the departments of heroic managers simply because these bosses are too busy to interfere in subordinates' activities, which permits the inadvertent option for the kind of development that comes from self-directed venturing into difficult areas.

The Developer must sweep away these tentative views of development in order to tap the full potential of a department. To achieve excellence, development must be continuous and intentional, a core activity of managing that serves both as a motivational spur to performance and an aid to making the shared-responsibility team effective. As the Developer works with each subordinate to improve the skills needed for making the best contribution to managing the total unit, the team's capacities increase. In turn, the participation of each subordinate as a team member creates situations that require sophisticated skills, thereby revealing developmental needs, allowing practice of the skills, and providing multiple potential sources of feedback about each member's performance. This cyclical interplay continuously operates to strengthen the whole.

The goal of development, for all subordinates, is not just the improvement of their technical skills. An equally vital objective is to develop those managerial, interpersonal, and problem-solving skills that they need to share effectively the responsibility for managing the unit. This emphasis on inter-personal and managerial growth does not preclude the kind of development that good Technicians and Conductors would elect. General coaching, assignment of challenging new tasks that stretch the subordinate's capacities, and constructive criticism can be helpful and welcomed by subordinates. But excellence is most fostered by increasing the subordinate's abilities to share in managing at the departmental level, while at the same time meeting the subordinate's need for challenge and growth. This coordinated idea of development is crucial in most units, since few managers have the luxury of being able to select all those under them, and few subordinates are likely to be completely ready to be full-blown partners in this expanded responsibility. Some will be expert enough in the specialty of the unit but poor team players, others will be extremely cooperative but unwilling to make tough decisions, while some will be so hard-nosed that they drive their peers into defensiveness. The most demanding facet of the Developer's role is building this collection of subordinates while getting the necessary tasks accomplished.

Such coordinated development is best accomplished through the day-to-day interactions on the job, and the power of the Manager-as-Developer approach is its integration: Fulfilling the task and developing subordinates aren't incompatible needs that require elaborate trade-offs. Instead, they often find simultaneous achievement. The manager can seek congruence, and further development, in a number of ways.

First, seeing what areas the employee has difficulty with when asked to share in overall responsibility gives the superior clues about how to customize development so that the type of tasks and amount and kind of assistance will be most useful. This observing can be augmented by individual discussions, which allow the supervisor to know each subordinate's areas of interest, undeveloped potentials, and career aspirations. Tasks are assigned not just to broaden the subordinate's technical capabilities, but managerial strengths as well. The choice of tasks a subordinate requests can give the manager valuable insights. Does the subordinate reach far beyond her grasp? Are his aspirations set too low? When these questions are used for discussion, more learning occurs, on the part of subordinates and manager.

Managers are frequently concerned about giving subordinates new tasks that will also be learning opportunities; they worry that excellence may be jeopardized. "After all, shouldn't particularly the important jobs go to the ones who can do them best?" This orientation assumes a direct relationship between how skilled an individual is and how well the task will be accomplished—that is, as illustrated in Figure 5-1, that the further away the subordinate moves from known skills, the lower the performance. The presumption of a simple, linear relationship, however, is false. It ignores the impact of motivation on performance. Research on achievement and motivation has demonstrated that most individuals (especially in the kinds of jobs we have been discussing) seek tasks that are possible but still challenging. (Only persons with low needs for achievement want the easy tasks they know they can solve 100% of the time.) Thus, Figure 5-2 is a more accurate representation of the relationship between prior knowledge and performance; there is no warrant for a trade-off between excellence and learning. But we would even go a step further in this analysis: By proper coaching, assistance, and support, you can move the peak of this curvilinear relationship even farther to the right on the subordinate ability scale. That is why a sink-or-swim concept—which no successful athletic coach would use—is so wasteful of subordinate talent. Of course, a manager must take care that the assistance isn't so excessive

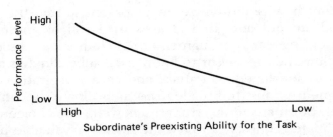

Figure 5-1   Presumed relationship between prior knowledge and performance.

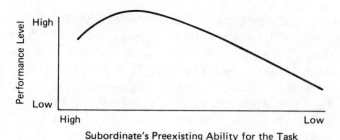

Figure 5-2 The accurate relationship between prior knowledge and performance.

that it removes the motivation of the job challenge (thus pushing the individual to the left side of the performance peak). Judgment and timing are required.

Full development obviously involves not only *what* has to be done but the *way* in which the subordinate goes about the task. Coaching and assistance can be very useful in pointing out new alternatives, political as well as technical factors, interaction style, and the like. Managers are often hesitant about allowing subordinates to take on new and challenging assignments, fearing *how* the tasks will be carried out. Is Ned's inability to gain the cooperation of his counterparts in other departments keeping you from giving him more responsibility? This question should be brought up, as you talk with him about job assignments, performance on current tasks, or a specific incident you have observed. Is Martha's timidity in setting priorities with demanding peers causing you to hesitate about allowing her autonomy? You can talk with her ahead of time and then discuss it at a team meeting including her and her peers. Is Michael's inability to see political ramifications of the technically correct points he makes reducing your ability to trust him as a departmental representative at important meetings? Before the next such meeting, discuss with him both the specific sensitivities of attendees and his general need to learn to think organizationally in order to advance beyond his present level.

Countless opportunities for helping subordinates learn are ignored by managers. For example, the management group of an accounting firm planned development by having some of the junior managers make presentations at their yearly planning retreat. But afterward, all they said was "Nice job" or "Well done." These comments were honest and appreciated by the subordinates, but consider how much more could have been learned if one of the senior managers had sat down with each presenter and specifically pointed out the effective and not-so-effective parts of the presentation. Most managers also forget that sharing what they know and explaining why they do what they do can be valuable for younger subordinates. Deborah Linke's success owed much to her commitment to seize development opportunities. Not only did she invite subordinates to her external meetings, but she debriefed each meeting afterwards.

Even the nature of the superior–subordinate relationship (and problems within it) can be used for development. Does Jo's tendency to express so much confidence about being able to handle a job make you doubt her judgment? Does Sam's constant focus on problems make you want to avoid him? Both Jo and Sam could greatly benefit from your feedback. Even Howie's defensiveness when you comment about areas he needs to work on can be the subject of a developmental talk. Pointing out how he responds to constructive criticism with denials (including his excusing away of the feedback you are now giving) may be the most important learning he has gained all year.

For the Manager-as-Developer, problems are potentials. What Manager-Technicians see in subordinates as fixed traits that limit effectiveness, or that Conductors view as weaknesses to be maneuvered around through compensating structures or personal finesse, Developers see as *opportunities* for growth. The need to utilize subordinate skills as part of the shared-responsibility team makes any incident or daily event an occasion to show the subordinate how to be more effective. The leader's comments can never fall to a picky or personally punitive level. Instead, the goal of all feedback is to make the subordinate as competent as possible.

The Developer is constantly thinking about how to interact with subordinates in ways that get the immediate problem

solved and help them learn how to deal with subsequent difficulties. Whether by questioning, direct teaching, sharing information and experience, giving advice, extracting lessons,
giving interpersonal feedback, or just keeping quiet while the
subordinate works it out alone, the Developer uses naturally
arising interactions to foster learning. It comes as no surprise
that almost universally subordinates also strongly desire such
coaching and feedback. The responses to our leadership style
questionnaire (filled out by the subordinates of the managers
who attend our workshops) consistently show the largest dis-
crepancies between what the managers do and what their subordinates want on the following three questions: "Has your
boss helped you to plan your career opportunities?" "Does
your boss give you timely and honest feedback on how well
you are performing?" and "Does your boss coach you in ways
that help you perform better?"

The thrust of our discussion thus far derives from two crucial assumptions. First, most subordinates want to learn, grow,
and take on the added responsibilities that the Developer style
demands, and second, most subordinates can develop. Although we believe that both assumptions are valid, certain
conditions affect these assumptions.

Increased responsibility and job challenge are motivating for
most subordinates in contemporary organizations, but it is neither automatic that all subordinates will want to make the effort to learn the requisite skills, nor guaranteed that they will
be committed to learn the particular skills needed by the unit.
The Developer must therefore work on another kind of development—of subordinate commitment to contribute to the
unit's overarching goal. The Developer reinforces the general
importance of the goal, but also helps each subordinate see
how his or her job, and participation in managing the unit,
aids in accomplishing the goal and in the person's career development. Subordinates need to be shown what's in it for
them at the same time that they are making contributions to
unit excellence.

Some subordinates may be incapable of such synthesis. Their
aspirations may be too far askew from what the organization

can offer, or they may be too committed to a specialist role to be willing to learn to think in a broad managerial way. Ultimately, such subordinates must leave the unit or be fenced off from mainstream activities. The recruiting specialist in a small personnel department, for example, who wanted to do only training and organization development work, was extremely frustrated when her manager could not promise that she would be asked to work only on those kinds of activities. The company wasn't large enough to have a full-time internal consultant. The boss was also frustrated, because he agreed that she was talented at her specialty and he did want to help her grow, but enough of the right kinds of assignments were not available. He knew she would leave the company (which she did), but he realized that employee interests and organizational needs cannot always be matched. After thorough efforts to make a match have failed, the manager at least has precisely identified the subordinate's limits.

Since the second assumption of the Developer model concerns learning capacity, which refers to behavioral rather than personality change, we are optimistic about how much people can learn when conditions are right. For every person fulfilling the Peter Principle—that in a hierarchy every person tends to rise to his or her level of incompetence—we see dozens more whose abilities are significantly underused. We do acknowledge, however, that at times a job expands beyond the individual's capacities to learn. This situation often occurs in high-growth companies, where rapid growth thrusts people upward before they have time to learn the basics. Three or four such promotions can leave some people on limbs so unstable that they can neither stand nor retreat. Sometimes ability is present but inexplicably motivation is not; some few people are afraid or unwilling to learn.

Nevertheless, an advantage of a developmental approach is that the same procedures that help most subordinates expand their competencies reveal those who cannot or will not grow. Interactions that assume developmental capacities also prevent subordinates from being able to hide behind past performance or to feel that they are being treated capriciously or punitively. It becomes clear who should move elsewhere, as described in an actual case later in the chapter. On-the-job continuous development works properly when there is a good working relationship between the superior and the subordinate, open to mutual communication and influence.

DEVELOPMENT DEMANDS DIRECT COMMUNICATION

Subordinates are reticent to disclose personal goals and aspirations if they are uncertain of the boss's receptivity. They will refrain from expressing concerns about their ability to do the job or from specifying personal learning needs, if they fear that the supervisor will use such information against them. They will not disagree with the boss's inappropriate suggestions if they fear they will be punished in return. Without adequate two-way communication, any actions taken by the superior that are counter to the subordinate's needs (even with the boss's best intentions) may be silently accepted by the subordinate but sabotaged in the execution.

An open superior–subordinate relationship increases the communication flow downward as well. A major block to development is the common reticence of superiors to give feedback on interpersonal and managerial issues, especially to their least effective subordinates. When the relationship is open, managers feel freer to let the subordinate know when improvement is needed.

If the relationship is not open, the superior's annoyance about a subordinate's way of operating is exactly what keeps the superior from sharing overall responsibility, from assigning the most challenging tasks, from providing the personal reassurance, and from wanting to work closely with the subordinate in coaching and assistance.

Most managers are reluctant to comment on ineffective or inappropriate interpersonal behavior. But these areas are often crucial for professional task success. This hesitancy is doubly felt when there is a poor relationship between the two. Then the manager is likely to say, "I don't have the kind of relationship with Brad that would let me comment on this" or "Sarah would just get too defensive if I mentioned these problems."

Too few managers have any experience in how to confront others effectively; generally they can more easily give feedback on inadequate task performance than on issues dealing with another's personal style. As one manager described his reluctance to tell a colleague that his passivity made it tempting to walk all over him, "I know I should talk to him, and I know what to say, but I don't like to talk about these things." Even when the boss does gather up the courage to raise an issue about a subordinate's interpersonal style, he either does it so indirectly and with so much sugarcoating that the message doesn't get through or with such anger and rejection that walls of defensiveness are thrown up. We frequently talk with subordinates who do not realize that the boss has tried to criticize them, even though the boss claims to have "let them have it right between the eyes." Alternatively, sometimes the subordinate is so crushed that he or she can't even remember exactly what was said.

We saw this scenario with a vice president of data processing at a large insurance company. He had repeatedly missed the subtle hints his boss had given him about his overbearing style and his habit of carrying on arguments for too long. He was stunned when he was bypassed for promotion. When he insisted on knowing why someone else had been selected over him, his boss unloaded so heavily that the words spoken could not even be recalled by the vice president the next day.

Many on-going learning opportunities have been missed because superiors didn't know how to give feedback in a useful way. When lack of skill for constructive feedback is compounded by the perception that the superior–subordinate relationship is not strong enough to withstand negative comments, it is small wonder that so little real development occurs. As we show later in this chapter, the skill of giving effective feedback can be learned, as can the skills of building more robust and effective working relationships even with very difficult subordinates.

DEVELOPMENT DEMANDS MUTUAL INFLUENCE

Open upward communication must have some force behind it. Subordinate development requires that the employee be able to influence the boss as well as the other way around. Balanced solutions are possible only when both parties can openly negotiate with each other.

A number of tough questions need balanced answers. Is sharing in departmental responsibility really helping the subordinate develop desired skills and career opportunities, or is it only postponing decisions the boss should be addressing? Are the tasks appropriately challenging, or do they push the subordinate beyond reasonable capacity? Is the boss providing adequate assistance, or overdirecting? These kinds of questions demand resolution that is balanced between superior direction and subordinate autonomy. It is all too easy to cross over the line from helping subordinates to helping the hell out of them!

In all situations it is mistaken to expect the superior to play god and assume total responsibility for an appropriate resolution. Subordinates best know their own interests and career aspirations, even if they may not always be able to articulate them fully. It is the subordinate who knows when enough direction has been provided and when more information is needed. Subordinates usually best know their own weaknesses and needs for learning. When subordinates trust the boss, they can make important contributions to shaping their own development and aid the boss in discussing sensitive areas.

How to give subordinates what they want while gaining their full commitment to the unit and participation in managing must be mutually negotiated between the superior and each subordinate. But such negotiations are shams if the subordinate has little power to disagree and argue back. Conversely, lopsided negotiations in which the Developer cannot exercise strong influence are also dangerous. The superior–subordinate relationship must be solid enough for each to push on the other without the exchange deteriorating into "Do it because I said so" or "Try to make me." An effective relationship is based on high mutual respect, trust, and concern.

THE NEED FOR EFFECTIVE RELATIONSHIPS
WITH ALL SUBORDINATES

Few would argue with the importance of feedback to subordinates on their interpersonal and managerial style. Life would be easier if managers could simply tell subordinates when they monopolize meetings, ram their ideas down others' throats, don't listen to other people's points, talk around the subject, or give up too easily when faced with disagreement. The problem is that it is easier to criticize those subordinates who least need it. But the Manager-as-Developer has to be able to make these kinds of comments to all members of the team. It is impossible for a unit to reach excellence using a two-tier system—an inner group the leader trusts enough to be open with and an outer group that is treated with benign neglect.

Managers have the most difficulty being open with those subordinates who would normally be relegated to the outer circle. The same interpersonal problems a manager displays in any dealings will be greatly emphasized in relationships with least-favored subordinates. Being disapproving of what the subordinates do, the superior keeps them at arm's length. Such distance prevents mutual knowledge and understanding, trust and concern cannot develop, and no learning can take place about how to influence one another. The more the boss avoids the subordinate, the harder it is for the boss to have a positive impact, and vice versa. Just as those who like and feel comfortable with each other spend more time together, building positive sentiment and expanding potential mutual impact, those who are uncomfortable with one another move away, decrease interaction, and lose the opportunity to influence each other.

The need for positive superior–subordinate relationships is clear; the problem is how to form them with those subordinates with whom the manager feels less close, but who generally most need improvement. Interpersonal problems are less likely to occur with subordinates who are close to the boss. They are more trusted, asked for advice, accorded greater influence, and assigned more important and challenging jobs. They already informally share in the managing of the department, or are at least included in the manager's thinking about such matters. Their relationship is secure enough so that they can say almost anything to their superior, including disagreeing with actions taken and decisions made. The superior feels the same freedom and gives feedback naturally when such a subordinate makes a mistake and praise when the subordinate comes through. In these effective relationships, the subordinate gets the information, assistance, and support needed to allow personal growth and development as well as a high level of performance for the unit, and the superior receives valuable information, advice, and support. In the absence of manager–subordinate closeness, interaction decreases, communication distorts, and relationships cool; the result is that existing talents are not fully utilized.

As consultants, we frequently observe the phenomenon of a wide range in the quality of the relationships among boss and subordinates. But when we talk with individual members, we have often discovered that this range of relationships does *not* closely reflect the actual competence levels of the subordinates. We do not find that those with low ability are close to the superior (although at times an insecure boss embraces weak sycophants); more often, people with high ability but irritating styles are pushed away and underused. "Brilliant but impossible" and "competent but defensive" are labels often used to isolate talented subordinates.

Such a situation, besides wasting human resources, causes another problem that prevents excellence from developing. For a Developer to seek to build a team of subordinates who assume many of the key coordination and managerial functions, everybody has to be on the team (or at least all those who have, or are interested in, more than individual contributor roles). For such inclusion to be genuine, the manager has to move from the traditional (distant) stance of informally rank-ordering subordinates and allowing only the best in the inner circle, to including all immediate subordinates as members of the team. The leader cannot ignore differences in ability, but differences should be seen less in a one-dimensional, good–bad, rank-ordering fashion, and more as an array of possibilities, so that different people are valued for different attributes. Complementarity is valued. Most important, despite

differences in subordinate skill and style, relatively little differentiation can exist in the quality of the various working relationships among superior and subordinates. That is, the
superior must build ties of open communication, trust, and
mutual influence with all.

BUILDING EFFECTIVE RELATIONSHIPS WITH DIFFICULT SUBORDINATES

It is one thing to say that open mutual relationships are needed with all subordinates and quite another to actually build
them, especially with those who are least compatible and at-
tractive to the manager. How, then, does one escape this dilemma, where the very behavior about which one wants to
give feedback itself prevents building the kind of relationship
that would make feedback easier and more effective?

We have developed a method of *supportive confrontation*
for building effective mutual relationships with difficult subordinates. The essence of this method is to focus on a way to
bring the other close enough—by learning more about the
other's needs and goals while avoiding negative personality
judgments—so that your feedback can have great impact, yet
not drive the other person away. We picture this as *putting
your arm around the other to pull him/her close enough to hit
hard (with behaviorally specific feedback) in a way that will
improve the relationship (and keep the person close).* Sound
difficult? Yes, but not as difficult as you might imagine. We
will analyze each part of this vivid model and explain what has
to be done at each step. Then some examples of managers using the model to deal with competent but difficult subordinates will make the lesson clear.

Put Your Arm around the Subordinate and Draw That Person Close

Just as a boxer cannot land a solid punch while backing away,
a manager cannot directly influence another's behavior from a
distance. For one thing, a distant manager will not have the

information that is necessary to develop an influential approach, will not know the other's concerns (what keeps the person performing below capability), aspirations, and interests. Furthermore, being "distant" frequently implies an adversarial relationship (which is how the boss is most likely to feel about such a troublesome subordinate).

People are likely to resist influence from anyone they do not feel is on their side. Thus, "by putting your arm around and drawing close," we are *not* referring to making sugar-coated negative comments. Instead, we are suggesting a process that enables the superior authentically to get to know and understand the subordinate. This process moves the leader from a rejecting position to a role in support of the employee's development not of the negative behavior.

How does a boss who is already locked into negative, rejecting feelings about the subordinate escape that rigid position? First, the superior must try to see past the subordinate's irritating behavior to the underlying causes. The goal is to *understand* the reasons for the other's behavior, which is not the same as *accepting* the behavior. In most cases, it is easier to be sympathetic when the intentions behind the behavior are known. Deborah Linke's approach (as described in Chapter 3) was to start with the assumption that a subordinate's dysfunctional behavior was due to inappropriate use of a *strength*— applying what would be an appropriate and skillful behavior in one situation to another, inappropriate situation.

A major barrier to achieving close understanding with a difficult person is the human trait of attributing negative personality traits to those whose behavior is not liked (Jones, et al, 1972). When Ted plays politics and keeps his cards close to his vest, the natural tendency is to leap to conclusions about his personality—he's a "sneaky bastard" or a "nasty wheeler-dealer." Once that label is attached to Ted's personality, it is difficult to see how to be close to him. "Once rotten, always rotten" is the way people reject closeness with someone whose behavior isn't up to their standards.

An alternative view of behavior—that, except for those who are pathologically unable to respond to their environment, persons are heavily influenced by the *situations* they find themselves in—casts a much more hopeful light on the prospects of achieving harmony with difficult subordinates. Although some of a person's behavior undoubtedly is caused by unique personality traits, a surprisingly high percentage of behavior can be explained by understanding the situation the person is in. Few of us behave similarly with our boss, spouse, and mother, for example. We adjust our behavior to fit the others around us, their expectations, our roles and responsibilities, the organization's demands, and so forth. In other words, *the situation* is also an important determinant of behavior.

If as a boss you have come to dislike or be annoyed by a subordinate, chances are you have attributed much of his or her "defects" to some kind or personality trait, and you are hooked into assumptions about the subordinate that prevent closeness. Try out this formulation: "Let me assume that this difficult subordinate is really a very competent, well-intentioned person. How then could such a nice, able person behave in such a negative way? What in the situation might be causing this behavior?"

By situation, we mean work setting, not life history or child-rearing practices used by the subordinate's parents. Even though nonwork factors always play a part in anybody's life, and in some cases overwhelm any work issues, we urge examination first of the work situation, because the most potent forces influencing a subordinate's behavior are usually found there. Furthermore, these are the forces a boss can more readily influence. For example, is there anything in the way rewards are allocated that might account for Ted's extreme caution? Does the system reward never making mistakes rather than risk-taking? Is there anything in the nature of what the task requires (Is Ted basically a nasty person or does his job of being responsible for quality control force him to behave in negative, suspicious ways)? Is there anything about the pressures that co-workers, his subordinates, or you have placed on him that could account for part of his behavior? Has a former boss forced him to "anticipate nasty behavior by laying low," so that he has pulled attacks from others which he must now maneuver around?

Such a situational analysis performs two functions. First, it produces a plausible explanation that can exist side-by-side with personality explanations, although we are not saying that personality is never the cause of dissension. Rather, we are suggesting that it is more profitable to check out a situational hypothesis because setting is easier to alter than personality. The second benefit from situational analysis is that it might reveal areas where you don't know the answers or pressures on Ted that you didn't know existed.

Both these outcomes from situational focus are crucial because they raise doubts in a superior's mind, which has the advantage of making it possible to move from an initial rejecting position into a direct data-collection mode, even if it is just to approach the subordinate and seek the information. An elaborate "investigation" is not necessary. Something as simple as dropping in Ted's office might be very productive: "You know, Ted, we aren't working that well together and I would like to do something about it. Furthermore, I realize there's a lot about your situation I don't understand. Could we have lunch together and start to talk?" Such an approach is more likely to move both parties from their entrenched positions than attempts to maneuver around the subordinate or avoid him whenever possible.

In the act of reaching out, you can gain the information needed to understand Ted's world. This world includes the situation that may cause some of the dysfunctional behaviors, as well as Ted's intentions, goals, and aspirations. Reaching out is your first effort to put your arm around Ted and draw him close, but this approach works only if you can truly unhook from having written Ted off. Otherwise, your behavior is manipulative game-playing, which most subordinates will be smart enough to read. Authenticity is a very powerful managerial tool and inauthenticity has great power to damage. If you successfully view the world through Ted's eyes, even briefly, the beginnings of closeness are established.

It is important to define closeness in terms of *understanding*, which is not necessarily intimate liking. The goal is to build an open, effective work relationship, not a close friendship. A boss's exploratory discussions with a subordinate are fact-finding about the intentions behind behavior. Often, the boss finds out that behavior that appeared to be nasty, aggressive, foot-dragging, lazy, or just plain inept was intended by the subordinate to be constructive. Good intentions don't excuse poor performance, but they do provide a mutual basis for dialog. After a boss has learned about the situations to which the subordinate is responding, the groundwork is laid for exploring the subordinate's goals and aspirations, valuable information is gained, the distance between superior and subordinate is decreased, and a setting is established for constructive work.

Above and beyond understanding some particular behavior, closeness is built when a boss can understand more of the general aspirations of the subordinate. Letting the subordinate talk about goals, short- and long-term objectives, hopes and concerns, not only provides useful information but also nurtures greater feelings of closeness. The subordinate is likely to feel closer to a boss who has listened with care, and the boss is likely to feel less distance after the context or background for particular behaviors is understood.

Finally, greater knowledge of the subordinate is useful for other aspects of managing. It increases the Developer's ability to determine what assignments the subordinate would find challenging or otherwise rewarding. The Developer can better judge the degree of autonomy suitable for the subordinate, how much "stretch" is likely to lead to excellent performance, rather than drowning, how to frame requests so that they fit with the subordinate's concerns. When it is useful for the Developer to push hard on the subordinate, the pushing can be personalized and focused. Successful achievement in getting close—a friendly version of knowing the enemy—makes the second step in supportive confrontation more potent.

So the Boss Can Hit the Subordinate Hard with Behaviorally Specific Feedback

"Behaviorally specific feedback" equals comment on the other's behavior and its effect on others in the unit. Two subtle but crucial distinctions must be kept clear. As suggested

above, the *intention* behind a behavior, and the *effect* that behavior has on others must be viewed separately. Mike may intend to be humorous, but others may find him silly. Sarah may
intend to be kind, but others may think her condescending.
Ralph may intend to be persuasive, but others may consider
him overbearing. Willie may intend to be flexible on issues,
but others may perceive him as vacillating.

The second distinction separates who is expert about the *intentions* of behavior and who is expert on its *impact*. There are
always two experts in matters of behavior: the person behaving and the receiver. The person behaving is expert on his or
her *intentions*, but can only guess at how that behavior *affects*
other people. Conversely, others are experts on how a particular behavior affects them, but can only guess about the behav-
er's intentions.

Many attempts at giving feedback, particularly around another's interpersonal style, do not work because the giver of
feedback doesn't stick with this area of expertise (how the behavior affects him), but moves into the other's area of expertise (the intention behind the behavior). If Harry has a
tendency to make negative comments that shoot down others'
proposals, he will be more receptive to feedback which comments on the behavior ("I've noticed a pattern; you frequently
begin discussions of proposals with a string of negative points")
and its impact on the receiver ("That makes me wary of including you in on new ideas"). This approach works better
than feedback that reflects on his *personality* ("You must be a
very negative person") or comments on his *intentions* ("You
are trying to show off how smart you are"). Even if the boss
could get inside the subordinate's mind and soul to confirm
such statements about personality and intentions, such comments are almost never useful and almost invariably arouse defensiveness.

When the superior links "putting an arm around" with "behaviorally specific feedback," the message can be very strong.
If through getting closer, a boss learns the intentions and goals
of a subordinate (through asking, not by guessing or psyching
out), then a boss can intervene helpfully when there is a dis-

crepancy between the subordinate's intentions and the effects on others. For example, if it turns out that Harry's negative comments are intended to be helpful, to save others from traps he has anticipated, the boss could say:

> Harry, that really is too bad. I now see that you intend to be helpful, but your continual focus on the negative aspects of issues makes it hard for me and others to acknowledge your help. Despite your good intentions, people are tuning you out. We aren't listening to you, but it's your own actions that keep you from reaching the goals you want.

If the boss is truly on Harry's side (that is, has an arm around him), alternative behavior will be suggested that better meets Harry's goals:

> I think what you want to do is very important and I really support it, but I think there is a more effective way you could go about it. Why don't you practice looking for three positive responses you could make before criticizing? Or perhaps you could put your criticisms in more constructive form, adding suggestions about how to solve the problems? This approach might make it easier for others to listen to you.

In a Way That Will Improve the Relationship (and Keep the Person Close)

Often, the Developer doesn't have to provide specific solutions; accurate feedback that points out the discrepancy between the *effect* of the behavior on others and the person's *intentions* can in and of itself be very useful.

Most important is that feedback be caring and genuinely aimed at being helpful to the other. If your honest intention is to provide useful information because you want the other to succeed, your choice of words has little significance. Technique is less influential here than genuine desire to understand the other's aspirations and join him or her in the improved performance that will achieve them.

Knowing the other's goals and aspirations and linking improved performance to them is the best way to demonstrate that you are on the other person's side while still being influential. The Developer carefully uses what was learned earlier about the subordinate's aspirations to show how the subordinate's behavior is affecting his or her achievement. Positive feedback shows the subordinate what behaviors are likely to further goals. Although emphasizing the positive is no less necessary than pointing out deficiences, it is easy to overlook the assets of someone who is generally irritating. But even the irritating subordinate does something well and will be more willing to hear about an area needing improvement—after being reinforced for a strong point. Whether to reinforce strength or to highlight deficiencies, feedback works best when the receivers perceive that you want them to succeed in meeting their goals, which makes them willing to provide valuable data on how they have been doing.

The trick, of course, is not just to get the person close and hit hard, but to do it in a way that sustains or builds the relationship. If you punish, or play "gotcha," with a person you have convinced to allow you close, a second chance at an effective relationship is rare. Hitting just to hurt, or to demonstrate your own strength, or to get even for past irritations only results in anger and retaliation. If a subordinate believes your feedback is punitive, he or she will sometimes retaliate overtly, with direct attempts to hurt you back, but the most damaging reaction is indirect. The person may adopt a passive attitude, especially if you hold the higher formal position, following orders literally, but only those orders you remember to make explicit. "Working to rules" is a time-honored way for lower-power people to drive their bosses crazy and to bring the organization to a near standstill.

Alternatively, the subordinate can retaliate by omitting upward information not directly requested, standing by while you commit an error that the subordinate had the knowledge to prevent, or even, in extreme cases, providing misinformation or "accidentally" making costly mistakes. A determinedly negative subordinate can make a boss's life miserable, and if the person is half-clever, can do it without ever risking a formal rebuke.

Such problems are bad enough when the subordinate is doing routine tasks that can be closely monitored, but the subordinates we have been discussing are doing the complex, sophisticated tasks that require their *commitment* to be done well; their hearts must be in these tasks in order to perform even reasonably well. To capture subordinates' hearts, and commitment, you must be credibly concerned about their welfare, their aspirations and values, and their learning, not just your own position. When your genuine concern comes across, you can be very tough without driving a subordinate away. Remember that only the subordinate can be sure of his or her intentions, and cannot be sure of the impact of the behavior. As the person who has been affected, you have data that the subordinate can only get from you. It is an act of real caring to offer observations on the impact—especially the impact on you—so that the subordinate can benefit and learn from your involvement.

EXAMPLES OF SUPPORTIVE CONFRONTATION

How successful managers use supportive confrontation to handle the dual issues of developing a relationship and achieving task objectives illustrate the process we have discussed.

Stan wanted more complex and challenging work than his boss, Karen, had been willing to give him. Karen was hesitant, because Stan had a tendency to feel he could take on anything. Furthermore, Stan's style was to accept only the minimum of assistance before going off on his own. If he was later questioned about how things were going, his response was always positive; Stan would never admit difficulties or approach Karen with problems. His tendency was to hide difficulties that he couldn't solve. After a problem could no longer be hidden, he had a dozen excuses why it wasn't his fault. Although Stan usually came through as required, bits and pieces of this behavioral pattern showed up frequently enough so that he was getting the reputation of being a bit of a con artist. His peers and Karen increasingly doubted Stan's ability to come through on promises.

Karen believed the problem would come to a head soon, because Stan was finishing a project and had let it be known that he wanted the responsibility for an upcoming assignment that would be a major step for him (as well as an important project for the department). Karen raised the issue at their next meeting, as a two-pronged problem. She mentioned the lack of comfort she felt in giving such an important assignment to Stan and the increasing difficulty she saw Stan's style causing in his relationships with co-workers. Since the assignment would require that Stan work closely with her and others, she believed they all had to work out a better relationship.

Stan immediately denied there was any problem, gave excuses for the specific examples that Karen cited, and maintained that everything was fine. After several similar exchanges, Karen pointed out that he was actually enacting the pattern that she had identified. Stan became more resistant and claimed that the problem was hers and reflected her difficulty in delegating. The meeting was at stalemate, and it appeared that no breakthrough could be achieved. But Karen realized that problems, especially important ones, can't always be neatly tied up in one session, so she ended the meeting by saying that before she assigned the project, Stan had to work out a plan of working with her that involved his sharing any job-related concerns, promptly identifying areas where he needed assistance, and coming in to her when problems first develop. Realizing that Stan really desired greater responsibility, Karen made clear to him that she could grant him more responsibility only if he was willing to be forthcoming in talking through plans and issues. She also suggested that he check with other co-workers to see if they saw the situation in the same way she did.

In the following week Stan did talk with a couple of his colleagues, who confirmed what Karen had said. Receiving such general confirmation of Karen's straight message, Stan became more open to finding an alternative way to work with his boss. The two of them then spent a profitable hour negotiating the specifics of their new working relationship.

In this case, the success of Karen's confrontation depended in part on the willingness of her subordinates to be honest with each other. If the norms of the office had been highly protective of co-workers' feelings, her approach could easily have backfired. Effective subordinate development, therefore, may involve changing the norms and practices of the department as well as the specific superior–subordinate relationship.

Karen might also have developed her team so that they could publicly discuss each other's interpersonal styles. Five or

six colleagues pointing out to Stan the problems with his behavior would carry a lot of force. But for such feedback to be
helpful rather than coercive, a mature team has to be developed (a topic we explore in chapter 6).

Not all supportive confrontations require the direct help of
other subordinates.

For example, John, a white manager, dealt with Frank, a recently hired black subordinate, in a way that protected privacy.

In an attempt to discover Frank's interests, goal aspirations, and underdeveloped skills, John had tried on a couple of occasions to have informal
conversations with his new subordinate. Frank had been highly regarded in
the recruitment process, and although pleasant and agreeable, seemed to
his boss to give only "socially acceptable" answers. John had pressed him
about what he wanted to do and where he wanted to go in the organization, and he believed that Frank's responses were textbook-perfect examples of what an employee would think the organization would want to
hear. Rather than taking Frank's responses at face value, John sat down
with him after several of these polite "minuets" and said, "I am not comfortable with our relationship. We can only work well with each other if
we level and tell the other exactly what we think and feel. In your answers,
I think you are telling me what I want to know, not what you really feel."
Frank's eyes narrowed slightly, but he said, "Of course it's a good idea to
level with each other. What makes you think I don't?" John replied, "Because you don't show any feelings, no matter what I say. You retreat behind your glasses into a glassy stare, and even when I criticize, I don't get
anything but politeness from you." The always-present smile faded from
Frank's face and he quietly responded, "Does it make any difference what
I want? I was mainly hired to fill a quota, not for what I could do."
The ensuing discussion, although difficult for both parties, cleared the air
and laid the groundwork for their future relationship. John did not allow ra-
cial difference to serve as a barrier to talking directly to Frank. That
allowed Frank to go beyond the polite distance he used to protect himself
in his token status. They were able to talk about the difficulties for both of
them in working out an honest relationship, where Frank could be perceived as an individual not just a representative of blacks and be expected
to level with his boss. Subsequently, the discussion moved beyond improving their relationship to John's helping Frank develop his interpersonal skills
in dealing with others. Since Frank treated all whites in the same friendly
but distant manner as he had John, John coached him on ways to be more

direct (and therefore more effective) in other relationships within their free-wheeling organization.

People are justifiably guarded about being open in communication. Most have personally experienced, and all have observed, cases where the "messenger is killed for the message." People have learned to exert great self-censorship, often more than is needed. A manager must be aware that cautious subordinates will closely watch and test the superior to see if honest communication is really being called for before they can consider being responsive. A subordinate watches for certain clues to the boss's intent: how the boss responds to opinions that differ, the extent to which subordinate comments are listened to, and the degree of personal feelings the subordinate is encouraged to express. The subordinate will also judge the climate for communication by observing how open the boss actually is. Does the boss only give socially desirable responses, or is there willingness on the superior's part to be open about difficult issues?

But this guessing game (with its accompanying danger of misread clues) can be short-circuited if the manager explicitly states, as John did in the preceding example, that an open relationship is wanted. The manager must follow up by supportively confronting the subordinate until open communication is achieved.

Unfortunately, however, even the best relationship-building efforts may not result in improved performance. Sometimes difficult subordinates are difficult because they are unable or unwilling to function in more satisfactory ways. The process of supportive confrontation, however, can make even termination a cleaner, more mutual process, as reported by a sales manager a few months after attending our leadership workshop.

During the conference when we were discussing difficult subordinates, I realized that I had completely written Mike off and had stopped any effective communication with him. Mike was a 53-year-old sales representative who had been with the company over 12 years. He was well liked by the central office staff but had not met his salesplan for five of the last six years. Furthermore, I was starting to hear complaints about him from some of our clients.

I first tried to put myself in Mike's shoes. What must it be like to be near the end of one's career and starting to go downhill? If I were Mike, how receptive would I be to criticism? I might then be able to understand one of his habitual behaviors that had been particularly annoying to me: his tendency to look only to external factors for his failures, to blame "bad luck," the market, competitors who used unfair tactics, and the like.

Still, before meeting with Mike, I did two things. I considered what would be a reasonable goal for him in six months—what exactly did I expect of him in terms of sales level, generating new business, and the like. Then I thought, "What is it in Mike's behavior that would cause him trouble in making sales? Is it something in his style or is some knowledge lacking?"

I then sat down with Mike and began by acknowledging that our relationship had deteriorated, that I had been dissatisfied with him but hadn't confronted him before, and also that I probably hadn't helped him as much as I could have. Mike immediately blamed me for everything that had gone wrong. It was fortunate that I had thought this out before, because my first response was defensive, to attack back. What helped was that I had already thought about why Mike must be hurting—clearly his pain was greater than anything I was now feeling about his comments.

After Mike had vented his feelings, I repeated that I wanted to change our relationship so that I could be more helpful. In return, we needed to get agreement on some specific goals for Mike. Although I would help him, it would be his responsibility to meet certain objectives. He was to be accountable for them, and if he failed to meet or substantially reach them in six months, he would be placed on probation. We mutually negotiated these goals. When I felt he was setting them too low, I pointed out what other sales personnel would do. We ended up with my original list modified, but in a way both of us could live with.

I then asked Mike what he thought might cause him difficulty in going about reaching his goals. In what areas did he need more training, and were there ways he behaved that caused problems? (I also asked him to discuss what he thought was easy for him—what his especially strong areas were.) As he shared his self-perception, I also shared my perception. I tried to point to specific behaviors at specific times that illustrated the problem areas I saw. At one point, he got very defensive and offered external reasons why the problems I identified were not his fault. I used his response as an illustration of what I was pointing out in his behavior.

In this discussion, we agreed to specific areas in which he could benefit from training. I sent him to a training program to work on his time-management problem. Also, we set up regular meetings (every two weeks) when we would review progress. I said that I was always available if he had a question, but that the initiative was up to him.

Mike did not meet the goals at the end of six months. I placed him on probation, with notice of termination in three months. I again met with him on a regular basis to offer assistance and coaching. Seven days before the end of his probation, Mike came in and said that the fit between him and the job was not right and quit.

As a result of this process, there was minimal reaction by the office staff (who had very much liked Mike). There was neither a decrease in morale nor a rise in paranoia among others. Mike found another job in an area both of us had discussed as being more in line with his skills. Perhaps most gratifying to me, he expressly thanked me for my concern. He is doing well in his new position and is much happier.

The important theme throughout this incident was that the superior was able to become unhooked from a punitive, rejecting position. Also, the relationship became work-focused (what had to be done by when), as well as more supportive. The boss didn't set the subordinate up to fail, but was on his side. Finally, the conclusion didn't find the boss deciding that the subordinate was inadequate or incompetent; rather, the subordinate also realized the poor fit between his talents and what the job required.

Was this process an expensive waste of time—letting nine months pass before the termination of an underperfoming subordinate? Perhaps the answer is yes in this case, but the waste is certain when a problem is written off without any attempts to find a solution. In a department led by a Developer, situations seldom get this bad. The attention to continuous development would have long since forced attention to dealing with Mike. Furthermore, the cost of tolerating deadwood, as often happens under traditional managers, is also high. There were many benefits gained from the nine-month process just described—beyond the obvious result that the manager, and probably Mike, felt good that every reasonable option had been tried. This approach dramatically demonstrated to subordinates the manager's commitment to high standards and to subordinates' well-being. Emphasizing only the first commitment often encourages resistance and low risk-taking in subordinates.

The orientation of the Manager-as-Developer is to work actively with all subordinates to make them included and integrated in the department. Individuals near the periphery of the unit must be brought into fuller functioning with the unit. However, if this integration doesn't work, the ties can be cleanly cut. The key subordinates who report to the boss should all be included close to the boss (as well as to each other) in a cohesive team, or they should be removed. It is not helpful to have subordinates at a distance—too removed to share influence effectively, but connected enough to be a source of irritation. Removal, however, should occur only after the failure of genuine efforts to understand the subordinate, build the relationship, and use the relationship to enhance mutual influence and develop full potential.

FUNDAMENTAL ASSUMPTIONS FOR DEVELOPING INDIVIDUALS

Behind the model of continuous development for all subordinates, which utilizes supportive confrontation as a central developmental technique, are three key assumptions.

1. *Most people can change, learn, grow.*
2. *Influence between boss and subordinate can be mutual.*
3. *Most managers can learn the necessary skills.*

Most People Can Change

The example of the sales manager and Mike, the unsuccessful older salesman, could be interpreted as proof that "you can't change a leopard's spots." Many managers believe that truism, so they aren't willing to invest in time-consuming, intense, interactive developmental activities. The natural difficulties encountered by subordinates are viewed as separating the strong from the weak and teaching something along the way to the survivors. This kind of passive management-by-hurdle is regressive: A manager will not get the best from people by making it difficult for them to succeed. Managing should be the creation of conditions that increase the likelihood of success for even average subordinates. Anyone can make it hard for people to succeed, then cling to the survivors. It takes a good manager to get the best from everyone. But if the Mikes of the world can't produce, what is the use in managers' knocking themselves out? It is true that some percentage of subordinates in any organization will not make it, no matter what the boss does. However, it is impossible to know who can make it under good conditions—appropriately stretching assignments, coaching, supportive confrontation, full inclusion—unless those conditions are provided. No matter how many subordinates actually can't grow or don't fit, you need to manage as a Developer in order to find out. In fact, this system has the advantage that either growth is promoted or those who genuinely can't make it, such as Mike, are revealed.

Several of our workshop participants have reported similar outcomes: After supportively confronting a poor performer, they have seen the subordinate volunteer to leave, with gratitude for having been given a chance. This result is far cleaner, and more equitable, than the usual melange of mixed signals, foot-dragging, hard feelings, and eventual firing or shunting aside.

Nevertheless, in our workshops and consulting, the majority of those who are being managed developmentally live up to the highest standards, rather than fail. Even some subordinates who had previously been written off by their organizations have come to life, surprising everyone.

Such change should not be so unexpected. After all, we are talking about behavior change, not personality transformation. Adult personality is relatively fixed, but as we have pointed out, behavior is largely situationally shaped. Change the conditions—tasks, information, rewards, support, feedback, and the like—and the behavior will, more often than not, change accordingly. Since behavior is not innate, it can be modified; being learned means that behavior comes as much from specific experiences and the present situation as from deep-seated personality factors. Is Linda brusk with subordinates and co-workers because of traumatic childhood experiences in the first six years of her life? Unlikely. It is more probable that she was rewarded for such behavior as a rising manager, when her bruskness compensated for the insecurity of youth and kept others from confronting her.

Interestingly, the belief that few can grow is self-perpetuating. If a manager holds to this notion, he has little reason to confront supportively a poorly performing subordinate (or the meeting has little conviction). But behavior change can be spurred when people are made aware of the dysfunctional effect of their present behavior, shown alternative behaviors, and rewarded when these alternative approaches are elected. Such concrete steps are manageable only when you believe in a widespread capacity for persons to grow or you manage as if you did believe. Your positive attitude increases the probability of growth occurring and allows for mutually decided departures if the growth proposition turns out not to be true in specific cases.

Managing as if all subordinates could develop has some other advantages. It allows you to set high standards, since quality work can be expected of competent people. Thus the manager is not faced with "task success" and "concern for people" as incompatible pressures. Instead, these objectives can be brought together—especially for the type of work and type of subordinates found in most complex, contemporary organizations. Evidence suggests that expecting high performance from others actually induces it, so that treating all subordinates as if they are capable of excellence increases its likelihood. (Rosenthal, 1968; Livingston, 1969)

Influence Between Boss and Subordinate Can Be Mutual

We have argued that the Developer needs to share responsibility, and therefore power, with subordinates. The subordinates are encouraged to disagree, push for their own needs, and get into a joint problem-solving or negotiating mode with the superior rather than to carry out orders obediently. Despite the persuasive evidence for such an approach, many managers will be ambivalent about moving in this direction. They frequently believe they have little enough power now, that their authority is not commensurate with their responsibility. Furthermore, managers report increasing difficulty in being able to influence subordinates; it is no longer possible just to order them around. At the very least, subordinates now demand plausible explanations, and, more often, they want to direct the nature of the decisions. This description particularly fits the highly trained employees in most contemporary organizations. Under these conditions, managers are understandably ambivalent about increasing the power of subordinates.

But such reluctance makes sense only if you assume that the amount of power is fixed (so that by sharing some with subordinates, you end up with less) and that subordinates will use their increased influence to block the attainment of departmental goals. From one point of view, both assumptions are valid. After all, power includes the ability to say no, and if the superior and the subordinate are in a dispute that only one can win, increasing the subordinate's power may be to the boss's disadvantage. But if power is defined as the ability to get things done, then there can be *enabling* power as well as *restrictive* power. Power can derive from saying yes as well as no. A Developer uses power and influence by increasing subordinates' work responsibilities and assisting them to be more competent.

A manager must understand the two faces worn by power and influence. If the emphasis is on restrictive power—on increasing the discrepancy between the superior's level of influence and the subordinate's—the final effect may be to *decrease* the amount of *leader* influence. On the other hand, if the leader places primary importance on enabling power and seeks to increase the ability of the subordinate to be influential, the final effect can be to *increase* the leader's power. The explanation that clarifies this apparent paradox rests in the fact that most healthy adults seek to avoid being dependent (Argyris, 1957). They are willing for others to have more power and influence than they themselves possess, but only when they still have sufficient autonomy to exercise some control over their own activities. Most people resist when the power discrepancy increases beyond conditions of interdependence to dependence. Their initial response may be an attempt to increase their own power. This resistance may be in the form of constant disagreeing with the boss or counterattacking, either of which acts to decrease the superior's power. If the resister's attempts to increase power are not successful, he or she will likely withdraw—either overtly (leaving for a new job) or covertly (withholding commitment and involvement). The leader's power is further reduced. Another way people in low-power positions reconcile their objective world with their need for autonomy is by restricting the number of areas in which they are willing to be influenced. Early research on performance appraisals supports our observations. Subordinates are less likely to accept the supervisor's recommendations for change when there is a high power discrepancy between them, and more likely to accept such suggestions when there is low discrepancy (Blake and Mouton, 1961). When people feel that they have some control over what will happen to them, they are more willing to be open to influence attempts. Thus, ironically, willingness to be influenced is often directly related to a person's ability to resist influence.

When the reverse process occurs (that is, the superior increases the influence of the subordinate so that the power difference is decreased), the overall power of the superior can increase as well. The subordinate is more likely to consider the superior's ideas than to resist automatically. The possession of influence and responsibility increases a subordinate's commitment. Since the employee now views the boss as helpful, he or she is more likely to be committed to the superior and the department goals. Finally, if power is defined as the ability to get things done, a subordinate will increase in influence as the subordinate's competencies develop. A group of very able subordinates who are working toward a common goal can lead to a more powerful department than the most influential leader could produce alone.

How can a subordinate's influence and power be safely increased? How can a leader be sure that more influence for the subordinate doesn't mean less at the top? The discussion has now come full cycle, because the answer is "through an effective relationship and through the job." Insofar as the superior listens and considers the subordinate's requests, encourages the subordinate to disagree, and moves away from a unilateral decision-making mode to a joint or negotiated one, the subordinate will have increased power. But that also frees the leader to be powerful. It is not necessary for the leader to accept passively everything the subordinate requests; a strong subordinate means that the leader no longer has to hold back influence for fear of overwhelming a subordinate. Instead, both leader and subordinate may be as strong as they wish, because both are competent, willing to try to influence the other, and willing to be influenced by the other in return.

Thus, increasing the power of the subordinate can lead to an overall increase in the leader's power. Power can accrue to a leader from the sense of obligation the subordinate feels for the effort the leader has made to assist subordinate development. Insofar as leaders go out of their way—to understand the person and fit assignments to the subordinate's interests and aspirations or give extra coaching and feedback so that a subordinate can be more successful—the more credit is built up that the leader can call on when extra effort is needed.

There is a further way subordinate development can increase a leader's influence. Knowing better what the subordinate wants means that assignments can be made in a way that decreases resistance. Instructions and assistance can be given in ways the subordinate can easily accept.

A third way that this style of management increases superior influence is by putting the leader on the subordinate's side. From that perspective, a leader can make demands in a manner more likely to elicit cooperation than conflict. When the leader's feedback is linked to the subordinate's aspirations— how the behavior the leader is asking is related to how the subordinate can accomplish personal objectives—the leader is positioned so as to increase collaboration.

Most Managers Can Learn the Necessary Skills

The Developer model undoubtedly demands a great deal from any manager. The developer must employ a wide range of interpersonal skills that are often assumed to be possessed only by human resources specialists. The Developer needs to be empathetic; skilled in building relationships with all sorts of subordinates, including those who are most irritating; able to be highly influential yet influenceable; and mature enough to handle comfortably all disagreement and conflict from subordinates. How many managers can claim these qualifications? How many managers have both the skills and self-confidence to carry out these functions? In addition, the Developer manager might seem disturbingly reminiscent of the heroic manager, since the discussion imputes a great deal of responsibility to the Developer.

It is certainly true that the role of an effective developer of subordinates requires skills that many managers have not foreseen. But as employees become both more expensive and more important, the interpersonal skills we have discussed will have to become a standard part of every manager's repertoire. Otherwise, adequate performance can exist, but not excellence.

The Developer approach also demands a great deal personally from the leader. As Developer, you must be willing to become more vulnerable, if there is to be an open relationship with your subordinates that allows all of you to talk about things that are interfering with performance. Also, risks a subordinate takes in terms of accepting new assignments, are your risks as well. In these senses, the Manager-as-Developer is a very demanding role: You have to give up the mantle of heroic invincibility.

But in today's complex organizations, the Developer's functions are truly less demanding than traditional heroic activities. Building a climate in the department that stresses development would be futile for the heroic leader to attempt. In an atmosphere that fosters learning, it will be considered natural for the manager also to learn. Although sometimes managers need to appear certain and unshakeable in order to provide security to anxious followers in a crisis, or to sell an idea, most of the time managers need to convey the message that learning is all right.

Only a leader who is clinging to heroic notions is embarrassed to admit to learning needs. When managers own up to what they are struggling to learn, subordinates of the kind we have been discussing breathe huge sighs of relief—after all, they usually have a good idea of what the boss doesn't know!— and pitch in to help. Most people want their boss to succeed, and given half a chance, they will try to help the boss learn. After our workshop participants have returned to their jobs and been open with their subordinates about what they now admit they want to learn, their subordinates have almost invariably responded positively—so long as they are convinced the manager means it.

At our workshops we have repeatedly worked with managers who discovered they needed to listen better, to learn to understand difficult subordinates, or to find ways to give tough feedback supportively, who were then able to practice those skills and get a good running start in a few days. Though it takes genuine skill and repeated practice, half the battle is deciding to try. Then, with a little help from your friends, you can rapidly increase your capacities.

Furthermore, inherent in a shared-responsibility system are numerous learning mechanisms. You will not be totally on your own to determine the best ways to manage. Altered departmental relationships will establish feedback loops to you from subordinates. Finally, the Manager-as-Developer mode makes life easier because of its built-in expectation that everybody shares responsibility for making things work well. Thus, effective individual subordinate development is a two-person responsibility, not the sole burden of the leader.

But even with shared responsibility and mechanisms for superior development, it is a great deal to expect that most managers can be objective and fair with all their subordinates. Even the best-intentioned bosses have biases. In spite of your best efforts to be concerned about all subordinates, you will find it difficult to be empathetic with everybody. But there is another shared-responsibility mechanism built into this model of leadership—the cohesive team. As we have suggested, and further explore in the next chapter, a mature group can also assume some of the responsibilities for development. Peers often know more than the superior about what others are doing well and what areas need improvement. Peers, probably more than the superior, can exert strong pressure (and provide strong support) for change. Thus, one of the goals of the Manager-as-Developer is to construct a team that supports enough openness of communication, trust, and mutual influence so that the group can assume some of the responsibilities for individual growth and development.

INTRODUCTION

Achieving excellence demands the development of a high-performance team. Such a group produces high-quality solutions, provides coordination among members, and is the vehicle for shared responsibility in managing the department. Such a team, although still a relatively rare phenomenon, can now achieve a level of departmental performance far beyond what can be expected from leaders with an heroic style.

There are several reasons why an effective team is now crucial to producing excellence. First of all, when subordinate tasks are complex, specialized, and changing, it is almost impossible for a leader to know all the relevant information. Behavioral science research has revealed that groups make superior decisions when issues are difficult. (Maier, 1970)

However, the highest-quality solutions are of little value if they won't be implemented. Conditions have to be such that all the members are willing to work together in carrying out decisions. Few, if any, managers could single-handedly accomplish all the necessary coordination in a busy department. For tasks to be accomplished well and on time, subordinates must interact with one another—consulting, checking, cajoling, and confronting—without always going through the boss. As every manager knows (and as substantiated by numerous studies of organizational life), informal negotiation among peers is a common occurrence. It has to exist, because organizations couldn't function if all members limited themselves to what was in their job descriptions and complied with a formal chain-of-command system. But rather than seeing this informal organization as an aberration that must, at best, be tolerated, the Manager-as-Developer recognizes its value and incorporates it into the formal structure of the department. Not only does this inclusion legitimize such interactions, it also serves to improve their effectiveness. If the department group can be developed to take collective responsibility for coordination, work will be accomplished more rapidly and the inevitable tugs and pulls among people committed to representing their own area interests can be cooperatively balanced by members who assume a stake in the outcome and hold needed information.

In all areas, quality will be higher and implementation more likely if members can confront each other when problems are being hidden, information withheld, positions overstated, or other games played. Members, more often than the astute leader, are in the best position to know what is actually going on. In conventional groups, members shy away from direct dealings with each other. They tend to sit by and observe, waiting for their chance to argue for resources, time, favored information, or consideration. Their manager must carry the roles of prosecuting attorney (to see that all the facts are brought out) and judge (to decide among competing views and force cooperation). This process, in turn, tempts subordinates to "present best cases" and reduces their incentive to make accomodations with peers (since there is always the chance that the boss can be won over).

Thus, what is for the boss a tough coordinating job just from sheer complexity and the range of knowledge required becomes even more difficult. On the other hand, if the drive and energy of subordinates could be channeled into team effort, with the team managing the individualistic and competitive tendencies of its members, performance is enhanced.

Not only is a shared-responsibility team likely to achieve greater coordination, it is also more likely to utilize the range of member resources. In a fully developed team, individual strengths are recognized and supported, rather than perceived as threatening. Members can accept help from each other without fear of seeming weak or dependent. Each person's particular strengths are available to the team, not only for answers or direct performance, but also to help others in the team learn.

Developing a shared-responsibility team sets the stage for further individual development, which occurs when the team is collectively performing many of the managerial functions. Participation in the tasks of running meetings, building the team effort, understanding others enough to integrate their functions into the central departmental thrust, and managing the problem-solving process provides constant practice of valuable skills. Team members need these skills in this setting, but they are also practicing the same techniques they will need as managers.

Groups also help members learn through direct feedback. Remember the distinction drawn in the previous chapter between intentions behind behavior and the *effects* of that behavior on others. The group represents more "others" who can give their reactions. (Deborah Linke, for example, incorporated learning and development as a standard part of staff meetings by having members evaluate, at the end, how each meeting went.) Expanded feedback is a valuable source of information and a powerful impetus for change.

A vivid example of this feedback effect occurred during a meeting of a maintenance department. The group included one member, Alfred, who had posed particular problems for his boss and co-workers. He was a mediocre performer and a nuisance at meetings. He repeatedly made excuses, tossed out smokescreens and red herrings, and obfuscated any issue that approached his territory. In the middle of one of Alfred's fog attacks at this meeting, another subordinate turned to him and said, "You know what, Alfred? You are full of bullshit. You have more goddam excuses than anybody I know, and I am sick and tired of hearing them all the time." There was dead silence, but no counter-statement from Alfred or any of his co-workers. He knew this was the general consensus and just listened. All the boss had to do was reassure the angry peer that in this team, peer confrontation was allowed. The discussion went on with a chastened but more cooperative Alfred.

Managers are often hesitant to permit this degree of confrontation for fear their "Alfreds" couldn't take it. Feedback, however, does not have to be as punitive as in Alfred's case (but since the language fit the norms of this blue-collar department, the remarks were not as abusive as they might be in other settings). Indeed, one of the key tasks of the Developer is to help subordinates improve their skills in giving and receiving feedback constructively.

As the members learn from each other and the group becomes increasingly proficient at sharing responsibility, performance will rise. Consequently, the department's influence with other parts of the organization will rise (as Deborah Linke found). Also, since subordinates are assuming more of the managerial responsibility, the leader is more free to deal with the external environment, take on larger tasks, and thereby become more powerful relative to other management. Managers who can create effective subordinate teams can deliver more to the organization, which builds their reputation and the likelihood of their receiving further important assignments. These are not insignificant by-products.

A MATURE, SHARED-RESPONSIBILITY TEAM

Despite the potential advantages to creating a shared-responsibility team, many managers express strongly negative sentiments about teams, groups, committees, and meetings. They associate teams with delays, endless talk (or false, constrained politeness), avoidance of responsibility, and other unpleasant outcomes. Indeed, too few management teams now function in ways that could produce enthusiasm and encourage emulation.

Suppose, however, that your direct subordinates could function as a team with the following characteristics:

* Everyone knows his/her own and others' tasks well enough so that nothing falls through the cracks; everyone knows who is, and who should be, doing what.
* Trust is so high that the group does not need to meet on every issue. Because all members know, and are committed to, the same overarching goal and know each other's attitudes and positions on issues, any member can act in the department's name when necessary, without seeking everybody's approval. Each member is confident that no one, including the boss, would act without consultation unless there was a good reason—such as prior general agreement, special expertise, legitimate time pressures, or unavailability of affect-

ed parties. And the person who does act would know that
others would back any action.

- Such a group would not be very "group-y" or clinging and
would not waste time meeting on trivial issues or limiting
those who had taken individual initiative. A lot of individual
work would be assigned to be done outside meetings, with
reports and recommendations brought back to the team.

- Members who were clearly more expert than the others, in
certain areas would be given great latitude to make the decisions on those matters.

- Nevertheless, if issues cross several areas or affect the department as a whole, members would seriously address the
issues together, fight hard and openly for their beliefs, insist
that their concerns be addressed, yet also pay attention to
the needs of the department as a whole. Everyone would be
comfortable wearing at least two hats, one for their area and
one for the department.

- Although skilled at persuasion and willing to fight hard over
important differences, members would feel no obligation to
oppose automatically initiatives from other members or the
manager. There would be no competition for competition's
sake. Members would enthusiastically support the positions
or ideas of others when they happened to agree. Furthermore, when they were in opposition to one another, the battles would center on issues, not personalities. Differences
would be considered legitimate expressions of a person's experiences and job perspective, not indicative of incompetence, stupidity, or political maneuvering.

- Despite members' willingness to fight when necessary, the
climate is pervasively supportive, encouraging members to
ask one another for help, acknowledge their mistakes, share
resources (people, information, or equipment), and generally
further everybody's performance and learning.

- The group pays attention to successful task achievement and
to individual member's learning; members are not restricted
to areas where they have total competence and hence can't
acquire new expertise, nor are they so overloaded with

learning experiences that group performance seriously suffers. Cautious members are pushed to venture into less secure areas, while overreaching members are reminded that
new opportunities can't supplant ongoing responsibilities.

- Perhaps most important, the group has self-correcting mechanisms; when things aren't going well, all members are
ready to examine the group's processes, discuss what is
wrong, and take corrective action. Whatever the problems
—overly lengthy meetings, inappropriate agenda items,
unclear responsibilities, lack of team effort, overly parochial
participation, or even poor leadership practices—the group
takes time out to assess its way of operating and to make
mid-course corrections. Individual members as well as the
manager feel free to raise questions of team performance.
Nevertheless, the group is not so overly self-analyzing that it
neglects its main tasks. High task performance remains a
central concern.

Does this team profile sound too ideal? Is the well-developed team a fantasy projection that will remain frustratingly
out of reach in the real world of petty politics, indirection,
waffling, and hushed-corridor cabals? Deborah Linke's group
quite rapidly developed similarities to our well-developed
team, and we have seen other successful teams often enough
in our research and consulting to know that exceptional leaders and special subordinates are not prerequisites for the creation of excellent teams. Two examples further illustrate what
shared-responsibility teams can look like. These groups took
time to develop and require maintenance effort, but they
demonstrate some of the potential of the mature team.

Ted's Team

Ted is a plant manager. His team is composed of the production
manager, treasurer, head of sales, quality-control manager, plant-
maintenance manager, head of engineering, and director of personnel. The
eight of them meet every Wednesday afternoon for two and a half hours to

identify problems and make operating decisions; they meet for the entire afternoon one Friday a month to make larger decisions on policy, budget, capital expenses, and similar larger concerns (or more frequently if an emergency arises).

A recent meeting began with everyone (including Ted) reporting the problems they were encountering both within their area and with other areas. Ted as chairman was listing problems on the board in preparation for the group to decide priorities. Some problems needed to be handled at once; others could be put off, assigned to one or two individuals, or allocated to the monthly Friday afternoon session.

As the discussion progressed, it became clear there was a problem in the maintenance department. Several of the other areas complained of inadequate service. "We never know when you are going to come to repair something; we put in an order and we don't know when it will get taken care of until just before your men come over." "Your department will start a job, get it half-completed, and move off to start another one, leaving a mess behind them until they come back three to five days later."

As this list of complaints grew, the plant-maintenance manager became more and more defensive. At each complaint, he had an explanation that either took the blame off him or sent it back to the complainer—for example, "But you put in an order and then changed it once we started work!"

After a few minutes of this pattern of accusation and defense, the plant manager stepped in. "Joe, we aren't getting anywhere with your explaining away every problem. Our purpose here is not to put you down, but to find out what the real difficulty is so we can correct it. We are hearing symptoms of the problem, and we need to get them out, but then we need to find out what the core problems are."

The discussion continued, as the plant manager checked with everyone else present about any difficulties they might have had with maintenance. These problems were listed on the board, along with the problems Joe said he had with the other departments. The defensive tone of the meeting slightly dissipated as people started to adopt a more problem-solving orientation.

After all the problems had been listed, the group collectively started to explore causes. After a few minutes, it became clear that there wasn't an adequate prioritization system to handle requests for maintenance. Apparently, under the recently retired previous maintenance manager, a laissez-faire system had grown up where crew leaders could select the jobs they wanted. They tended to pick jobs that were more interesting, repaid old debts, or could be used to build new obligations.

As members started to explore alternative methods, one pointed out that it wasn't the best use of their time to work out the mechanics of a new system. "Anyway, that is Joe's area, and it isn't our right to tell him how to do his job. We should just tell him what our needs are from plant maintenance." After this was shared, Joe was asked to come up with a procedure that would try to meet these needs. He was asked how long it would take. When he estimated two weeks, the discussion was put on the agenda for that meeting.

Before the group went on to the next item on the agenda, the production manager volunteered, "Joe, if you want to, let's get together next week. My area is the heaviest user of your department, and I have some ideas about how this could work well for us all."

Although Ted's team still has areas for improvement, its meeting was characterized by important team skills: the capacity to share problems, not hide them; a rather unusual willingness to confront a peer about alleged poor performance in front of the boss; a readiness to shift from blaming to problem exploration; a boss who neither cut off differences nor encouraged personal attacks; genuine helpfulness extended from one peer to another; collective input to the agenda setting and prioritizing process; and considerable subordinate initiative. Although many of these characteristics are not often found in management teams, they are typical for Ted's team, because of the effort and time that were spent building the necessary climate. A different team, operating in a different setting, can show us further instances of good team performance.

Arnold's Team

This team of seven people included Arnold, the hospital director of a major medical center, and his immediate subordinates, the directors of nursing, finance, and the clinic, the head of personnel, the facilities manager, and the assistant hospital director.

For the past two years, the hospital had been under probation by the state accrediting agency; this year there was the danger of losing even that conditional status (which would have severe financial repercussions). The state agency had cited problems with below-code facilities and inadequate procedures and record-keeping.

In preparation for the accrediting team's visit, this administrative group had set up a crash program nine months earlier to deal with the major issues. They had initially listed 96 areas that needed attention, which they had narrowed to the most crucial 19. And during the past nine months, in addition to their normal work load, the group had been steadily chipping away at this "must do" list. Success in those efforts required a high degree of cooperation and a willingness to take initiative and move beyond individual job descriptions.

At the time of the meeting to be described, the accreditation visit had just occurred and the group had learned unofficially that the evaluation would be positive. Not only had they avoided suspension, but a two-year accreditation would be granted. The administrative team knew they would also be given a long list of recommendations to deal with, but they would have two years to do so, which eased the pressure a bit.

Arnold had called a special meeting to share this information and for the group to assess how they had worked together during this crisis period. The pressure had been too high during that time to allow this sort of examination, and Arnold felt that it would be useful to help them learn from this experience and to get them in better shape to handle the remaining items.

The first half-hour of the meeting was spent in some well-deserved mutual congratulations. Members shared examples of how their departments had solved the impossible problems. They also related comments of the accreditation team, which had expressed surprise and pleasure over the progress made.

Then the group started to explore in detail how they had worked together. They focused not on what jobs had been done but on how the different individuals and their respective departments worked together. As one would expect, the initial comments were mainly complimentary, but soon they became more balanced. For example, "It was easy working with you when you could make the decisions, but when it required your putting pressure on your staff, then decisions took much longer."

Although positive and negative comments were made about all members of the staff, including Arnold, there became evident a convergence of criticism about Arnold's administrative assistant, Paul. "You would promise things to be done, but deadlines would slip." "I couldn't count on you to come through when you promised," said Betty, the head of nursing. "I didn't have that problem," the facilities manager commented. "That's because he does everything you want," Betty and others exclaimed.

The last comment led to heated denials from both Paul and Jim, the facilities manager. "You are just imagining that," they charged. Arnold came in at this point and said, "Let's see if we can identify specific incidents. Were there times Paul didn't come through when Jim asked him to? Conversely, how many times has Paul not come through when you asked him? The issue isn't 'good–bad guy,' but whether there is something in our style of operating that we need to look at."

As they started to explore the specific interactions, a pattern emerged. Paul did tend to be overly responsive to what Jim wanted, at the expense of others. When Arnold and others tried to look at the causes, it became clear that much of it was due to Jim's style of making requests. Jim tended to come in very sharply, with a manner demanding immediate action. He said he didn't mean to be autocratic, but that's what worked well with his crew leader and workers. "Anyway, that's the way I am; you guys can demand things, too."

Arnold pointed out that Jim was saying his style was unchangeable, but was recommending that others change their style: "What's sauce for the goose is sauce for the gander." In the discussion that followed about how much people could, or wanted to, change, the following agreement emerged. Jim would try to differentiate his demands and not treat each as an emergency, while others would be more direct in their requests. For the most part, however, members acknowledged the different styles among them. For example, Jim was told, "As long as we know that when you say, 'It has to be done,' you mean 'within a week,' we can handle your requests."

Again, although this team can do more, its willingness to take the time to celebrate a success, then review the way it had come about, explore unresolved issues, and work toward greater understandings and acceptance of mutual work styles, is relatively rare. Too often teams continue frustrating patterns, even though all members know individually that things are not working well. Typically, they tell each other in twos or threes what is wrong with other team members or the boss, but they do not face the issues openly or constructively.

Why, when the advantages of advanced team effort are so clear, is that state so seldom achieved? What prevents excellence? Why do so many team meetings end inconclusively, without clear decisions and clear responsibilities assigned for implementing decisions? Why do some team meetings leave the subordinates resentful of having been subtly manipulated and the boss frustrated at subordinate foot-dragging? Why do decisions apparently settled at meetings subsequently reappear as full-blown problems, just when least expected and most inconvenient? And why do so many issues that should be settled out of meetings creep into them, while issues that need collective discussion, decision making, and implementation fail to get proper attention?

A variety of barriers can block effective teamwork, including poor procedures, inappropriate goals, poor management of the problem-solving process, and failure to see how groups must be developed over time. We will discuss each of these problems, but underlying all of them is a more fundamental difficulty—the attachment to heroic images of managing.

Heroic managers believe that they are totally responsible for their unit's success and must therefore be in control of everything. A skillful Technician or Conductor who feels confident dealing one-on-one with subordinates will often be far more worried about dealing with a group of them. It is far harder to control everything in the geometrically more complex network of six or seven people interrelating than when the boss faces only a lone subordinate. Concerns about losing control— being ganged up on, having poor ideas proposed from below and attached to by subordinates with limited perspective, conflicts raging out of bounds and hurting individuals—keep many managers from allowing or helping a potent, active, committed team to develop.

Managers preoccupied with control fail to see that a group operates on a set of laws and dynamics that differ from one-on-one guidelines (and that must be managed differently). A group is more than the sum of the individual members. The interaction among members that heroic managers fear because it might get out of control is exactly the potent force that can be harnessed to increase quality and implementation of decisions: the group's latent potential for mutuality of control, initiative, and responsibility. As mentioned earlier, successful team development hinges on managerial guidance and group work in four main areas: procedures, goals, problem solving, and progression by stages.

PROCEDURES GOVERNING THE TEAM

Many managers fail to attend to the team's composition, structure, and meeting schedule. Procedural matters should be settled early in the development of a team, or serious problems can develop. For example, careful attention must be given to membership—who should belong as regular members, how many members will be enough for diversity and coordination but not too many for necessary participation and commitment, what links are to be established with persons not in regular attendance, and how to tap nonmember expertise when needed.

One plant manager struggled with the question of whether to include the management information system (MIS) and personnel managers as regular members of his team even though they were not his direct reports. They were dotted line to him and direct functional subordinates of bosses at headquarters. After he thought about it, however, he realized that since his team would have to create new information systems and would be faced with a ticklish set of labor-relations problems, the team would be making decisions that needed the ideas of these persons early in the process, not after the plans had begun to take shape. The department (and the team) couldn't function properly without their continuing participation and commitment.

Another manager, however, came to the realization that her team was just too large and unwieldy. She had representatives from all the areas ultimately responsible to her coming to every meeting (partly because her predecessor had so ignored their needs that it had been necessary for her to include people as a symbol of concern) and the discussions were too cumbersome. In a rare display of bravery, she raised the subject with the group, talked it through, and collectively they decided to reduce membership but increase pre- and postmeeting exchanges with the excluded members. She even polled the group for suggestions about who should remain as the core team and used their suggestions as a basis for decision.

Whether you choose to allow potential members to argue for their inclusion or whether you think it is best for you to make the decision autonomously, you must thoroughly think through the implications of membership composition. Should a direct report who is a star individual contributor, but who hates group meetings and has no management aspirations, be forced to attend? Either way, your failure to think through how to utilize the subordinate's talents can damage team effectiveness.

Similarly, it is important to work out a regular meeting schedule, with appropriate time blocks reserved for differing purposes. How many times have you been at a team meeting that ends with everyone pulling out calendars and struggling for 15 minutes to find a common time for the next meeting? Or sat through a three-hour meeting that could have taken 30 minutes, then found that at another meeting only 45 minutes was allotted to major planning or strategic issues? Also, newly formed teams need extra time to work out relationships and procedures, but managers who aren't convinced about the value of teams often make early meetings very short—to "avoid wasting time until we see if this team thing can work here."

GOALS OF THE TEAM

The length and frequency of meetings should depend on what is supposed to be accomplished at meetings of the team. Team meetings are a problematic area for heroic managers. They generally treat meetings with their subordinates as information exchanges, where they make a series of announcements and then gather information from subordinates on recent operating results. Often these show-and-tell sessions are lethally dull, only livened up when the manager plays detective with subordinates who try their best to gloss over problems.

Meetings are costly in terms of people's time (a two-and-a-half-hour meeting of eight people consumes 20 person-hours—the equivalent of half a work week). Transmitting and talking over decisions the manager has already made are not effective uses of time.

Another common purpose of meetings is to "advise and counsel" the manager. These appear to be highly participative activities, as members jump in to offer their opinions and push for solutions. Careful observation, however, reveals that there is one key person to influence—the leader. Even though there will be a semblance of having everybody buy into the decision, no solution will be acceptable without the full agreement of the manager.

Such a meeting has several advantages over pure information transmittal. It allows more give-and-take, because the group is grappling with problems rather than just sharing information. This greater involvement taps more member resources and produces a higher quality solution than the leader deciding alone.

Another attraction of a consultative meeting, and the reason why it is favored by so many managers who want to be participative, is that while increasing the chances for subordinate input, it keeps the ultimate control in the hands of the leader. Even when the manager doesn't come in with a prearranged solution and is open to a range of alternatives, there can always be the fear that subordinates will push for something that the manager finds unacceptable. But in this type of meeting, where the leader holds veto power over the final answers, any movement of the group in an undesirable direction can be blocked. This leads easily to a kind of pseudo-involvement of members, as when a manager introduces a topic as if it were open for discussion but by many subtle and not so subtle signals makes it clear that he or she already has the solution in mind. The discussion, and the meeting, can't end until others discover the manager's solution and "accept" it.

Thus the attraction of consultative meetings is also their main limitation. Advise and counsel sessions do not make full use of subordinates' abilities and therefore prevent the attainment of excellence. When the leader holds on to the final veto power—when that is the person who has to be convinced—then the responsibility for the quality of the outcome and the success of the department remains on the leader's shoulders. Lacking full responsibility, subordinates are more willing to push their own parochial interests, withold or distort information, or settle for a solution they know is less than optimal.

Then what is the alternative? Instead of maneuvering the group to predetermined decisions, asking for advice on carefully framed alternatives, or announcing decisions made elsewhere, managers should view team meetings as an opportunity to make joint manager–subordinate decisions on key issues. The decisions are made by consensus, in which all people, and not just the leader, have fully expressed their views, feel satisfied they have been heard, and can support the final decision even if it is not their opinions.

The distinction among these decision-making styles in groups is an extension of the research by Vroom and Yetton (1973) on different ways that managers typically make decisions. Figure 6-1 describes these styles.

Vroom and Yetton found that effective managers use all three decision-making styles depending on a number of situational factors. Nevertheless, we have seen that there is usually a predominant style for crucial departmental problems. The Manager-as-Technician tends to use an autonomous style, the Manager-as-Conductor tend to use the consultative mode (although it is often presented to subordinates with a verbal overlay of "this is our decision"), and the Manager-as-Developer uses a joint style. These decision-making styles vary along the dimension of participation. The rule of thumb is to have greater involvement when subordinates have crucial information or abilities and a quality solution is needed—both are important criteria for the Manager-as-Developer in dealing with crucial departmental problems. This orientation does not, and should not, preclude the Developer's use of autonomous or consultative approaches for other types of problem.

Autonomous. The manager makes the decision, either on the basis of information already held or after gathering information from subordinates. The role of the subordinates is not to generate or evaluate solutions but to provide information.

Consultative. The manager shares the problem with subordinates, getting their ideas and suggestions. Although there may be attempts to have everybody buy into the solution, in the last analysis the manager makes the decision.

Joint. The manager shares the problem with the subordinates and together they generate and evaluate alternatives. Decisions are by consensus; the manager does not try to impose his or her solution on the group but is willing to accept any decision that has the support of the entire group.

Figure 6-1 Decision-making styles. Vroom and Yetton's original labels were Autocratic, Consultative, and Group. We retitled the first to remove the pejorative tone, which is not a necessary ingredient when leaders make decisions alone, and changed the third, since all three of the decision-making styles can occur in a group setting.

If you are like many managers, you are probably thinking, "Wait a minute, my department isn't a democracy; this is business and I'm the one who will make the decisions. The buck stops here." Yes, you have ultimate responsibility. But the issue isn't democracy—that's a political, not a managerial, issue. The question is whether you want excellent performance. Groups (and individuals) can't achieve that standard if they don't address issues of significance and work through them together. Otherwise, the necessary commitment, willingness to provide information and level with one another, and determination to make the decisions work cannot be gained. The manager need not throw all decisions to the group and sit with hands tied while the group gets carried away; shared responsibility definitely includes the manager. Certain decisions will have to be retained by any manager, for reasons of relative expertise, political considerations, confidentiality, group readiness, and so forth. Nevertheless, meetings must have the resolution of important issues as a core goal, with the sharing of information and announcements a subsidiary goal. Through addressing the issues that matter members simultaneously become committed and develop their skills.

THE PROBLEM-SOLVING PROCESS
IN THE TEAM

Even when teams are working on fundamental issues, managers consistently fall into heroic assumptions about their own role in the discussions: "I have to decide what the real problem is, be responsible for getting all the relevant data out, and extract possible solutions, and then I have to choose the best one." When we explore with managers—even those who are committed to being highly participative—what they do in running a problem-solving meeting, we often see a variation of this super-responsible approach. Given this kind of model, certain managerial behaviors tend to appear.

The leader often starts by defining the problem (which may not be the real problem or the one subordinates consider central).

The leader takes on the responsibility for the meeting's quality control. Through raising objections, the manager pushes for quality answers. With such responsibility lodged firmly in the boss's corner, subordinates decrease their commitment.

Seeing that subordinates are willing to settle for any solution that meets minimal standards galvanizes the leader into more checking and more questioning.

The alternative to this self-defeating cycle is not to give up responsibility but to find ways to get it shared, which can begin with your reconception of the leadership role in discussion. Your function is not to be the one who must extract all relevant information and provide the answers—that is being a Master Technician. Likewise, your job is not to keep your hands permanently clenched on the reins to make sure that subordinates stay on track—that perpetuates the Manager-as-Conductor.

Instead, your role is to develop the group so that they too feel responsible for seeing that an effective problem-solving process is being used. This managerial function is an active role, not a passive one. The effective Bob Young (in chapter 3) was quite active in holding the problem in the forefront and forcing members to deal with it. Deborah Linke was active in helping the group restructure its function and procedures. When a group is starting out and members are not yet skilled, sometimes Developers have to be active in running the meetings. Although this involvement may resemble the role taken on by a Conductor, the purpose is fundamentally different. The Conductor does it to maintain control, the Developer does it to model appropriate behavior with the expectation that members will soon take on many of those functions.

A manager must adopt a very active leadership stance to get subordinates to share in the success of the group. Most people have been thoroughly indoctrinated to leave that responsibility to the leader.* But excellence is more likely if members feel they have the duty and the authority to intercede when the discussion gets off track, the problem is incorrectly defined, the solution is superficial, or commitment to implementation has not been given. Changing members' expectations and increasing their skills will not occur if the leader sits back passively.

The Developer's role is no less influential than the heroic one, but it uses different means. Rather than exerting constant hands-on control to provide the specific answer, the Developer seeks to influence the group's norms and the members' ex-

---

*To show how firmly ingrained the roles "leader" and "member" are, we recommend the following experiment. Take five people and give them a problem to solve collectively. All will jump in, make suggestions, give ideas, and help the group move toward a solution. Then tap one person on the shoulder and say, "You are the leader of this group." That person immediately leans forward and the other four lean back. The number of comments (especially ones that are controlling) made by the leader will dramatically increase, whereas those by the members will decrease. In such simple ways, subordinate commitment is decreased and their resources lost.

Stage of Group Development

Behavioral or Skill Area	Membership	Subgrouping	Confrontation	Differentiation	Shared Responsibility
Atmosphere and Relationships	Cautious, feelings suppressed, low conflict, few outbursts	Increasing closeness within subgroups, cross-group criticism, false unanimity	Hostility between subgroups	Confident, satisfied, open, honest, differences	Supportive, open, expressive, varied; disagreement resolved promptly
Goal Understanding and Acceptance	Low, fuzzy	Increasing clarity, misperceptions	Up for grabs, fought over	Agreed on by most	Commitment to overarching goal
Listening and Information Sharing	Intense, but high distortion and low disclosure	Similarities within subgroups not as great as perceived	Poor	Reasonably good	Excellent, rapid, direct
Decision Making	Dominated by active members	Fragmented, deadlocks, to the boss by default	Dominated by most powerful, loudest	Based on individual expertise, often by the boss in consultation with subordinates	By consensus, collective when all resources needed, individual when one is expert (not necessarily the boss)
Reaction to Leadership	Tested by members, tentative	Resisted, often covertly	Power struggles, jockeying for position	General support, individual differences in influence	Highly supportive but free to disagree on issues
Attention to Way Group Is Working	Ignored	Noticed but avoided, discussed outside meetings in small groups	Used as weapon against opponents	Alternates between uncritical or overcompulsive discussion.	Discussed as needed, to aid work accomplishment; anyone can initiate

Figure 6-2 Common operating characteristics of the stages of task-group development.

Adapted from Cohen et al., *Effective Behavior in Organizations*, 1980, and Obert, *The Development of Organizational Task Groups*, (1979).

pectations, to develop their skills, to prevent avoidance of the key issues, and to see that analysis is rigorous, discussion thorough, and standards kept high. Such task-focused groups are not wishy-washy bull sessions that drift among issues. The leader encourages members to address each other on the issues because they share responsibility for working, implementing, and living with the decision.

Although the Developer role is active and controlling, it is less often a decision-making role. When the discussion concerns key issues on which the manager does not have clear differential expertise, the focus must be on the group's collective judgment in order to produce good answers. The manager undoubtedly will contribute directly to that discussion also, but he or she will be equally concerned with helping the group function effectively so that members can jointly create a quality decision that all will implement.

TASK GROUP DEVELOPMENT OVER TIME

A final barrier to effectiveness is raised when managers fail to take into account the need to *build* the kind of group that is desired. Effective teams do not spring full-grown from collections of individualistic and competitive though competent subordinates. Task groups must go through fairly predictable phases to reach fully shared responsibility, but the phases are often so nerve-wracking to the manager concerned about remaining in charge that all real hope of working effectively together is abandoned in an early phase. The erstwhile team is frozen forever into impotence or ineffectiveness. The early demise of the team's potential only serves to reinforce the manager's bias that subordinates can't be counted on anyway; soon everyone is complaining about the excessive or infrequent, boring or hostile, useless meetings—including the boss who runs them.

As a start toward finding ways out of an unsatisfying stalemate, we will examine the difficult stages that task groups inevitably have to pass through—even teams that are eventually very successful. Understanding what is likely to happen—and why some difficulties along the way are necessary before shared responsibility is arrived at—should make the journey easier to undertake. There are five recognizable stages in the development of work teams, which we will call (1) member-ship, (2) subgrouping, (3) confrontation, (4) individual differen-tiation, and (5) shared responsibility (Obert, 1979). Although not every group progresses in exactly this sequence, and many groups do not get past stages 2 or 3, each of the stages is com-mon enough and the issues fundamental enough, so that the model serves as a useful approximation of reality. (You may find it amusing to see where the teams in which you are a member or leader fit.) The common operating characteristics of the stages are summarized in Figure 6-2.

New work teams struggle most with *membership* issues. At the beginning of any work group's life, members try to decide how much to invest themselves. They ask themselves how valuable the team's efforts are likely to be, what their place on the team will be, what role they will be allowed to play, whether their views will be respected, how the boss will do things, what the other members will be like, what the team is supposed to do as a team, and so on. Since no one can be sure about the others, initial meetings tend to be cautious and dis-cussions superficial and polite. Think back to the first few meetings of a new task force to remember what this initial stage feels like—the frustration at apparently aimless drifting as members struggled to figure out what the game was going to be and how they would fit in.

Since everyone is isolated, considerable attention is paid to sizing others up, deciding who might be compatible and who is likely to be a difficult opponent. The formally designated manager is under no less scrutiny, and scrutinizes in return.

As members start to identify who is "like" them—who holds similar views, has a comfortable style, shows common interests —the group moves into the *subgroup* stage. Members are struggling to find support and seeking it in this group. No one wants to have the experience of saying something controversial and having the whole group turn against him or her. The isolated individuals are so relieved to find someone with something in common that they cling to any birds of a feather—even if the feathers aren't quite as identical as they're advertised. Once a few people make common bond, others move rapidly to find their most common ally; the group quickly fragments into clusters of twos or threes who eagerly support their comrades in the cluster. These alliances can make for very peculiar and constrained discussion, since newly found birds of a feather must be careful not to squawk in ways that would mark them as imposters of another species. Meetings can take on the quality of wading through molasses, as opinions are ventured cautiously and only in accord with known positions of fellow subgroupers; most that is important is reserved for conversations in the safety of the corridors or private offices.

Some persons, emboldened by having allies in the meetings, will exert more effort to try to shape the goals and to capture influence, but most attempts at power will be indirect and covert, with a few sniping and hit-and-run attacks across subgroup lines.

When a team is at the subgroup stage, a lot of eye-rolling occurs among subgroup members when a person from another subgroup speaks, together with other nonverbal signals designed to reinforce newly found solidarity. From each subgroup's perspective the others are inferior—too verbose, too covert, too biased toward marketing or production or research or some other speciality, too naive, too political, too narrow, too philosophical—in short, not "like us."

In some organizations all teams operate in subgroups. Norms in the organization discourage open conflict; there is little expectation of genuine collaboration, so no one pushes hard to go beyond the fragmentation and distance. Members of such teams expect little and often come to have a highly cynical view of groups.

When members become frustrated with the inability to engage vigorously the issues the team should address, they often move beyond polite subgrouping into *confrontation*. The underlying question they are asking is whether they will be able to have sufficient influence on the issues. The confrontation, however, tends to be across subgroups, with previous sniping turning into more open, noisy warfare. Discussions are angry and heated, with intense mobilizing of weapons such as information and resources. Struggles ensue for control of the team's destiny, its goals and fundamental thrust, its basic operating philosophy, and procedures. Since the action is so heated, however, with coalitions fighting other coalitions, even trivial issues take on symbolic importance as to who is "ahead," gaining, or behind. Thus anything can be fought over, including time and location of meetings—details that have no impact on performance—and other insubstantial matters that are significant only insofar as they represent relative power and status. Subgroups overstate their cases and cannot let themselves accurately perceive the positions of others, for fear that they might become convinced and let down their allies.

Although meetings of groups in this stage can be chaotic and hostile, they at least are energetic and vital. More important issues are raised and fought over, which increases member commitment. In fact, with rare exceptions, only when a team is able to fight in this way can it can break through everyone's resistance against buying into the team's overarching goals, which might be at the expense of their own subunit's comfort and wishes.

Few groups can survive being frozen in confrontation, especially hostile confrontation, but some fighting is necessary to heighten investment in the team and in one another. As one middle manager commented about the year-old team of which he was a member, "We've got to take the gloves off sooner or later; all this pussyfooting around makes it impossible to get to know each other well enough to ever resolve our differences —or find out that we actually agree on some things."

We have seen a few work teams get stuck at the confrontation stage—and even seem to enjoy the fireworks and drama —but more often teams quickly move forward into differentiation or fall back to subgroups. The teams that retreat are frightened by the intensity and release of energy that comes with confrontation or are pushed backward by the manager's concerns about people getting hurt or meetings getting out of control. Successfully managed groups move forward toward *individual differentiation*, which is about as far as most teams get. Progressing to that stage is not to be devalued; a stage-4 team can be highly productive.

At stage 4, members no longer need the permanent support of their subgroups, or, more accurately, shifting subgroups have developed whose composition changes depending on the issue. Knowing that they can find support, members also see that they will find recognition for their individual contributions.

As members begin to loosen their subgroup allegiences and respond to issues on their merits, the team can handle more important issues. The limitation to this fourth stage is that people's loyalty is more firmly attached to their subareas than to the department as a whole. Meetings are seen as occasions to work out interarea issues rather than to problem-solve collectively around the management of the unit. Members know what their individual jobs are, what to expect of one another, and what the team can do. The team's goals are reasonably accepted and most members want the work to get done.*

Groups that reach stage 4 usually become businesslike, doing their duty by attending meetings, but tending to parcel out individual assignments and to get through the agenda quickly, with the expectation that all will carry their own weight. Members only vaguely perceive any great benefit from collective action, and if they do, they doubt whether such a collection of individualists could ever agree on anything requiring intense commitment and collaboration.

---

*Occasionally, out of relief that the fighting is over, groups at this stage will become overly attached to each other and romanticize the good fellowship of being together. Meetings can proliferate, and too many issues that appropriately should be decided by individual members or the boss are brought to the group for decision. Poor decisions are made because everyone is reluctant to disagree for fear of upsetting the hard-won harmony.

This stage is not bad for getting the necessary work done in an adequate way; indeed, many managers would be delighted if they could bring their groups to the differentiation stage. Yet, it is possible to go beyond this adequate level into the shared-responsibility, collaborative, high commitment, and high intensity mode described early in this chapter.

In stage five, *shared responsibility* is achieved, and individual uniqueness and collective effort are both valued. The team addresses the issues vital to successfully managing the department, and members keep each other informed without wasting time and trust one another to act, but fight hard and fair over issue-based disagreements. A team can soar that is truly dedicated to its overarching goal, able to move freely between individual and collective effort, willing to confront and support members, dedicated both to performance and learning, and increasingly willing to take on management functions. Such conditions make work joyous even when serious and pull even greater dedication from those on whom the manager depends.

HOW TO MOVE TOWARD
A SHARED-RESPONSIBILITY TEAM

How can a manager, convinced of the desirability of creating a shared-responsibility team, initiate movement in that direction? Is a heroic effort needed to prepare a group for a postheroic style? We believe that any reasonably competent middle manager is capable of developing a shared-responsibility team. Managers have reported that just being aware of this model of stages of group development is helpful. Rather than seeing the cautious participation of members as timidity, the leader can recognize that such behavior is natural in a necessary but passing early stage. Rather than being wary of conflict, the leader can identify conflict as crucial to the movement toward group maturity. If the manager knows the major theme in each stage, he or she also knows what actions can be taken to promote movement to the next stage. For example, one leader who recognized that his team was in a subgroup phase had members work in pairs that cut across the subgroups on agenda items for the next meeting. Another manager began to encourage disagreements when she realized that more conflict was needed to move past the polite discussions of key issues.

Although awareness is important, it is also crucial that managers acquire specific skills. In our workshops, we have seen managers practicing and learning the team-development skills that are necessary not only to manage as a Developer, but to manage at all in contemporary organizations. Running meetings, dealing with conflict over goals and procedures, supporting those with good ideas but reluctance to speak out, initiating discussions about important, department-wide issues, and keeping people focused on the tough issues—any manager needs these skills.

The most potent way to work on team development is by having the group actually grapple with real and important departmental problems. Deciding central issues forces team involvement; members won't sit on their hands when the topic directly affects their areas. Tasks that encompass the entire department put teeth in the concept of shared responsibility when the decision is made jointly by the members and the leader. Among possible issues, there are many that do not require full group participation; some issues are beyond subordinates' competencies or readiness, others require instant action, and still others are too inconsequential to bother with. Such problems are better left for the manager to resolve autonomously, perhaps after consulting relevant individual subordinates. But there are many important issues that can best be solved and implemented by joint effort among members and the manager. The goal is to have increasingly more challenging problems before the group. We recommend the *15% rule* —problem difficulty should be 15% ahead of the point of group comfort. In other words, such issues as setting the annual budget, determining core departmental policy, introducing

new products, and appraising performance in each other probably should not be assigned when the group is in the first two
development stages. However, some of these issues can be
used to move the group into stage 3 and beyond. We saw one
team move fully into maturity when they were asked to dis-
tribute the yearly bonus among the members.

The Developer must work concurrently on three separate
but related areas: to increase systematically the importance of
the problems the team deals with; to move from a consultative
to a consensual joint decision-making style as problems increase in importance; and to change the norms and develop
members' skills to succeed in their expanded responsibility.

The last function is part of what makes the Developer's role
an active one. The Developer is active in moving from being
the leader conducting the meeting to having members take on
more and more of those functions. The Developer must also
pay careful attention to how the group is working and must
come in and comment when necessary. Have members spent
enough time defining the problem or are they only dealing
with a symptom of the underlying issue? Do they really have
agreement on the issues or is there strong group conformity
that is coercing a minority into acquiescence? Are they collecting or utilizing appropriate data about the problem? Have
they marshaled data in a way that precludes possible options?
Are they considering enough alternatives before converging
toward a solution? Have they anticipated the consequences of
their most favored alternatives? Do they know what criteria
they will use to judge a positive outcome?

All these issues involve generic problem-solving abilities that
a manager can use to help a team make a better decision, to
help subordinates be more effective team members, and to
teach subordinates the skills that will enable them to perform
better and coach their own subordinates. A manager does not
have to practice rigid adherence to a theoretical problem-solving model in order to be useful; a manager who pays attention
to the thoughtfulness and thoroughness of the discussion rather than concentrating on its correctness is likely to encourage

a higher-quality decision. Such managerial attention also helps the group get past some of its difficulties, no matter what stage it is in, and it reinforces the centrality of the team's *work*, by constantly focusing on the quality of the decision processes. High-quality, joint decisions are thereby placed at the forefront of the group's time together, which allows the manager to insist on excellence without predetermining the specific answer to get there.

There are of course times in the discussion when the manager has specific information or expertise that no one else has and appropriately contributes directly to the discussion. As we have suggested, team development does not have to render the manager impotent or silent (although occasionally leaders who decide not to rush in are surprised to discover how much their subordinates can contribute). One manager, who returned from our workshop with the resolution to stop dominating his own group's meetings, decided that he had no reason to add anything to the discussion at a subsequent meeting. When a subordinate asked him after the meeting if something was wrong because he'd been so (uncharacteristically) quiet, the manager burst out, "Not at all; best damn meeting we've had in a long time." It is not so important for the manager to aim for abstention; rather, the manager's activity should center on helping the team address the issues.

In all team activities, it is important that the manager makes the boundaries very clear. Any limits or untouchable areas should be made explicit. When it is a given that there will be a new compensation scheme, for example, the manager must make sure that the question under discussion is *what* the scheme will look like and *how* it will be implemented, not *whether or not* to have it. There are also times when a manager must express reservations. "Do we really have the resources to deliver in that area?" "Do we want to go to the mat on that issue?" This managerial input is important information for the group to have (and speak to). The group will develop best when a manager openly shows concerns. Your managerial objective must be to develop the group so that it will become

strong enough to let you wade in with your opinions and arguments without pulling punches and without fear that you will
inhibit free discussion. When members can fight back on issues
(and not just to get the boss), then you can be a full participant, gaining as much influence over decisions as your opinions merit, but no more. And for those issues where you can't
live with any but one particular decision, it is still possible—in
fact, desirable—that you make the decision. Attention to the
group's problem-solving process on selected issues does not
substitute for responsibility and it is not a license for abdication. In fact, the manager's involvement reinforces what is all-
important—the need for excellent, well-thought-through decisions to which all are committed.

The focus on the problem-solving process thus occurs within
the framework of work accomplishment. The leader who is
attempting to build a shared-responsibility team still needs to
exercise judgment about when to make decisions directly,
when to consult with the team first, when to enter into joint
decision making, and when to delegate completely. Trade-offs
between making a particular decision "correctly" or using it as
a developmental experience will sometimes have to be made.
But a manager must remember that a technically correct decision isn't worth much if it requires the cooperation of subordinates who resent having been excluded from the debate or
who do not fully understand why it has been made. On the
other hand, there are many decisions that subordinates can
happily implement without having participated and other decisions that do not require intense subordinate commitment to
be effective. The important thing to have in mind is that excellence can be achieved only by a cohesive team that is increasingly ready to take on the managing functions for the
whole unit, and that therefore you need to be looking for every opportunity to work toward the creation of such a team.
Whenever possible, rather than providing answers or maneuvering the group to arrive at circumscribed, predetermined
answers, the group's efforts to solve problems should be used
to expand the group's problem-solving, managerial capacities.

SPECIFIC ACTIONS TO MOVE THE GROUP THROUGH THE FIVE DEVELOPMENT STAGES

Direct use of the problem-solving process is a central way to foster team learning, but the manager can also use awareness of the stages of task-group development to aid in movement toward shared responsibility. Beyond the basic need for the manager to be patient through the time-consuming processes of each stage, the Manager-Developer can ease progression through the stages. At each stage members have a characteristic set of questions and concerns, and by tuning in to those concerns and taking straightforward measures to respond to them, the manager can gently foster progress or help unfreeze a group that's ready to move but stuck.

The first stage, *membership*, has members wondering about their place in the group and their positions relative to others. Activities that ease the exchange of information about one another—including meetings around meals to allow informal chatting—can help ease tensions. Similarly, giving subassignments to mixes of members can help people new to working together make linkages.

The second stage, *subgrouping*, is marked by members' relief at finding allies but also their great caution about venturing away from subgroup positions. Members worry about whether they will be isolated if they break rules. When a team is in this covert, sniping stage, it needs to tackle controversial issues with overlapping responsibilities for taking positions. The object is to *heighten* tension and differences rather than diminish them, to legitimize exploration and fighting. A group stuck at stage 2 needs help in getting to confrontation, even though conditions may temporarily be more unpleasant.

Once a group has moved to stage 3 and *confrontation*, however, where there are plenty of chances for members to stake out and defend positions, the team must then be moved beyond preoccupation with issues of power. A group struggling over whose ideas/positions/proposals will triumph cannot develop creative, win–win solutions. Here, cross-subgroup assignments can help to break down barriers and stereotypes. Longer off-site meetings organized around larger, long-term issues can also be helpful in providing sufficient time and perspective to allow subgroup members to explore new combinations.

Once the team has reached stage 4 and *differentiation*, it can be difficult for members to give up some independence in the interest of collaboration and fully shared responsibility. Members want to protect their hard-won independence and trust, and they can be very resistant to movement toward collaboration. A manager who now spends time tracing the ways in which decisions in each person's area have impact in other areas can be the stimulus that leads members to see the benefits of working together. Reminders about the overarching goal for the unit, especially as a standard for assessing whether decisions are producing excellence, can be useful. If the manager persistently points out the seriousness of particular issues and insists that the team address those issues, members can be pulled past their investment in operating relatively independently. The desired collaboration still leaves room for member individuality; the only conformity requested is to the overarching goal. How everything else is carried out can still allow members considerable individual freedom.

Thus far, we have concentrated on basically task-oriented methods. All of these techniques, along with team problem-solving methods, should be familiar to and within the generally accepted norms in most organizations. The methods are focused on getting work done better and do not call for extraordinary psychological or behavioral-science skills. All of the methods have been used effectively in many organizations. Nevertheless, perhaps even more important than reaching a perfect state of harmonious *shared responsibility* (stage 5), is the need to establish self-corrective mechanisms to deal with the inevitable times when the team loses effectiveness. No manager or team can ever "get it all together" permanently; like marriage, it takes work to keep a complex set of interrelationships healthy and productive.

For this reason, it is important, early in a team's life, for the manager to work to legitimize the team's ability to talk about how it's doing. Such discussions need not be frequent or overly personal and self-revelatory; they should be highly task-driven. Whenever a team experiences unusual difficulties, it must be able to stop and examine its processes. A look at the team's effectiveness and what might be done to improve it can do wonders for creating joint ownership of the team—provided the manager is willing to take the group's concerns and suggestions seriously and is not defensive when some of the suggestions hit home.

Evaluative discussions are very different at different stages of the group's development. In the early stages, process discussions are likely to be as cautious as the other discussions. No one wants to say anything that could possibly increase vulnerability, so process discussions about deeply held feelings are unlikely and inappropriate. But direct discussion of the cautious atmosphere, the way agenda items are set and discussed, and the difficulties with getting accurate information or full participation can all be legitimatized as topics. The simple question, "What's going on in our meetings?" or "What could we do to improve our meetings?" can be helpful in establishing the manager's willingness to examine process. Similarly, simple, uninterpretative process observations can be helpful—for example, "We seem to be having trouble discussing this fully; what's holding us back?" or "Does anyone besides me notice that issues we supposedly had settled keep coming back up?"

As the group moves to later stages, the processing, when necessary, can become more intense. Discussions can take on the team norms that hinder effectiveness or the lack of listening or support and begin to move toward examination of individual style and its impact. Not only do such discussions help improve performance and move the group through the stages, they also determine conditions for more direct, impactful processing during the shared-responsibility phase. By then, the mature group can not only discuss and alter its operating procedures; the group can talk openly about each other's strengths, weaknesses, learning needs, and strong accomplishments.

It isn't easy, and certainly not automatic, to get to stage 5, but once it arrives the manager's job is far easier. Members share in the responsibility for the unit's management and for making the meetings run well, as well as helping each other's individual talents develop. As peers they know a great deal about one another that isn't usually accessible to the manager, or else is discussed only behind closed doors, and their willingness to talk openly about what they know and believe aids in their growth and in team performance.

With a stage-5 team guided by a commitment to the unit's overarching goal, it is possible to achieve a level of performance excellence in which the work of the department is coordinated through a collaborative team, individuals are developing, and the manager contributes to the building of the human system while taking on higher-level functions.

A few notes of caution are necessary, however. A shared-responsibility team is not synonymous with a team that meets incessantly. Although more meeting time may be necessary in early stages of development, a reasonably well developed team can get a great deal done in fairly short order. Such teams often do a lot of business on the fly, briefly touching base with the appropriate members, but mixing it together with rapid information exchange, good humor, and the willingness to pull everyone together when issues are difficult and far-reaching.

Similarly, the shared-responsibility concept does not mean that the Developer is unable to take charge and make decisions when necessary. In fact, well-developed teams allow the boss *more* latitude to decide things without having to explain or justify minutely. We have seen many units whose bosses are so mistrusted that everything is an uphill battle. Even the most innocent suggestion is questioned, picked at, and resisted. Such situations reflect a lack of shared responsibility, not a surplus.

Finally, a shared-responsibility team takes time to build. Initial meetings will not be filled with subordinates gratefully falling all over you for releasing them from bondage. When subordinates have never experienced a genuinely collaborative team, they are understandably suspicious of anyone who says that by taking on more responsibility things will get better for them. Their reactions will vary, depending on the group's stage—from discomfort in stage 1, suspicion in stage 2, hostility in stage 3, to foot-dragging in stage 4—but the reaction will seldom be unalloyed enthusiasm. However, a manager should not be discouraged by such reactions, but take them as indicators of how important it is to move the group beyond where they are at present. We turn now to a more extensive look at how to begin implementing the Manager-as-Developer system. Where can you get the right leverage for movement?

INTRODUCTION

Leadership theories that describe what should be often have limited usefulness. Although the description of an idealized state can serve as a goal to strive for, practicing managers wonder how they are supposed to exchange their present set of headaches for the depicted utopia. "Yes," they admit, "this description of an ideal manager with an ideal department is highly desirable, but is it attainable?" More pertinent, "Is it attainable for me in my situation? You don't know my department and how unrealistic it would be for me to practice those leadership principles. How can I move toward collaborative problem solving when all my subordinates are protecting their own interests? How can I delegate responsibility when I have no confidence that subordinates will act responsibly? How can I give up monitoring quality when I think most of them are satisfied with just getting by?" If the manager does not know how to move beyond adequate, a description of excellence remains a tantalizing mirage on the horizon, no matter how desirable.

The Manager-as-Developer model has the unique advantage of providing both a vision of what to strive for and a plan for how to get there. Although the approach works best when all subordinates are fully trained, the group is mature, and members are totally committed to the departmental goal, the model also works to create these very conditions for moving from adequacy to excellence.

A second advantage is that the basic orientation of the Developer is the same at the beginning as it is when the members and the unit are fully developed. The central function of the leader is to develop the conditions and subordinate capacities so that subordinates increasingly share in the management of the unit. Certainly the specific actions of the leader vary with the skills of the individuals and the maturity of the group, but whether it is the first day or a year later, the manager is asking the same question: "How can each task be accomplished in a way that further develops my subordinates' competencies?" This question shows the leader's simultaneous attention to current work demands ("how to accomplish the task") and the future abilities of subordinates ("in a way that further develops subordinates' competencies"). Task accomplishment is not sacrificed for people, nor are people sacrificed for work. This is the developmental function: The task is accomplished today so that tomorrow the subordinates will be a little more able to take on increasing responsibilities.

The Developer approach has several important implications. First, it changes the leader's attitudes toward problems. For the traditional manager, problems are problems—they are nuisances and barriers to effective work. But to the Developer, problems, while still not desirable, are also seen as opportunities—as leverage points that can be used to build further competence. The same difficulties that cause the traditional manager to hold back from making fuller use of subordinates are used by the Developer as the vehicle for improvement—of the subordinate and of the unit's performance. For example, take the all-too-frequent situation of staff meetings where members withhold the real issues and hide problems. In these meetings, the traditional leader is not likely to bring up crucial department issues, yet that "problem," of hidden issues, could be the catalyst the Developer uses to confront the group on their behavior and help them move to a higher stage of development. This mind-set of "problems-as-opportunities" gives the Developer much more freedom; the leader is no longer as constrained by present imperfections.

The Manager-as-Developer orientation also implies that tangible benefits can occur immediately. So often, the concept of development requires present investment for delayed rewards, and for managers who are under constant pressure to produce today, such deferred return appears to be an unaffordable luxury. But in the Manager-Developer model, the process of providing more challenge, tied to important goals and reinforced with team interaction, is immediately rewarding and can stimulate extra effort. In many instances, subordinates know what to do and how, but have been held back by unnecessary conditions that block skill utilization. The manager's attention to development brings obstacles to the surface; when they are then removed, subordinates can often make significant and early contributions.

This chapter will show how you can move toward excellence using the Manager-as-Developer style. We will illustrate each step of the way with examples from former participants in our leadership workshops, who agreed to tell us how they had gone about using what they had learned. We have supplemented their accounts with examples from our consulting experiences with a variety of upper-level managers who have improved the performance of their departments. Although there exists no single way to go about developing a unit, you will see the important elements of the model and the general sequence that others have followed. Like other managers we have worked with, you will want to fit the model and your implementation strategy to your own setting. Some parts or sequences may require alteration or omission.

We begin by describing seven steps for building toward excellence. To get a feeling for the entire sequence, think back to what Deborah Linke did (described at the end of Chapter 3) in developing her department. In discussing these seven steps, we will make the connection to her actions as well as describe other types of actions taken by leaders who managed as a Developer.

SEVEN STEPS IN DEVELOPING A HIGH-PERFORMING SYSTEM

What Deborah Linke did to develop excellence was determined by the specific characteristics of her office, the nature of the task, and her own personal leadership style. Clearly, there cannot be one way for the Developer to lead; the approach will vary with each leader and situation. Nevertheless, from our data we can determine some underlying dimensions that all Manager-as-Developers must take into account when moving their units from their present status to excellence.

We have identified seven important components of building an excellent department: (1) assessing appropriateness for change; (2) conditioning the turf; (3) building readiness and acceptance with subordinates, peers, and superiors; (4) building mutual-influence relationships with difficult subordinates; (5) developing a shared-responsibility team; (6) developing individual subordinates; and (7) identifying and gaining commitment to an overarching goal. For analytical purposes, we will be ascribing a logical sequence among these components, but in practice, we have found many variations. Some managers have started with actions we have ranked sixth or seventh (as Deborah did). Furthermore, in almost all cases, these are not discrete steps with clearly delineated boundaries between each stage; a great deal of overlap usually occurs, and most managers worked on several categories concurrently. Successful implementation, however, appears eventually to encompass all of these steps.

Step 1: Assessing Appropriateness for Change

At the very beginning, you need to ask two questions: "Do the conditions in which the Manager-as-Developer model works best presently exist in my department?" "Even if they are present, is this the most appropriate time to implement this model?"

In terms of the first issue, we have repeatedly stated that this managerial approach is most appropriate when: subordinates have complex and interdependent tasks; they are working in a changing environment; and they are reasonably competent. Note that these conditions were certainly met in Deborah Linke's department. But there are many managerial situations in which conditions are not right—tasks may be simple and routine, change may be quite slow, and subordinates may presently be working at the limits of their potential. In those situations, a manager with high technical competence who still best knows what is to be done and how to do it will get better performance from a Manager-as-Technician or Conductor style.

An example from one of our workshop participants, where most of these conditions were met, illustrates how vital one

missing condition can be. Ted headed a research-and-development lab doing metallurgy work for aircraft engines. People in
his department were highly competent engineers and scientists, who did complex work and faced constant change in
technology and customer demands. Their work was interdependent within a project, but not between the several projects
going on in the department at the same time. Thus the project
supervisors (who reported to Ted), did not feel interconnected
with the other supervisors even though they too had complex
tasks and worked in a changing environment. As Ted explained:

> I encouraged the supervisors to come to the weekly meetings with
> their own agenda and to take charge of the meetings. Rather than my
> previous style of giving orders, I limited myself to asking questions so
> as not to interfere with their activities. (But, if results weren't forth-
> coming, as they had promised, I asked close questions.) This ap-
> proach did not work well. They did not wish to assume departmental
> responsibility. They continued to view the department as an arbitrarily
> arranged group of separate fiefdoms and did not wish to accept the
> challenge of changing old ways. In fact, one of my subordinates re-
> signed because he was sure that my efforts to share management re-
> sponsibilities were only an admission of my incompetence.

In another case, the manager reluctantly realized that her
subordinates were not sufficiently competent to allow the department to achieve excellence. Her organization had grown
rapidly over the last couple of years, and the tasks in her department had become increasingly complex. More than half
her supervisors lacked technical training, but had learned on
the job when conditions were simple. For her to expect more
out of them than they were presently giving would have been
untenable. Furthermore, they would have been traumatized if
they were asked to share in the responsibility for managing
the department; they were struggling to keep their noses
above water just fulfilling their present job duties. If this leader were to use all aspects of the Manager-as-Developer approach, it would have been necessary to replace many of her
staff (which she eventually decided to do), since she had ample

evidence that they did not have the educational background or capacity to learn the new skills.

The first question (are the conditions right) can have an affirmative answer while the second (is the time right) is answered negatively. There are many legitimate reasons to postpone introducing the Developer approach. One of our managers held off because his unit was three-fourths of the way through its yearly budget cycle and his group could only focus on meeting those goals. The introduction of a major change in how the department was to be managed could only have been felt as disruptive. (That manager prudently waited until his unit was in the first-quarter planning stage for the next year's cycle before modifying his leadership style.) Another manager was confronted with a reduction in workforce mandated by top management. His staff was suffering so much uncertainty and anxiety over their own futures in the company that it would have been impossible for them to take on increased responsibilities. The leader had to wait until all reductions had been made before he could ask for the increased involvement demanded by the Manager-as-Developer style.

In our experience, however, the major factor determining the appropriateness for introducing a Developer approach rests not with the subordinates or the department but with the leader. It is common for leaders to put the blame on subordinates—"They aren't competent to take increased responsibility"—or on the organization—"This approach is not compatible with my boss's style"—rather than admitting their own reluctance. Generally, manager willingness or unwillingness most determines whether this leadership style will be tried (and whether or not it will be successful). Managers' reticence may be due to their being under too much stress to handle the effort of dramatically changing their leadership approach or to their not being enough dissatisfied with their present heroic styles.

Whatever the forces ruling the organization, the department, or the manager, it is necessary to assess whether this is an appropriate change to make and an appropriate time to make it. Discretion may be the better part of valor in this decision, because there are major costs if you decide to start down the path with the Manager-as-Developer approach and then do not follow through. False starts can raise subordinates' expectations, just to dash them into great cynicism. Those who bought into the new goals of producing excellence will feel disillusioned, and those who were fearful of change will feel validated for having resisted; both reactions will make it that much more difficult the next time you propose something different.

Note that this point of suitability applies to implementing the entire approach, as Deborah Linke did. It is possible to introduce bits and pieces from the Manager-as-Developer model —such as improving relationships with individual subordinates, introducing a career-development program linked with task assignments, or improving the meeting effectiveness of your team. But each of these changes done separately, although likely to produce some benefit, will not have the major effect that a concerted effort will have. Not only is there synergy when each part builds on the others, but the Manager-as-Developer model is more than a collection of parts—it is a mindset that produces a wide array of developmental activities.

Step 2: Conditioning the Turf

Although we have suggested assessing readiness as Step 1, we do not mean that everything has to be perfectly lined up before a beginning can be made. Rarely is a department so ready for the Developer approach as Deborah Linke's unit (and rarely are managers as unambivalent about producing change as she was). In most cases, some tasks are simple while others are complex, some work is interdependent while some is not, and some subordinates are relatively highly skilled while others have a lot to learn. It is misleading (and limited) to assume that all conditions have to be perfect before one can move as a Developer. The normal problems that exist in most departments should not be excuses to stay in the heroic mode.

The question is not whether all conditions for a postheroic style presently exist, but whether they can be made to exist. That is, can jobs be made more complex and more interdependent, and can subordinates (and teams) be developed to take on this increased responsibility? It is not a matter of making things more complicated for the sake of fitting the model. Instead, in most of the organizations we have been describing, task complexity and work interdependence already potentially exist and have been either designed away or around. One of the reasons why managers' jobs are so harried is because subordinate task simplification has driven decisions higher than necessary. Much of what managers do can be pushed downward to subordinates who are closer to the problem, which increases job challenge and task interdependence—perfect conditions for a development management style.

Frequently, the Manager-as-Developer approach could be effectively utilized if some important preparatory actions were taken—perhaps restructuring the office, changing or expanding assignments, designating a team where none had existed, or building relevant systems and procedures. As one example of such conditioning, let's return to Ted's problem described in the previous section. His subordinates' resistance to collaborative effort was due to their having separate fiefdoms. Ted's actions focused on changing his department's structure.

> We restructured our research projects so that there was one department-wide project under the direction of a project manager (who was chosen from the senior engineering staff). This meant that the entire department had a technical goal in common, which has had rather good results for department collaboration. There are now numerous opportunities for the individual sections to build on the activities of this common project as well as a forced requirement for each to use some of the other's work to gain their own objectives.

Subordinates' jobs can often be enriched, by giving them new work assignments, by delegating downward important (technical and managerial) tasks (as Deborah did), or in various other ways. In many cases, the question of creating complexity, or forcing it, is not the issue; the development approach permits the increased complexity that earlier had been denied. Too many organizations have tried to apply the scientific management technique of breaking jobs into small, manageable pieces to jobs that inherently demand wholeness, intelligent thought, and judgment. Likewise, as we have noted, it is often less a matter of "increasing task interdependence" (since such work interdependence may already be required by the nature of the unit's tasks) than of pushing coordination problems down to the subordinates most directly involved. Finally, it is less often the case of "inadequate subordinates" than that their abilities have not been fully developed. Having more challenging jobs augmented by on- and off-the-job training frequently brings subordinate competence up past the minimal level needed for a Developer style to work.

These forms of "conditioning the turf" do not preclude the more common (and more drastic) actions of changing personnel, restructuring the department (so that the right players are on the key team), and modifying outdated or inappropriate rules and procedures. All can be useful. Nevertheless, everything does not have to be perfectly in place before one manages as a Developer. In fact, one of the best developmental activities can be to involve subordinates in making some of these changes (a point we will return to in later sections).

Preparing the Turf with Your Boss and Peers

A very important "turf" to condition is your own superior. Bosses do not like surprises. Even a boss who has been hoping you would change your leadership style in exactly the ways we prescribe will have become used to certain patterns of interactions with you and your unit. It can be disconcerting to your superior if, without proper briefing, he or she finds that your subordinates have decision-making power that they did not have before, are representing you and your department on external task forces and committees, and have an increasing role in managing the department. Cueing the superior in ahead of time usually eases these problems. And as Deborah Linke found, it is often possible for bosses to be supportive when sub-ordinates utilize a different leadership style if they understand the changes and see that they are for the mutual goal of im-proving departmental effectiveness.

Most of the workshop participants who went back planning changes in their department, first talked with their superiors to explain the reasons for the changes and what they hoped to gain. Several managers even showed their superior their ques-tionnaire results, a gutsy move since the scores included the skills the manager's subordinates thought needed improve-ment. For several people, "conditioning the turf" entailed a direct effort to improve their relationships with the boss. One manager, for example, felt that he had too little influence with his boss (a problem the subordinates had strongly pointed out in their questionnaire responses) and went in to change that situation (an influence act in and of itself!).

Another turf area likely to need some conditioning is your peers. For a variety of reasons they have an interest in your leadership style; it may affect your ability to deliver what they need, how your subordinates respond to their requests and those of their subordinates, and how you look to upper man-agement compared to them. Since you probably can't do your job without the cooperation of your co-workers, you need to get them ready for what you're up to.

With those closest to you, you can talk about what you plan to do and why and enlist their support. You might ask them to let you know if they see you slipping into the heroic mode in interactions with your subordinates or to pass on subordinate reactions they hear about through the grapevine.

For peers who are more distant or more clearly antagonis-tic, you might try to figure out what impact your department's changes will have on them. Then you could inform them about particular aspects of your changed department that will make life easier for them or service them better. You could ask them for information on current interdepartmental prob-lems and then involve your subordinates in the solution. Final-ly, you need to prepare them for any temporary alterations in your department's ability to meet their needs during "reorganization" and show how the changes will ultimately benefit them.

In general, for any attempt at change, it is useful to identify who will be impacted by or interested in it, what their stakes are, how they will be influenced in terms of status, discretion, resources, relationships, and activities, and what you can do to anticipate difficulties. This technique, called *stakeholder analysis*, is useful on any issue, but especially for making the kinds of changes called for by the Manager-as-Developer model.

Step 3: Sending Initial Signals to Subordinates

A change in your leadership style, with concurrent demands that subordinates change their behavior, will be more successful if it is clearly communicated rather than carried out covertly. When a manager states what he or she is trying to do (and the reason for doing it), clear signals are sent to the subordinates and paranoia is reduced. Nothing causes more consternation (and wasted effort) among subordinates than a significant (but unexplained) change in the leader's style. Note how clear Deborah/was about her intentions in her initial meeting with her subordinates.

Even though the articulation of new goals and expectations is crucial, relying solely on statements is not enough. People know that words are cheap, that the manager's speech doesn't prove he or she is committed to this new direction. Subordinates wonder whether the manager's new approach is a fad that will last only while times are good and be jettisoned at the first sign of difficulties. At some companies, subordinates joke about the "latest binder for the latest program," and make bets about when it will end up on the shelf. Insofar as this new approach makes significant demands oñ subordinates, they will be rightfully hesitant to give their full commitment before they are convinced of its substance. As another of our participants reported: "There was tremendous doubt that my goal would last more than a month—the ignore-the-boss-and-he'll-forget-it syndrome. I've recently noticed some discomfort on the part of some of my subordinates who realize I haven't forgotten it!"

It is useful for the leader to plan some tangible action that conveys both the reason for the change and a personal commitment to this new direction. Such signals can take many forms. In some cases, internal events provide an appropriate rationale. Typical examples are: the development of a new product, or the department taking on a complex and important project; a consultant's report that reveals morale or performance problems; a major crisis in operations; falling sales or increased costs. All these events give credence to a leader's saying, "The way we have managed before won't suffice for these new conditions." The manager we mentioned earlier, whose subordinates were not competent to handle the Manager-as-Developer approach, sent clear and strong signals by transferring or counseling out several members of her immediate subordinate group. She knew that this unusual toughness would help make clear her determination to raise the unit's performance. Thus, "conditioning the turf" can be one way to send clear signals.

External factors can legitimize changes in how the department is to be run. Such events as a mandated reorganization or a change in the unit's functions are excuses for changing the type of leadership used in the unit. The interesting suggestion in this idea is that crises may be the best time to introduce a Manager-as-Developer approach. Managers often tell us "there is too much going on in my department for me to introduce such a major change in my style." Yet it is often under conditions of crisis when change can most easily be brought about! (Cohen, 1982). Whether the problem is internally or externally derived, such events can be the rallying force to pull people away from their provincial concerns into a common effort. In a sense, participants at our workshop had an unusual advantage, because they could use the results of the Leadership Questionnaire to gather this common effort (see appendix). Subordinates knew that their scores had been summarized for their managers as part of the workshop, so they were ready to hear the results upon the manager's re-

turn. The majority of our managers used the opportunity to report the results and begin a discussion about what they had
learned.* But even our workshop managers did not consider
such discussion a low-risk venture. They expressed many
worries: "Will my subordinates still respect me if I talk about
my deficient areas?" "Will they use this opportunity to really
jump on me?—this could end up being pretty vicious." "What
if they expect instant change and I can't live up to their expectations?" Nevertheless, results were positive in all the cases
reported to us. Respect went up, not down, because subordinates saw their boss's openness as a courageous act. They felt
relief that behaviors of the superior that had bothered them
could now be openly discussed. Generally the tone of these
meetings was collaborative. As one manager described it:
"Subordinates recognized my problem and offered support to
me—we jointly prepared a plan to achieve change, and it
worked very well." These positive outcomes do not deny the
stressfulness of this experience for the managers. Discussing
one's leadership style—the problems as well as the assets—before a group of subordinates is not easy.

This kind of vulnerability on the part of the leader has impact because it concretely demonstrates the leader's commitment. Being willing to take the risk of openly discussing one's
style, encouraging comments (and criticism) from others, and
considering modifications of behavior are actions taken only by
a person who is serious about improvement. As a second benefit, the leader actually demonstrates, or personifies, the type of
changes he or she is talking about. Deborah Linke could talk
about her goal of wanting to be more open about receiving
feedback, but her credibility was underlined when she asked
her subordinates to expand on the Leadership Questionnaire
results. This approach also has the benefit of setting the norm
that behavior is to be openly discussed. Central to the Manag-

*This kind of meeting parallels the team-building sessions run by organizational con-
sultants who collect data on how the department is doing and then feed the results
back to the manager and the subordinates. See Cohen, Fink, and Gadon (1979) for further descriptions of this approach.

er-as-Developer approach is the legitimacy to talk about how individuals (and groups) are operating. Again, just making the statement is platitudinous, but encouraging discussion of your leadership style demonstrates the statement and illustrates the benefits from openness.

Setting a norm for open discussion made it easier for our respondents to talk later to subordinates about their work styles. It doesn't feel quite fair for the leader to say, "*I* am committed to improvement, but *you* go first." When the leader starts, it is that much easier for subordinates to follow. Finally, this discussion tended to clear the air between subordinates and manager. By airing their complaints, leaders and subordinates transform adversarial relationships into collaborations, which builds commitment.

There may be situations, however, that don't favor the leader who comes to subordinates with the goal of joint improvement. For example, the operating officer in a small organization asked one of us for help because the morale was low. He had tried a joint-improvement approach before, but he had not followed through on modifying the problem behavior that his subordinates had pointed out. He said that he would be willing to hold another meeting to discuss problems with his operating style, but his subordinates refused. "We can't do it again. We feel burned out with the process and don't have the energy to raise these issues with the possibility that nothing will improve." Although it appeared that the manager was for the first time firmly committed to change, his subordinates could not be convinced. The manager had gone to the well once too often. He had to come at the problem from another angle—to begin with more concrete changes in his own behavior, without the support of a collective commitment to change.

Another manager discovered a different problem with open discussion of leadership style with subordinates: She couldn't carry through on being open. As the feedback continued and she became increasingly defensive, trying to explain away all criticism directed at her, her subordinates closed up and became convinced that she would never change. These examples reinforce the point we made earlier about first assessing your own willingness to change. Promising improvement but not following through causes problems that come back later to bite.

In general, whether the manager uses an external event, an examination of how the department is doing, or even an examination of his or her own management style, subordinates require a tangible sign that statements about change are to be taken seriously. Furthermore, for change to persist, the new direction must be reiterated frequently. In his work on how chief executives produce change, Peters (1979) found frequent use of signs and symbols, often just small actions that were repeated time and time again, which signified that the change had top priority. Deborah Linke used the printing and distribution of her unit's overarching goal as such a symbol. When her subordinates themselves posted the goal, this further increased its symbolic and real power.

Step 4: Building Mutual-Influence Relationships with Difficult Subordinates

Of the three components of the Manager-as-Developer model, usually the easiest to begin with is the building of effective subordinate relationships. Working one-on-one to improve working relationships is likelier to produce beneficial results quickly, is another sign that things will be different, and yet is less risky than taking on the entire team at once. If you can't improve your relationships with difficult individuals, you are no worse off than before you tried, and you probably earn credit for effort.

Working with individual subordinates to understand the problems and to improve the relationships is a source of crucial information and a start at getting all subordinates heading at least roughly in the same direction. A leader should listen carefully to disaffected people; they may speak for others in the department who are more reticent about expressing their views. The interest you demonstrate by listening is likely to start to alter the negative feelings.

Working with individuals first also reduces the risks of getting negative group reactions. You don't want to open up loaded issues in a group that includes resistant subordinates who might gang up against you.

If you can start to find some common ground with the difficult subordinates, they are less likely to try to sabotage your efforts later in group meetings. Similarly, subordinates who feel estranged from you may not feel free to speak up in a group—not only might you retaliate, but other members could turn and attack. Thus, for the sake of both the superior and the (difficult) subordinate, the wiser choice is often to open up communication on a one-to-one basis. Each can start to understand the position of the other and work toward common expectations.

In Chapter 5 we explained how to use supportive confrontation to deal with problem subordinates. Some variation of that method—understanding the other's goals sufficiently to get close enough to give powerful feedback in a way that builds the relationship—will help foster a better working relationship. Deborah Linke found that changing her mind-set from its constant negative focus helped her gain a more satisfying relationship. Others decide to begin by directly asking the subordinate what they as managers have been doing to make the subordinate unhappy; they thereby demonstrate their readiness to alter managerial behavior in order to clear the negative atmosphere. The important goal is to make it possible for all subordinates to contribute to their maximum potential.

Variations of this approach allowed several of our past participants to break through their dissatisfaction, or even antagonism, with particular subordinates. In some cases, the employee made an about-face to become a very valuable contributor to the department. In other instances, as with the underperforming sales rep reported in Chapter 5, both parties soon realized that the employee's talents did not fit the job and mutual agreement was reached that the person should leave.

If the manager can create sufficient understanding with each of the key subordinates, so that each is willing to work in a cooperative way, the stage is set for the next step in building

a shared-responsibility team. If these individual connections
have not developed, then a manager faces potential problems
in moving into team building. In addition to the possibilities
we raised earlier (members can clam up in group meetings or
coalesce against the leader), subordinate resistance can undermine the group development effort. Building a mature team is
difficult enough without having members dragging their feet
or lobbing in hand grenades at inopportune moments! On the
other hand, a manager skilled in managing group process and
capable of diffusing the obstructive tactics of resisters can use
team meetings as a place to improve individual relationships.
We recommend this technique only if you feel comfortable
with considerable openness and tension.

The following scenario exemplifies some of the problems
that can develop when a leader moves too quickly into team
building, without taking at least the first steps in building a
working relationship with a difficult subordinate. Nick had
been promoted to head the administration department, a position that Sally had wanted. Sally's reaction to being passed
over was not helped by the fact that Nick was almost 20 years
younger and a rising star in the organization. Their different
styles further compounded the problem; Nick tended to be aggressive and confrontative, whereas Sally was more supportive.

Nick wanted to build a cohesive team with Sally and the two
other persons who reported to him, but the first meeting—
where they were to explore how they wanted to function and
what departmental problems to handle—was a disaster. Everything that Nick suggested, Sally argued against, and she
couldn't get a complete sentence out of her mouth before
Nick interrupted. Unfortunately, Nick became highly defensive, and since he lacked the group skills to stop their downward spiral and work on their relationship, the meeting broke
up with the two at loggerheads and everybody frustrated.

Fortunately, Nick had the courage to walk in the next day
to Sally's office to try to improve the way they worked together. The meeting was not easy; Sally fully expressed her dissatisfaction with Nick's style and her feelings of being ignored (by
him as well as the organization). Nick was tough too,

expressing his unhappiness with her lack of full commitment and her tendency to put things off and be disorganized. But both of them stuck with the discussion, which they ended, not as friends, but being able to listen to each other and work out mutually accepted agreements.

The next staff meeting was far different from the first. Tension still existed between them, and they had to make extra effort not to get hooked by the other. However, the more competent they became in their interaction, the more the tension receded. In the months that followed, the two had to meet several other times to continue work on their relationship. Although that initial confrontation session didn't (and couldn't) produce a perfectly smooth relationship, Nick and Sally had established ground rules that allowed them to interact productively on department problems. The way they worked together slowly but steadily improved.

Step 5: Developing a Shared-Responsibility Team

For key reporting subordinates to share in the responsibility of managing the unit, there must be an enabling vehicle, that is a cohesive team. In the process of developing the team, meetings change from information-transmittal sessions to occasions of joint problem solving on the main departmental issues.

The difficulty comes, of course, in moving from the former condition to the latter. It is one thing to announce that the group will now deal with the core departmental problems and another to have all the subordinates accept that additional task. Several of our respondents reported that acceptance of this expanded responsibility was difficult for subordinates who "just wanted to be told what to do." Even when subordinates were willing to take on increased responsibility, managers worried about whether their subordinates had the necessary skills, or the group had the appropriate norms, to be successful.

Managers have often made use of the various team-building activities conducted by organization development professionals, which usually involve offsite retreats with a variety of training exercises based on data collected from members about barriers to team effectiveness.* These retreats can be beneficial, especially if the culture of the organization is compatible with such activities and a competent professional is utilized. Nevertheless, a manager often doesn't need outside help to accomplish team building, and most of our managers developed their teams on their own.

We suggest that you do not separate team development from the normal day-to-day activities of your department. Use your group's regular meetings as the place to deal with increasingly important departmental issues. This approach often feels more natural—especially to a group that has not had experience with organization development activities—and dealing with real-time issues reduces resistance. Several managers discovered that when the group dealt with important issues, subordinates felt they could not afford to withdraw. "There's nothing like having the group decide personnel assignments or even budget allocations to pull participators out of the woodwork."

The leader must first act to make the meeting belong to the group, not to the leader. This may sound unimportant—after all, managers almost all say, "It is for all of us." But subordinates almost universally say, "It's the boss's meeting." And it is the boss's meeting if the manager decides the agenda, runs the session, and retains veto power on all decisions. It is contradictory to expect subordinates to share in the responsibility for running the department if they do not also share the meeting. Certain questions can identify how widely the ownership of the meeting is spread. Does the boss or the group set the agenda? Who prioritizes agenda items? Does the manager automatically run each meeting or do staff rotate the responsibility? Does most discussion occur between the manager and each of the subordinates or among all members fairly equally?

---

*Relevant readings on team-building approaches are Beckhard (1972); Cohen, Fink, and Gadon (1979); and Dyer (1977).

Is the key person to convince always the boss or the people who have to implement the decision?

Obviously, you can expand meeting ownership by modifying the dimensions suggested by these questions. In addition, a specific event often signifies that responsibility is to be shared. At a session where a manager, Ruth, was negotiating new roles and norms with her staff group to produce a shared-responsibility team, someone asked, "How do we handle it when a person can't make the meeting?" "We'll hold it anyway," was the quick response from the group. Then the point was raised about making decisions that might influence the absent member. After some discussion, Ruth suggested, "How about the rule that if you are not there, you agree to live with the group's decision?" "Does that apply to you too?" one member shot back. Ruth swallowed twice and agreed. There was a burst of laughter and members kidded that she had better watch out. But Ruth firmly replied, "If you are going to share in the responsibility, you also share in living with the consequences of your decisions." That interaction, which so well symbolized what shared responsibility meant to her, dramatically changed the tone of the meeting.

Group development also benefits as the centrality of the issues tackled increases. As members have more agenda input, issues naturally take on more importance for group members, but you can help by bringing in crucial issues to set the tone. The range of problems that respondents brought to their teams was large. Some introduced task issues: the closing of a division (and reallocation of management personnel in that facility); reconciling engineering problems between the design, drafting, and records department and cost accounting; deciding whether to open satellite offices in nearby communities; and negotiating quality performance standards for each of the subordinates' areas for the coming year. Other managers worked on policies and procedures: setting up a control system to monitor progress on projects; developing a two-way appraisal system for the manager and the group members; modifying the management by objectives system (MBO) so that rather than leader-determined goals, each subordinate proposed goals and negotiated them with the group.

Working on policies and procedures is related to a previous point: It is not necessary that all systems (such as scheduling, financial and control systems, and performance-appraisal programs) be in place before starting to implement the Developer model. When a procedure is lacking, jointly creating it can develop the team.

Many managers hesitate to go this far with an undeveloped group. Although moving too fast can be dangerous, foot-dragging can create missed opportunities. When problems can be openly discussed, failures in group performance can be utilized for developmental purposes. This provides the needed quality control while helping the group to grow.

This dual approach—linking team solution of important issues with further development of the team—can also work with a totally new group.

> Soon after I came back, the company reorganized the staff in my division in a way which involved numerous changes in personnel and reporting lines. In order to build the team spirit and get the members working with each other, I assigned them the task of developing promotional and motivational programs for the local retail operations (people under them). I gave them no direction, other than parameters as to the group of employees and operations to be targeted, time limitations and a dollar budget. The creation of the specific program was left to the group. The result was a solid program that combined new ideas with parts from previous programs. It also involved less paperwork and administration time than previous plans that had been developed by home office. The extra benefit was that it familiarized the new group members with each other and helped to grow the nucleus of their team effort.

Another way to move a group toward a shared-responsibility team involves a conscious change of the manager's role in the group—from problem-solver to builder of the team's capacity to solve problems. This transition was difficult for many managers. They had trouble putting aside their past tendencies to focus on personal solutions for problems (as Manager-as-

Technician) or on personal control of the discussion to produce predetermined answers (as Manager-as-Conductor). The experiences of three managers illustrate the range of managerial solutions for role transition.

> At first, before the meeting, I would figure out an answer I could live with. If they come up with a better answer, I'd buy that but if not, I had my back-up. Then I realized I was doing all this extra work ahead of time, and it put them in the stance of having to convince me rather than convince each other. Realizing that, I have learned to back off. It is hard, but it's working.

> I've taken a much less visible position at most of our meetings. I have had to learn to sit back and let the fur fly—it's a matter of letting conflict come out. Conflict on a controlled basis really gets people listening to each other. But to work, it takes a group who know each other, respect each other, and realize that only the "room" knows what went on.

> I call meetings to resolve specific problems and announce that I am not going to make the final decision. I then walk out of the meeting at an appropriate time to leave them to develop their solution.

These managers found they could move away from a Manager-as-Technician or Manager-as-Conductor role only by temporarily becoming less active than they had been before. Their solutions probably testify to how ingrained their heroic tendencies had become. Nevertheless, it is not a good idea to change from being active to being passive. The opposite of being on top of every point being discussed does not have to be keeping quiet. Shared responsibility, as discussed in chapter 6, requires active managing, not abdication. Otherwise, as the manager who started walking out of meetings reported: "I sometimes felt out of control because I didn't know about the problem solution until after it was implemented. I also had some difficulty explaining to superiors what was going on, and they, at times, accused me of abdicating my responsibility."

Furthermore, withdrawing, verbally or physically, robs the group of important skills you can provide—helping the members be more effective problem solvers—which is not the same as solving the problem yourself. You need to be engaged, but engaged in building the group's capacities and willingness to share responsibility, not in figuring out the problem, determining the solution, or trying to sell it to subordinates. Deborah Linke, for example, was quite active. She changed the purpose and procedures of the group by modifying how meetings were run and expanding the domain of the agenda. She worked to change the norms of the group about open conflict, and she helped members become more skilled in working in groups. All of these interventions were intensely active.

The question again rises. Is the Developer model just a refurbishing of the old heroic model? A substitution of the heroic manager who knows the answer to how the group should operate for the old hero who knew the answer to task issues? Although the Developer model does require some team skills and willingness to examine the way things are going, the responsibility for development does not rest solely on the leader. In fact, an important developmental action involves modifying the norms and procedures of the team so that the members can decide how the group can improve. Managerial initiative may set the wheels in motion, but the Developer does not continue as the group's sole driving force. Deborah Linke's team, for example, spent time at the end of each meeting examining how the group was working and what was needed to improve. When the whole group can openly examine how they are doing, development increases exponentially.

Sharing the responsibility for managing the unit frees the leader from having to know all the answers. This frequently leads to better solutions and removes a burden from the manager's shoulders.

As part of my job, I was supposed to "control" the systems projects, which was difficult for me since I didn't have the necessary technical knowledge. But the task was crucial because many of these projects were in some danger of going off course.

Using skills learned from the leadership workshop, I called a group of project managers together and said that they knew how to control these projects and that if they would share their knowledge and ideas with each other they could improve their control. They would then be in a better position to answer my questions and to insure their early knowledge of projects in trouble.

At the meetings where we developed a procedure, my role was to control the process but not to get involved in the task itself. At the first meeting, they selected a group of problems that cause projects to go off course. After that meeting, I distributed minutes that included this list. At the second meeting, they refined the list and brainstormed for possible solutions. They then weeded out solutions which were clearly impractical. I summarized their conclusions but before locking into them, I charged them to go out and test the solutions to see what actually worked.

So I control the process and the minutes; they control the content. The outcome has been very good. They are the owners of this procedure for controlling our projects.

My vice-president for operations suddenly quit due to ill health. We were faced with the question of how to manage the eight branch operations units, coordinate the interface between the branches and the three product divisions, and with corporate headquarters. Since we are a relatively small operation, we were short of management talent and needed a thorough external search to permanently fill that position. My first inclination, as in the past, was to step in and handle it myself.

But I thought, "If my executive group is going to share with me in the responsibility for managing, I should throw them the problem." We had a two-hour session in which we collectively grappled with the issues. I didn't try to push my solution on the group; instead I saw my role as making sure that the tough issues were raised. This was probably the best meeting we have had—and even though my initial plan would have worked, their solution was far superior. Not only did they accept the responsibility for solving the problem, but they took on the responsibility for implementing the solution as well. And their approach had the benefits of increasing Branch-Division communication (a past bottleneck) while moving us far along the path of regionalization—a move we had been wanting to make, but that I thought would have to be postponed until a new V.P. of operations was permanently in place. I left that meeting feeling as if 16 pounds had been lifted off my shoulders!

Step 6: Developing Individual Subordinates

The development of individual subordinates is the step that most easily can move forward or be carried on concurrently with other steps. It arises naturally from the ongoing work of the unit, since it flows out of individual assignments and interactions. "Developing others" has too frequently meant either sending people to off-site training programs (where what is learned may have questionable relevance and transferability to job performance) or throwing new assignments at them without careful thought about whether they fit their needs, interests, or talents. Although either of these approaches is an improvement over keeping a person dead-ended in the same job, they are still far from what is needed to make maximum use of the subordinate's (potential) abilities.

The managers we trained, like Deborah Linke, began developing mainly on the job, with off-site programs augmenting but not substituting for on-line, real-time learning. Furthermore, the process became continuous and joint. It was continuous in that it occurred through such ongoing activities as assigning tasks that were stretching, coaching so that subordinates could learn from these tasks, and regular feedback on performance. It was joint in that most of the tasks were negotiated between the manager and each subordinate. As a result, assignments approached the boundary of each person's ability—challenging enough to have a "stretch quality" but well enough within the range of the subordinate's competence so that success was probable. The negotiations worked to identify a common ground between individual interests and organizational needs.

Note that development can occur within the negotiation process itself. If the subordinate sets expectations too low, the superior is in a-position to point out underused skills. Conversely, if the subordinate aspires for tasks presently beyond reach, the superior can indicate the further knowledge and skills needed in order to be able to take on that expanded assignment. Virtually all problems can be used for learning.

In dealing with individual subordinates, the Manger-as-Developer must constantly ask the question: "How can I increase my subordinate's competencies while getting the task done?" The Developer thus promotes significant expansion of the subordinate's job responsibilities.

I set up a system whereby each individual had much greater choice in his or her own development. I had each person select a project from a list of available projects, rather than my making the assignments. Unless a certain project was of utmost importance, the individual had complete freedom of choice. That person also became responsible for defining any training needs for that assignment; my role was to ensure that the subordinate could get the desired training (from me, from somebody else in the unit, or through a formal program).

For each project, I negotiated higher standards than I had done before (these standards are reviewed quarterly with each person). I also became more open with my staff and shared much more information than I had in the past (technical information, political information, and information on what I wanted and how I felt). I became much clearer on my expectations of each person and where I stood on issues. I regularly discussed each individual's progress on an open, one-on-one basis.

The results? Quality of work increased almost immediately and the documentation standards were exceeded in a very short time—in fact, on the very first project. Improvement in quality of work was much higher than anticipated. Also, every critical project we had over the past year was completed on time or ahead of schedule. Trust between me and my subordinates rose dramatically and the group became very close. There was no turnover during the past year in my department, even though the overall rate was 20% for comparable units.

Managers in a developmental mode tend to do two things concurrently: set higher standards (and be tougher on their subordinates) and provide more assistance (and be more supportive). Toughness and support do not have to be antithetical; it's as if managers say, "I think you are capable of quality work

and I want to provide the assistance so you can attain it." The
higher-quality work often means that superiors delegate tasks
they previously would have taken on themselves.

> Chiefly, I have tried to enable "subordinates" (awkward term for me)
> to work to their highest capacity. For example, my assistant recently
> did most of the preparation work for some printed materials—work-
> ing with the lay-out people, details with printers, some rewriting of
> copy, contact with persons involved in providing the information, and
> so forth. Not only is the end product very satisfactory, but she feels
> good about being a part of it. Previously, I might have thought I had
> to do it all myself.

But toughness has a part in seeing that people come
through. One general manager was having trouble with two of
his plant managers. The plants were 400 miles distant, and the
plant managers had been using this separation to go their own
ways (often to the detriment of the entire organization). The
general manager grew firmer in setting limits through using
the management-by-objectives and career development processes to set explicit standards with consequences for nonper-
formance.

For many of our managers, "toughness with support" turned
out to be an excellent way to deal with subordinates who had
been performing at a substandard level. Rather than writing
such people off as incompetent, several managers, in a firm
but nonpunitive way, jointly developed high but attainable
standards and then provided the assistance needed to attain
them.

This approach was not without problems. Many managers
reported that it was still hard to give negative feedback—especially to subordinates whose poor performance had been tolerated for years, so they could justifiably claim that "nobody has
mentioned this before." There were also pitfalls on the other
side—in giving so much support and assistance that discretion
was taken away from the subordinate. As another manager
said, "I have spent considerable effort in coaching my managers to expect more from their subordinates, but I have to

watch myself constantly to keep from moving from 'helping' to 'helping the hell' out of my people." Others reported similar difficulties in knowing when to intervene with struggling subordinates. "When do I come in when I think I have the answer and when do I hold back and let them work it out—it's still confusing for me." This is a core issue in helping others grow.

No cookbook answer can be provided for this question of when to step in. The amount of direction, degree of support, and amount of positive and negative feedback require judgment, not formulas. We can only suggest two guidelines. First, the superior who assumes that subordinates are willfully lazy and generally incompetent will be much less "developmental" than one who respects the subordinate's abilities and intentions. Optimistic assumptions help create higher performance (Rosenthal, 1968; Livingston, 1969). Second, the manager must establish a relationship that allows for joint negotiation about the development process. The subordinate has to be able both to ask for help and to indicate when there is too much. And, as happened with Deborah Linke, subordinates have to be able to confront the boss about being too negative (or too positive). It would be a heroic regression to expect the leader to know exactly how best to develop each subordinate. Instead, the leader must be postheroic in setting up conditions that support both parties' working on the subordinate's development.

Several managers found that just communicating the expectation of continual development was enough.

A couple of my subordinates captured the spirit of shared management quite quickly. One of them took the initiative to develop a work plan for one of the unit's major projects. She subsequently called meetings, monitored progress, and updated the plan as work proceeded. Although there was a higher level of conflict than when the same project was done in prior years, the project was completed earlier than ever before and the work was of higher quality. Another subordinate asked to participate in developing the budget and progress reports for the unit. This was done as part of a developmental plan to prepare that individual for managerial responsibilities elsewhere in the organization.

Step 7: Identifying and Gaining Commitment to an Overarching Goal

Although Deborah Linke and others have used work on an overarching goal as one of the initial actions in building an excellent department, we have placed it as the final step because it appears to be comparatively difficult to implement. Determining a central direction that genuinely shapes action can be a struggle, which can be eased by lining up other elements first. Nevertheless, when conditions are favorable some managers have been able to utilize the idea of one central goal to focus and energize their unit early on. A few respondents found this approach particularly easy since their departments were in the middle of working on next year's objectives, and they found the exercise of identifying their unit's central unique thrust to be helpful in tying together the various specific performance goals.

Another manager used the idea of an overarching goal to change the focus of his subordinates, who were area supervisors responsible for clusters of retail stores. Mike wanted more of a sales thrust; he took that, and the conditions necessary to achieve it, as his unit's goal. Given one central theme for all divisions, subordinates did alter their attitudes about what issues should be central. For other managers, the attempt to identify an overarching goal helped to reveal that no real agreement existed about the unit's central thrust (even when members thought there was). "I reviewed my own ideas and sounded out their reactions as to the feasibility of this goal. I found we needed to reconsider, renegotiate, and refocus."

The general consensus among those who applied the concept of an overarching goal to their department was that different perspectives were surfaced, which then led to building a common point of view. As one manager reported: "The exercise was good because my managers began to see what everyone else was trying to do and thought was important. They better understand my point of view and each other's, as a result of these discussions."

Gaining greater agreement about direction is certainly a significant improvement over having members define it in different ways; but it does not represent the potential benefits of a challenging, exciting, and central overarching goal. Our workshop participants had more difficulty implementing this aspect of the Manager-as-Developer model than the model's other parts. Relatively few used it as extensively as Deborah Linke did.

Yet we believe an overarching goal is a crucial ingredient a manager needs to produce excellence. Like the afterburner of a jet, it produces a final boost that allows the members (and the leader) to give their full commitment to a task that is exciting and worth the extra effort. What does it take to benefit fully from its implementation? In part, the answer is time. Time is needed to identify precisely and fully implement an overarching goal that subordinates find exciting, yet is within the capacities of the department, the larger organization, and the manager. It also takes time to gain full member commitment to such a goal.

Goal adoption also requires genuine commonality of departmental purpose, not just an arbitrary collection of several unrelated units reporting to one boss. A manager explained: "I have five relatively different groups reporting to me. Each group wanted their own goal and had difficulty committing to a more general statement." In another case, subordinates had become demoralized by trying to achieve what they felt were unrealistically high targets set by top management and had retreated into their individual projects. Their manager said, "I presented my view of the department goal, but it met only grudging acceptance. We discussed it at length, but they were not able to accept the idea of a departmental goal and they didn't think mine was attainable."

Managerial follow-up is absolutely necessary to the process of goal adoption. Some managers realized later that despite initial agreement the goal was not actively used. "I stated the goal to the group and asked if they saw it the same way I did. Several took shots at it and good suggestions were incorporated. I think we still have the goal, but we haven't expressed it recently—maybe I should."

Finally, and most important, the manager has to be willing to make an enthusiastic commitment to the unit and its goal. In our observations of those in middle and upper-middle management, we have been struck by their rationality and almost impersonal attitude toward their work. Although they want to do a good job, they hold back from seeing it as particularly special. They seem more focused on the day-to-day managing of "what is" rather than on leading the department to what "could be." Have our business schools and corporations produced too many managers and not enough leaders? Perhaps the professionalization of management over the last 20 years, with its emphasis on objective decision making, logical analysis, and controlling and monitoring, has had a stultifying effect. Perhaps such movements have inhibited the manager's personal involvement and excitement in the tasks, attitudes that can cause leaders to develop a vision of what their unit could be. It is as if managers feel that it is inappropriate for them to care deeply about their work.

Of course, company policies that rotate managers every 18 months to two years from position to position may also breed this detachment. A highly mobile manager has difficulty in identifying and becoming personally committed to the goal of any one unit; perhaps the only thing that manager can become invested in is his or her own personal development. Some movement spurs motivation, but overmobility may lead to disinvestment as a form of self-protection.

Even when rapid mobility isn't the problem, a manager can still be reluctant to become highly personally invested. Listen to the concerns that even a settled manager can feel about a department that is accelerating toward excellence. Bill was head of a large office (more than 200 professionals) in an international engineering firm. He had spent most of his professional life rising in the ranks within this office. He had called one of us in several years ago because he wanted to improve his managerial skills and overall office performance. With our help, Bill started to introduce a series of programs for his staff: a sophisticated strategic-planning operation; a quantitative management-by-objectives program that tied compensation to performance; quality circles; a new marketing effort; and a detailed management-training and career-development program for all personnel. The office became known as one of the most innovative in the organization and its profit figures placed it among the top five.

We were talking informally with him one day a few years later, and he said, almost apologetically, "You know, something is happening to me that concerns me. I have this strong emotional feeling about the office, like we're really special. It's sort of the feeling that you have for your family—that they are so important to you that you would do anything for them. I worry that maybe I am getting too involved. I always thought that it was dangerous for a manager to become that involved in the office. I'm worried that this office now means too much to me."

We did not share Bill's concern. Certainly there is danger if a manager is so ego-involved that all perspective is lost and the manager sees the business as an extension of self, as often happens to entrepreneurs who start their own companies. But we saw Bill as different from the president who confuses the firm with him or herself. His commitment was to serve the office, not to have the office serve him. His personal investment in these programs was necessary if they were to be fully embraced by the subordinates. They needed to know that he was fully committed to these new activities.

We think that managers will increasingly pay attention to how they can be personally committed to the core thrust of the unit. A number of recent books are evidence of a reassessment of the attitudes of detachment. The importance of building the appropriate culture (Ouchi, 1981; Deal and Kennedy, 1982) or organizational conditions (Kanter, 1983) and of identifying goals that challenge and excite (Pascale and Athos, 1981; Peters and Waterman, 1982) are subjects vitally important to the Developer. We are also encouraged by the

progress managers make in our training sessions in being able
to identify their unit's central thrust and convey it with increasing enthusiasm.

THE INTERACTION OF THE SEVEN STEPS

We noted earlier that the separation of these seven steps of
the developer model served analytical purposes. The world is
not so neatly ordered, and development is not a lock-step time
sequence. As suggested, under certain conditions you can start
early with the overarching goal; at other times, the goal should
come last. The same sequence possibilities hold true for developing individuals and building a team. Furthermore, one stage
seldom presents a clear demarcation before another phase begins. Instead, a high degree of overlap usually exists among development activities. For example, early informal discussions
between the manager and subordinates can introduce a possible overarching goal long before actual work commences on
setting a goal. Since group development is an ongoing process,
by nature this task will be concurrent with developing more
effective relationships with subordinates and with identifying
and gaining commitment to the goal.

The seven parts frequently interact so that the steps build
on and reinforce each other. For example, in Deborah Linke's
department, group development and the formulation of the
overarching goal went hand in hand. Activities of the group
and individual development can reciprocally build on each
other. In some situations, the leader has to talk alone with the
member who has been acting inappropriately during meetings. Other times, the group becomes a very powerful vehicle
for individual development by being a source of feedback to
members or pressure on them to modify negative behaviors.

Although keeping in mind these seven components can help
you build toward excellence, progress is more likely if you
view development as an organic flow, rather than a mechanis-
tic sequence. Again, we think the best preparation is given by

a mind-set, not a cookbook of rigid preconceptions. If you define the leadership role as "building the conditions whereby key subordinates can help me in managing the department," and when you are faced with problems you ask "How can this task be accomplished in a way that further develops my subordinates' abilities to manage the department?" you can be more sure that you will choose appropriate actions.

The proper orientation is also a good impetus for rapid development. Deborah Linke was able to make significant progress in a matter of months. For an integrative ending for this chapter, we present another case that shows how another manager combined several steps to produce significant change in a very short time.

Chuck was head of training for a sizable organization. He had five other professionals on his staff, and one of them was a particular problem. Dick did not carry his share in terms of the amount of work done but dumped it off on the other members; he was uncooperative and would not initiate work with new parts of the organization. Instead, he repeated the same old programs with groups he had worked with before, thus failing to meet one of the department's prime goals—increasing the visibility and impact of the training department on the larger organization. At our training conference, Chuck was unsure about how he would deal with Dick and how he would implement the ideas from the conference back in his unit.

I decided that I had to make dealing with Dick my first action when I returned. I sat down with him for about an hour to discuss his performance. It was difficult, because as I expected, he had a thousand excuses and soon turned the facts around to blame me for his not getting more work. At least I had opened up communication between us, although at the time the discussion didn't feel very satisfying.

Three days later, I scheduled a four-hour meeting with my staff. I shared with them my Leadership Questionnaire results, and we walked through it section by section. It proved to be a very good method of building the team and setting the stage for others to engage in a similar process, because here I was, their manager, being the initial focus point. Since I had gained some skills from the conference and some reassurance that I was not a disaster as a manager, I was reasonably comfortable in allowing five others to assess my work situation.

After about two hours of my getting feedback, the other staff became more comfortable and started to ask for feedback on their style. After three and a half hours of discussion, it became clear that we had not begun to resolve all the issues for each person (as well as issues dealing with us as a team), and we agreed to meet first thing the following morning for another session. The next day we were about an hour away from noon and the key problem still had not been addressed (which was the quality and quantity of Dick's work and the very defective relationship I had with him). He had participated very little in these two sessions. Finally, the rest of the staff challenged him on his behavior. The end result was that they said, in effect, that they wouldn't carry him anymore.

Had the staff not raised this on their own, I wouldn't have broached it. I feel that would have been unfair. But I think what happened goes back to the fact that I was willing to be honestly assessed by the group for the purpose of building a more effective team. Since they were willing to participate in my improvement for those goals, then they had to assess honestly their own membership. Shortly afterward, our secretary (who had been part of the feedback process) came in and said that he had never before worked in a situation where the manager would risk so much, and he appreciated the opportunity to be part of that process.

Three days later Dick resigned his position and I willingly accepted his resignation. We handled hiring his replacement in an opposite manner than I had handled hiring before. Rather than my doing the selection, I set it up like a Papal election. To save time, I interviewed some 20 candidates and selected seven who I felt met at least the minimum standards. The other staff then interviewed those seven. We all met and privately voted (no discussion was allowed before this vote), and we had about 90% agreement on the candidates. We then discussed our reactions and jointly selected the person—so we all share in the responsibility.

Without being profound, I think it comes down to "trust the process" and don't try to manipulate. Be willing as a manager to model the behavior you want. It is risky and it is time-consuming, but I found it a better investment.

To aid you in thinking about implementation, we have summarized in the following list the key questions to address before attempting each step. Chapter 8 deals in more detail with some crucial implementation issues in difficult circumstances.

Step 1—Assessing Appropriateness

1. Does my unit now meet the conditions (complex interdependent tasks in a changing environment with competent subordinates) in which the Manager-as-Developer model is most appropriate?

   If not, is there the potential for these conditions to be met?

   If not, are these fatal flaws?

2. Even if the Manager-as-Developer model would apply, is this the most appropriate time to introduce it?

   Can the department handle this modification of my leadership style at this point in time?

   Am I personally willing to make the effort and take the risk of introducing this style of management?

Step 2—Conditioning the Turf

1. Are there any changes I have to make in my department before using the Manager-as-Developer style (changes in personnel, how the office is structured, procedures, and so on)?

   Can these changes be made collaboratively with my subordinates as part of this new style, or do I need to make them autonomously?

2. What conditioning do I need to do with my superior? With my peers?

   Is it enough that they know about these changes, or are there some things I need from them to make these changes successful?

Step 3—Sending Signals to Subordinates

1. Are there any internal or external events to which I can link the change in my leadership style? What explanation can I give for "why the need for this change at this time"?

2. How can I demonstrate my personal commitment to these changed goals? How can I indicate that this is not just a passing whim of mine?

Step 4—Dealing with Difficult Subordinates

1. Are there some subordinates with whom relationships are strained, where communication is blocked or tends to get distorted?
   If so, how can I approach them to get beyond blame and start to build a more open, mutual-influence relationship?
2. Is there any (other) preparatory work I need to do with my subordinates so that they will support me in this new direction?

Step 5—Building a Shared-Responsibility Team

1. What changes have to occur in defining the purpose of our meetings, setting the agendas, and conducting the meetings so that responsibility can be truly shared?
2. What stage of development is the group at presently? What can be done to move it to the next higher stage? In this development, can I build-in the expectations (and procedures) so that the group can start to examine openly how it is working as a team?

Step 6—Developing Individual Subordinates

1. Do I have the type of working relationship with each of my subordinates so that we can be open with each other and influence each other? (If not, go back to Step 4!) (Can each of us openly discuss how the relationship is working?)
   If so, do I now need to sit down with each of them to find out about their career goals, aspirations, and underdeveloped abilities?

2. What changes in their job assignments (both technical and managerial) need to be made to have fuller use of their abilities while at the same time developing them?

Step 7—Identifying and Gaining Commitment to an Overarching Goal

1. Have I identified a challenging and exciting goal that captures the unique thrust of this department?
   If not, what is the best way to go about doing so?
2. How can I best go about gaining member commitment to this goal?
3. Again, am I prepared to demonstrate my own commitment to using the goal to attain excellence?

INTRODUCTION

Chapter 7 described the implementation of the Manager-as-Developer model in steps and how a variety of managers employed parts of the model. Although managers seldom found changing style to be as easy as floating downstream with the current and usually had to work to prepare people outside and inside the unit, few of the managers described had to operate under highly negative conditions.

Deborah Linke, for example, returned to a rather hospitable environment. She already had good relationships with her boss, co-workers, and subordinates. Those under her had already been assuming responsibility for managing the department in her absence, so the Developer approach was unlikely to be resisted since the changes were consistent with what had been going on. But if your situation is not so fortunate, this chapter is designed to help determine what actions to take if you have poor relationships with subordinates and the Developer approach represents a radical change from past leadership practices. The key problem facing a manager in such cases is how to move forward despite unhospitable situations.

A leader's efforts can be hampered if his or her boss is uncomfortable with the style changes proposed. Some superiors want those who report to them to emulate a similar style, whether or not a particular manager finds it appropriate or comfortable. This issue may be especially controversial in upper-middle management, where fewer, less tangible indicators of performance exist, so that managers may be judged as much by how they go about the work as by actual work outcomes.

Another barrier to implementation may be raised if the manager lacks the abilities needed to implement the model. These are skills that some managers would not describe as fundamental requirements for the management role. While they would admit that all managers must be able to understand and prepare budgets, to handle scheduling, and to organize and delegate work, they might claim that the skills we have described for the Developer are more relevant to the organization development consultant or the personal manager. Many managers are not prepared to lead groups effectively, let alone to develop a group into a mature problem-solving team. Many managers could not broach "development" with subordinates, especially those who appear disruptive and negative. Other managers have no idea how to identify the department's core goal or how to muster the enthusiasm to gain subordinate commitment.

A related barrier, more fundamental than lack of acquirable skills, is the demand the Manager-as-Developer model places on the ego of the manager who uses it. Particularly in early stages of adoption, a kind of selflessness appears to be demanded. Subordinates have to be allowed the satisfaction of solving problems and getting the credit for jobs well done. As one of our participants put it, "I guess I have some ego problems, because I like to be the heroic manager and leave the silver bullet. It's difficult for me to get a group together and let them work out a solution when I think I have one. I agree that I'm not making full use of my people if I use them only as implementers and that is why I am intellectually committed to the Developer concept. But I have some emotional reactions that lead me to hesitate—to want to retain control."

Finally, just as with any changed behavior, the essential problem involves institutionalizing the new methods. How can the change be sustained? Temporary improvements are relatively easy to produce in the first blush of a new program, but once the novelty has worn off, the momentum and stability of changes are difficult to maintain.

There is no magic solution to dissolve the barriers to successful implementation of the Developer model. Your determination to overcome any difficulties you face is more important in practice than any number of calculated strategies. Nevertheless, building on the experiences of managers like you, who faced inhospitable situations and personal doubts, this chapter offers some ways to approach implementation of the Developer model. We begin with another extended case from one of our workshop participants who had to operate within a very hostile environment.

DEALING WITH AN INHOSPITABLE ENVIRONMENT: THE CASE OF MURRAY GARSON

Murray Garson reported to the president of a sizable advertising agency. He was responsible for the internal creative operations, which included, among other supervisory tasks, the planning and preliminary work on two important new projects that would help the agency move into a new field. He had first come in as a consultant to the president, but he now worked full time (although he continued to be listed as a consultant because of certain tax advantages).

Murray called us before the conference to find out if the program would be beneficial for him. He had had no formalized management training, but he had learned about advertising many years ago as a protégé of a prominent leader in the field. After working with this mentor for several years, Murray struck out on his own as a consultant. Murray felt by and large that he had been very successful in his present job, but he was now facing increasing problems with his staff. His description of the nature of the work and his desire to produce a first-class operation sounded appropriate for the workshop. He said he would see us at the session in two months.

When the Leadership Questionnaires started coming in from Murray's subordinates, we became alarmed. His results were the most negative we had seen, containing such comments as: "Machiavellian," "always playing politics," "not to be trusted," "only out to build up his personal power," "interfering in subordinate's area even when he doesn't have the expertise," and "totally interested in being in control." His scores on the scales were also quite low. (To be fair, there were some positive comments, but even these raised questions about Murray's ability to implement a Developer style of leadership—for example, "He is the best there is in playing company politics to get what his area needs.") We were so concerned over these responses that we thought about not sharing all of them with Murray (something we had never considered with any of the previous participants). Would the questionnaire results make him so defensive that he would only want to retaliate against his subordinates? But we postponed that question until we could see him at the conference and make our own assessment.

During the first three days of the workshop, in the role-plays and exercises, we observed some of the behaviors identified by Murray's subordinates. He tended to be indirect and play people off against each other. On the other hand, he was consistently willing to consider the (often negative) feedback from the other participants. On the basis of these observations, we decided not to withhold the questionnaire contents. But before the morning session started, we took him aside to warn him that it would be bad news, although we thought he could learn alternative ways of managing and even possibly turn around his back-home situation.

Nevertheless, he was rocked by the feedback. During the scheduled half hour of reflective time, for people individually to examine their results, Murray went out on the balcony and stared at the sea. One of us joined him; he said it was even worse than he had anticipated. He talked for a bit about his old mentor, "a genius but a bastard." The person was well known for being extremely creative and innovative, yet unscrupulous, with a trail of enemies and lawsuits. Murray had learned his lessons only too well. Now he worried about finding another way. Although this style was giving him technical success, the costs were too high—for him and for others. He wondered whether he could change; we pointed out times from the previous three days when he had heard criticisms from others and successfully tried new behaviors. He concluded he had nothing to lose by trying.

That workshop day was built around fully understanding the subordinate feedback and doing some planning for the final two conference days. One activity was a 12-person group, where each individual could share some, all, or none of the subordinate feedback each had received. Most participants were selective about what they disclosed, but Murray shared everything: "What the hell, you may as well know me warts and all!" He asked if others had seen anything in his behavior during the previous three days that might lead subordinates to have these sorts of reactions. He also asked about alternative behaviors that would have met his action goals without such destructive side-effects.

During the remaining two days, Murray worked hard to practice what he had been learning. He decided that two of his subordinates needed special attention, and he made careful plans to improve his relationships with them.

We were not wholly optimistic at the end of the conference about Murray's chances. We knew that he was going back to a very difficult situation and that a few days at a workshop might not be enough to overcome his accustomed style.

Four months later Murray dictated a report to us.

It turns out that I have been able to implement tremendous change, which has had a positive effect in my organization and in my own career. And I have been able to continue to use this Developer approach.

In planning for the first week, I had an extensive list of goals. First, of course, was a report to my boss on what the experience was like and the general content of the course. I gave him the draft of your book plus my notes and explained to him all that I felt I had learned. I also talked about what I planned to implement with his approval and support. He was very supportive at that time.

A second step was a one-to-one report to various staff people, letting them know that I felt I learned a great deal and was looking forward to sharing that material with them.

My third goal was to develop a good working relationship with one of my key subordinates, Dave, who posed particular difficulties for me. There had been a lot of disagreement about what my role actually was and over my generally manipulative behavior.

My fourth goal was to deal with Ken, my art director, who was the other key subordinate with whom I had a very strained relationship. I felt that Ken defined his goals in ways that were incompatible with what I saw as the central goals for the department. My efforts were to try to get his behavior in line with those of others in this unit.

My fifth objective was to change the nature of the staff meetings that I had been running very much as Manager-as-Technician and Manager-as-Conductor, where I either had the answers or manipulated the staff to come up with my answer. I wanted more the model of their assuming the responsibility for solving the problems. I started this change immediately by saying that although there were some things I wanted to cover in the next meeting the following week, I wanted the staff to determine the rest of the agenda for that and future meetings. Since this was such a complete change from my previous style, I hoped it would signal that I truly wanted things to be different.

My sixth objective was to speak at this meeting about the feedback that I had received from all of them, about the general kind of polarization that had developed in the staff, and the problems that derived from confusion around my role in the company (Why was I still a consultant; what did that mean?). Also, at this meeting, I wanted to start to focus on some form of an overarching goal for the departments that reported to me, to try and move toward excellence in the type of products we turned out. Finally, I wanted to focus on building my staff into a team, which would include being able to process how we worked as a group.

In addition to these actions, I had a lunch set up with one of my senior creative executives to talk about her goals and career development and then set up another lunch with a junior staff member who had been feeling a bit lost and directionless.

Needless to say, this was a very, very busy couple of weeks. But I was able to implement every one of these objectives except with Ken, my art director. I was just too fearful of breaking out of my previous familiar mode and too unsure of myself about whether I could reach him, so I laid back on that and didn't push it. Interestingly enough, three weeks later, he resigned from the company. It is possible that I might have been able to forestall that, but I think that our positions were so polarized by then, that I was actually relieved. I have since been able to replace him with a much more qualified and trouble-free person.

On the other hand, my meetings with Dave were much more successful. I tried to get out of my previously antagonistic position and see the world as he saw it. I made it quite clear to him that I wanted ours to be a strong working relationship and that I realized that the way in which I had been managing him was not productive for him or for me. I explained that I wanted to change and needed and wanted his help in this area. Our relationship has improved—it is still rocky, but we have a 60–70% improvement over what it was. Certainly our day-to-day interactions are quite smooth.

There were two major problems I faced in carrying out these changes. One problem was me. I really sweated in that first meeting—it took quite a bit of effort on my part to be honest with my staff and to feel that by giving them power and influence, I was not losing it. But the results have shown that the model of "giving power gets power" is absolutely correct.

My position in the company, after a difficult period which I'll explain below, has been enhanced significantly because of my new management style.

The second problem is that, at first, people did not believe that I was capable of, or sincere about, this change. I anticipated this reaction and tried not to force the change down their throats but hang out with it and let them feel, through example and through experience, that I was sincere. I think this approach has been very successful. The main thing I didn't succeed in was dealing with Ken. I consider that the only failure in the whole experience.

An unexpected difficulty arose about two weeks after I returned from the conference. The president called me in and confronted me with what he described as serious staff problems. It felt rather odd to me that he was seeing it at this point since I had talked over these same issues with him when I had returned. But I guess that he finally digested what had been going on for the past couple of months and, until now, had not been able to see the causes of it—that is, to see that some of his own behavior had generated part of the problem.

He reviewed the business situation and pointed out the difficulty in my having responsibility for all our present accounts and for the development of these two new areas that are vital for the growth of the agency. He asked me to let go of the former, the present operations, and to focus on launching the new products that made up the latter thrust. He said that he was "removing me from the firing line." Furthermore, he said that he was very happy with my performance in many areas, but that he saw some problems in some of my management areas.

I was relieved, in that for a long time I had felt over-stretched, but I also felt like I had failed when I hadn't even been given a chance to succeed. It was like I had received a slap on the wrist and a kiss on the cheek at the same time. This reassignment would not change any of my reporting relationships since I needed the same staff on these two new important projects (also the staff could pretty much, now, handle the existing accounts on their own).

Shortly afterward, my boss resumed his attempts to get me to change my status from a consultant to a full-time employee reporting to him. The difference here appears to be psychological: around an issue of my "commitment." For me, the only difference in the change would be economic; it would have severe negative tax consequences for me. Psychologically, it didn't make a damn's worth of difference to me; I was highly committed to the work I was doing. But this confrontation really interrupted our working relationship. I found myself quite angry with him and I think he found himself angry with me. I wasn't clear whether he was trying to push me out or not. It was almost like he was saying that it should cost me something to stay on. It didn't feel good leaving it like this, so I went back to my boss a week later and told him that I felt bad and felt like I was being pushed out. He disagreed and said, "I want you 120%." We left it there. I guess I felt a little more reassured.

That incident occurred in the first part of November. Then in December, my boss raised the issue again and said, "We'll come back with a better incentive system that will meet your needs." He explained that he was bringing in a management consulting firm to develop a system that would deal with the financial issues that seemed to hold up my "joining the family." Unfortunately, in the ensuing two months, this incentive program has still not been implemented, or even designed, as far as I can tell. But at least he has moved away from his confrontation position. Still I feel alienated from him. I decided, however, not to let these feelings disturb my job performance and workday attitude. For the time being, I decided to lay low in terms of my relationship with my boss and with my role in the company. I didn't raise the issue any more with him and he didn't raise it with me. Instead, I turned my attention to the new projects and continued to implement my new leadership approach with my staff—all to very good results.

In terms of my present leadership style, I would say that I have become a coach, counselor, and advisor to my subordinates, rather than a hated and feared tyrant. That previous behavior had come out of my own fears, my sense of responsibility, and the unusually heavy work load I had been under. I have made up my mind to continue along this new course and to deal with my subordinates in terms of our goals and objectives. The old manipulation and personal power games that were my previous style are gone—that isn't part of my behavior anymore. Certainly, early on, I had to catch myself from starting on that old tack and then I would laugh and openly say, "Look at me, this is the old Murray. We don't want to keep on going this way—let's try to turn it around and work together on the problem." And this change really feels good to me.

All the parts seem to work. The difficulties are only those of patience and time. I was afraid, originally, that I wouldn't have the skills to implement this approach, but I have found that I do have those skills and as long as I am willing to take the risks, this approach is effective.

In terms of overarching goals, it was difficult to develop ones that all the members could respond to. However, I have continuously hit that chord in the staff meetings and finally goals are beginning to evolve—but different goals for different segments of the company. The one goal that we have in common, and it is the goal for these staff conferences, is to create a sense of community among the various creative people in the company. I have asked my subordinates to speak on what they saw as the goals for their individual areas, and although it is still in the embryonic stage, this whole vocabulary of goals and objectives is becoming institutionalized. I think that in another four to six months we will have a handle on something in which everybody can believe.

My major effort has been in developing and building a cohesive team of people, and I think that has been quite successful. That group has gone through the textbook stages of development. They were in the subgroup phase when I returned from the conference, but then I started to get cooperation between departments and getting people from various areas to work together on these new projects. One project is so large-scale that it involves everybody. Even though it is a demanding project, I have continuously kept it in the forefront of our meetings so that it continues to be a unifying experience for everybody. I guess, in a sense, that it is our "task" overarching goal that binds all of us and complements our "relational" goal I spoke of before. With the group feeling more comfortable with each other, they are more willing to disagree and directly influence each other on work assignments and policy decisions. I think they are feeling it is "their" group and not "mine" as it was before. They set the agenda and prioritize the issues for discussion.

Another function of our regular meetings is to acquaint this group with the rest of the organization. Just about every Wednesday at lunch, we invite an executive from another part of the corporation (finance, marketing, production) to speak to the entire group about their job areas. So my staff, which started out as a diverse and uncohesive bunch of relatively inexperienced account executives, art directors, senior writers, and so forth are now a community of creative people who have a real understanding of what the company is all about and how it works—from marketing problems to why their people are paid when they are paid. That has made a tremendous change in their attitudes toward the organization. It is not in the sense of what used to be called "family"—that is outmoded in this day and age—rather it is more of a "community" that has developed.

This greater commitment to the organization means that I don't have to be as concerned with constant hands-on control. In fact, what I frequently do is to arrange submeetings with those directly concerned with an issue. I directly lay out the problem as I perceive it and ask this ad-hoc group to come up with a solution, procedure, or policy that we could implement. In fact, I usually don't stay for the conclusion of the meeting, just receive a report from the chairperson.

I am still a little bothered by the experience I had with my boss when he moved me off the regular accounts. It is still not really clear to me what's going on here, and it is the only area where I have a sense of setback in implementing what I think is a better style. I have to maintain my sense of patience because I see this approach working; it is more effective and more comfortable to me. I'm no longer angry at the end of the day and feeling that my staff is not up to par. In fact, I'm beginning to feel challenged by them, which is what I think it's all about.

Overcoming Poor Subordinate Relations

Although Murray swallowed hard and leaped into a difficult situation with great success, one swallow does not a spring into excellence make. Nevertheless, we can draw some lessons from the way he went about launching the Developer model into full flight despite negative subordinates and traditions.

In general, learning theory has shown that people are most ready for change under conditions of moderate tension and anxiety. When tension is low, little need to change is perceived; when tension is high, rigidity and resistance tend to increase. Because Murray was faced with subordinates who were very tense and unhappy, unusual methods were called for. To overcome all the tendencies toward retrenchment and "drawing the wagons into a circle," Murray had to make a dramatic departure from business as usual. He had to take larger risks than usual in signaling new intentions, trying new behavior, and using a new style. He, more than most managers, had to work hard at creating a vision of what might be possible. Murray's success was extremely gratifying, but the kinds of major changes he attempted are never easy or instantaneous. As Murray found, subordinates are going to suspect that statements about "a brave new world" are merely rhetoric. To reduce such doubt, a manager must persist in the new behavior until subordinates can see the benefits.

Under more accepting conditions, the change may represent an evolutionary development, a logical extension of what has occurred before. You can point to present practice and say, "Let's do it better" (which was the approach Deborah Linke could take). Issues of blame are less likely to arise and fewer costs are levied against you if you regress into previous behavior. At the other extreme, however, the existence of core problems demands more radical changes. It is necessary to say, "Let's not do what we did before—let's make it a new and better ball game."

Each approach to change—the radical and the more conservative—has its own potential pitfalls. Less disruptive development may be seen as so continuous that change never occurs; people may be content using new labels for what are fundamentally the same old behaviors, so that the organization continues at a good level of performance but fails to reach excellence. On the other hand, since extensive change is more difficult and requires greater personal risk-taking on the leader's part, its success is fundamentally more in jeopardy.

Readiness to Risk

Let's look more closely at actions that increase the chances of success when conditions are adverse. Foremost is the leader's willingness to take major personal risks, thus giving a clear and unambiguous sign that "the future will be different." We have seen managers get into trouble when they have tried to keep both worlds, putting one toe into the waters of change while the other foot is firmly planted on the dry, but crumbling, ground of the past.

Murray recently reflected, "As a result of my own experience, I would underline the point that the manager must be ready for dramatic change and that such change is perceived as a very big risk by everyone involved. This stance requires courage, but it's interpersonal courage rather than corporate courage." The risks include opening yourself to subordinates and asking what you are doing that's getting in the way of their being productive. Or raising an issue with a difficult subordinate without knowing beforehand how it will turn out. Risk-taking might involve letting go of all hands-on control, even with subordinates who don't inspire your confidence. And finally, you must hold firmly to this new direction even though the first steps are rocky and subordinates are very suspicious. (Note that the one failure Murray reported involved the person with whom he held back from full exploration of differences.)*

The willingness to let go of old dysfunctional behaviors is hard won. In any circumstances, even when a person has "mostly" changed, actions that recall the previous style trigger strong reactions among others. You can take three steps that reflect a new approach, but if the fourth is a regression into the old, subordinates are likely to point it out quickly: "See, I told you so—this change isn't for real." But the solution is for leaders to acknowledge imperfection freely. Murray was actually able to capitalize on the times he regressed to his old style; he publicly pointed out his errors and asked for his subordinates' cooperation in helping him change. As we noted in the previous chapter, you need to assess your readiness to change. If you are so ambivalent that you can't essay a fully committed attempt, you should probably stay with your old style until you are sure you can give full commitment.

Avoiding Finger-Pointing

If you can make a full commitment to change, you must work vigorously on the problems without looking for anyone else to blame. When things go wrong, you must conquer the tendency to determine fault. Again and again we have seen managers initiate witch-hunts, which are always ill advised and invari-

---

*Our emphasis on risk-taking is not to suggest that the solution is always that "more risk is better." Sometimes discretion truly is the better part of valor. Sometimes it is necessary to back off from pressing a subordinate, to give more breathing room. The development of a group requires bringing in more difficult problems as the group is able to handle them—not necessarily throwing the most crucial problem at them in the first meeting. And the Developer can't institute all changes during the first week (even though it looks as if that is what Murray tried!). However, holding back should be done primarily for the reason that others need time to assimilate the changes, not to maintain your own comfort.

ably more damaging than the original problem.* Witch-hunting ignores several facts: Rarely is there one villain who causes the difficulty through personal incompetence or malfeasance. More often problems are interactive: The subordinate does something that causes the superior to act inappropriately, which in turn causes the subordinate—and so forth. Often the problem lies in the system and not in an individual. Is Caroline really disorganized or is her job structured in such a way that she receives contradictory demands from multiple sources? Even if it is possible to find one person who is more at fault than others, punishment does not necessarily correct the problem; more often punishment discourages subordinates from initiative and drives future problems underground.

Nevertheless, the tendency to find someone to blame is very difficult to give up. Murray could easily have blamed Dave, his art director, or written off his entire staff as resistant or incompetent. Instead, he defused the issue of blame by taking the responsibility onto himself. Rather than nitpicking about "who is at fault for which problems," he was willing to say, "I have done some things wrong in the past, but I want to start afresh." Although such willingness to own responsibility can be effective anytime, it is most likely to be crucial the more negative the original situation.

Framing Change within Organizational Goals

Another key aspect of successful change is exemplified in what Murray did: He placed the change attempt within the framework of larger goals, not in terms of his personal benefit. He explained to the group that he wanted this change so they could better meet the organization's goals, be more produc-

---

*The urge to faultfind is a frequent motive for organizations to change leaders under adverse situations. The new managers may be no more competent than the old, but the previous ones can be labeled as the causes of the problems, which gives the new leaders an unencumbered hand. Sometimes people should be replaced, but at other times they are just being used as a scapegoat for more fundamental organizational problems.

tive, and achieve the new projects that were important to the company. He did not just promote change for his personal comfort or aggrandizement. That the change might make his life easier was a secondary result, not the primary benefit. As we have discussed with the concept of an overarching goal, people are more willing to make sacrifices (and any change involves at least the sacrifice of adapting to new leadership style) for the sake of a larger good.

To conclude, the Manager-as-Developer approach is not limited just to highly compatable conditions, but can be implemented in adverse settings as well. For you to be successful under the latter conditions requires extra effort and greater personal risks.

IMPLEMENTATION UNDER A SUPERIOR WITH A VERY DIFFERENT LEADERSHIP APPROACH

Different sorts of implementation difficulties arise when a would-be Developer's boss has a very different management style. For example, if your boss tends to play things close to the chest, to exclude subordinates from important decisions, and to keep tight reins on what they do, then how easily can you be open with your subordinates, include them in the management of the operations, and let go of tight hands-on control? When your boss wants to supervise very closely and expects you to have all the answers whenever questioned, to what extent can you give autonomy to those reporting to you? When we have discussed the Manager-as-Developer approach, we frequently hear the question, "Doesn't the entire organization have to at least accept the value of a Developer style in order for a middle-manager to be able to implement it?"

A number of our workshop attendees mentioned style conflict with a boss as a potential problem, but on closer examination this appeared not to be the real issue. Several reported that their bosses considered them professional threats, but the boss's attitude hadn't inhibited their ability to act as Developers with their own subordinates. Several others commented that, on the basis of events in the workshop, they had realized that their relationship with their superior needed work, but they went back, discussed their concerns with their superior, and resolved these difficulties. Deborah Linke reported that her boss's style was different from the one she was introducing, but that fact appeared to cause no problems after she had explained the reasons behind her change, showed that her changes didn't demand that he change his style, and that the two could still work well together. These cases suggested that any incompatibility of leadership style between Developer and superior can be dealt with.

Then, one Saturday morning, we got a call from Murray. It was March, two months after he had sent us the tape describing how he had been successfully implementing his new management approach.

The Manager-as-Developer style continued to work better, but I have other news for you—I have just been fired. Yesterday morning my boss said that he wanted to meet with me at 5 o'clock. I thought it was about a disagreement we were having about an action he had taken. Instead, he said that he thought it was best that we terminate. He said that there was just such an incompatibility between our management styles that he felt it was impossible for him to work with me. I asked if there was anything specific that I had done and where I had failed. He said no, he thought I was doing a good job, but our styles were just too different.

As I told you earlier, after the disagreement with my boss over whether I should give up my role as a consultant, I turned my attention to the special projects that were now my main concern. Oh, by the way—I never did give up the consultant status, because he never implemented the new incentive system that he said was "being developed." But we didn't talk about it anymore, and I just thought it was on hold. As I told you, I built up my staff group to be more of a decision-making team, where people could bring up their problems and we could deal with them together. Our practice of bringing in executives from other parts of the company gave my staff a much better understanding of the total picture and let us know about problems in other areas that might affect us and vice versa.

The trouble was that the more my approach succeeded, the greater the separation was between my boss and everybody else, and between my boss and me. It also became clearer and clearer that the boss was the problem in this office. Before, I had been blamed because of my style, but as my style changed and improved and better fit what subordinates wanted, it became evident that it was the boss who was the problem. Before, the boss had managed in a very casual style, which had set up his subordinates—the executives—as the bad guys.

As it became more apparent that I wasn't the problem, my power increased with my subordinates, because we saw ourselves as having common problems around difficulties with my boss's style. As this became clearer to me, it was doing nothing to increase my confidence either in my boss or in the future of this job, so I started to send out preliminary feelers —obviously not telling anybody—about the possibility of jobs outside this organization. During this time, I didn't say anything to my boss. I felt nervous about talking to him because of the distance between us. Every so often, my boss did raise the question of when he was going to be invited to our "lunch group" (that's what we called the times when we had outside executives come in). I kept putting it off and saying "Well, sometime in the future."

Things came to a head in our staff meeting on Wednesday. We were discussing some further problems we were having with my boss. He had just recently purchased photos without discussion with the art director: People were saying they were angry, didn't know what was going on, and that we should confront him. I tried to mediate the situation, and the group suggested that I talk with him. They voted unanimously for me to go; they bought into that solution. They also brought up several other issues that they wanted me to raise with him.

I decided that the best thing would be to take him out for dinner rather than go charging into his office. I realized that I had to build more linkages with him so he could really hear this information. The next day, Thursday, I mentioned to him that I wanted to have dinner with him and he agreed, but the dinner never came about. And then there was our Friday final meeting.

Murray reported that his feelings were very mixed—flattened by being fired but also a bit relieved to be out of the situation. When asked whether he felt the termination was really due to an incompatibility of styles, he thought for a moment before answering.

No, I think it was really due to two other factors. Before the change in my style, I and the other executives really protected the president; we were playing the heavy role and taking the heat. When I became a more effective leader and did the job I should be doing, it exposed my boss's style for what it was. Second, in reflecting on what I did, I don't think I am entirely blameless! There was part of me that wanted to turn my group against him. I wanted to build a cohesive team that excluded the boss.

What, then, does this turn of events say about the issue of incompatible subordinate–superior leadership styles? Does this demonstrate that all those who have nondeveloper bosses should quietly tuck this book into the deepest recesses of their inactive files and find a safer way to manage? We think not. The problem in Murray's case was not so much incompatibility of styles (although that was a graceful way for Murray's boss to have expressed the problem) as it was the issues of subordinate disloyalty and lack of respect. In almost all cases, problem relationships between a boss and an employee grow from these issues rather than from differences in style.

When we talk to superiors about what worries them in a subordinate, the issue of loyalty places a close second to general competence. "Will the subordinate try to undercut me, do "end-arounds" to my boss and others higher up, point up my faults in public?" Even though fewer managers these days tell subordinates that they demand respect, we have observed that managers quickly notice and react to even the smallest sign of disrespect. Conversely, when a superior feels that the subordinate is competent, loyal, and respectful, then the subordinate has a great deal of freedom to disagree, to raise a variety of issues, and to work independently. Even though the subordinate may never be explicit about not feeling loyal or not respecting the boss (as Murray felt but never disclosed to his boss), usually the superior easily senses such attitudes, with the results that the subordinate has less autonomy, needs to be very careful about what is said, and persistently runs into problems with the boss.

Subordinates can never safely ignore differences between their leadership style and that of their boss. Differences in approaches do not necessarily lead to problems; when differing styles inhibit communication, then problems can flourish.

For example, one of our managers began to delegate a lot of important decisions to his staff without preparing his boss and was subsequently seen by his superior as "abdicating his responsibility." You should not allow your boss to guess about why you are using an approach different from his or hers, because the boss can easily interpret your actions as a sign that you do not respect the superior's approach to management.

Thus, most of the managers who wanted to modify their leadership style after our workshop first talked with their superiors. They explained quite fully what they wanted to do and why they wanted to do it. They knew that bosses don't like to be surprised, and they wanted to make sure that any changes in their behavior would be understood by their superior. Many of these managers also shared the results from their Leadership Questionnaire, thereby providing a rationale for their change. (And none of these managers reported difficulties because the Developer style they wanted to use differed from the approach used by their boss.)

In other words, the greater the differences in leadership style with your boss, the more clearly and fully you should communicate. When there is great similarity in style, then much can be unsaid—after 'all, you share the same set of assumptions. But when your superior doesn't delegate and you do, you need to communicate that you are delegating to achieve the goal of higher performance, not because you don't know how to manage. You need to communicate that differences in style do not signify disloyalty or disrespect. You need to convey the following message: "Your style lets you manage best. But people are different, and my style lets me perform best—each of us has to find our own way to have a high-performing department."

How can you tell when it is necessary to work out clear expectations with your superior? Most situations that require careful attention to this issue are clearly flagged by danger signs. That was certainly the case with Murray. The anger, alienation, and uncertainty that he felt were clear signals, as was the ambiguity in the president's actions. Why had the president placed so much emphasis on Murray's giving up consultant status? Why was commitment such an issue for him? Although Murray did initially try to work on their relationship (after the boss took away some of his operating responsibilities), he stopped short of offering his boss a full explanation of the issues. Murray also didn't take advantage of several other opportunities to raise questions about how they were working together and then to negotiate mutually acceptable expectations.

However, even after a clear negotiation has been achieved between you and your superior on your mutual expectations, the boss will still occasionally want to influence how you manage (After all, isn't part of the boss's goals to "develop the subordinate?"). Even though you can accept many of your superior's comments as valuable, what about those occasions when the suggestions seem excessive and inappropriate? Do you necessarily have to go along? Can the boss's suggestion be declined without conveying a lack of loyalty or respect?

We think such suggestions can be declined—with care. In Chapter 5 we stressed the importance of a *mutual*-influence relationship between superior and subordinate. In such a relationship, you can increase your influence without alienating the boss or blocking his or her influence. First, fully explore the concerns of your superior that led to the suggestion—the concerns may be valid even if the suggestion is not. Both parties can then enter into a problem-solving situation to work toward a solution that sidesteps the problematic *suggested* solutions, meets the superior's *concerns*, and is *compatible* with your style.

Let's examine how this approach could have worked with Murray and his boss. When his superior first suggested that Murray give up his consultant status and become a regular employee, Murray did not explore why this was important to his boss. Instead, he dismissed it out of hand by saying that the difference in status was "only psychological." If he had probed further, he may have found that his boss had grave questions about his commitment to the organization and to the boss. With that information, they would have had the basis for some excellent problem solving. Did other actions of Murray convey lack of commitment? Could there be other means by which he could show commitment (other than by taking a severe economic loss)? If not, were there ways the boss could otherwise compensate Murray for the monetary loss?

"But," you may say, "the world isn't always that rational. What am I to do when I feel my boss's concerns are invalid or have led to too much interference? How can I get the boss to back off when I feel I'm being inappropriately told how to do my job? Won't differences in style cause problems in such instances?"

These kinds of problems can be effectively handled if you focus on the difference between means and ends and agree on the ends in exchange for autonomy in means. That is, the subordinate should first determine what ends (or goals) the boss wants. "You want my department to do X and Y by such a date, right?" With that knowledge, then the subordinate can agree to the ends, but ask for autonomy in the means. "Boss, I want to give you the results you want, because that is what I want also. But in order to do that, I need to have the freedom to manage my unit the way that lets me be most effective. I can commit to giving you what you want, if you will give me that autonomy. Then it's my head if I don't deliver." Most bosses would be delighted with such a statement, because it puts the emphasis where it belongs (on goals) and is an agreement by the subordinate to be held accountable on the basis of performance. Note also that no questions of disloyalty are raised—after all, the subordinate is being very loyal to the core performance goals of the boss and the organization.

Astute readers (or at least ones with long memories) will note that what we are suggesting vis-a-vis relating to the superior is very similar to what we suggest in chapter 5 for dealing with the subordinate. The same principles hold: You want first to find out how the other sees the world and what is important to that person and then take action to solve problems so that the organizational objectives are met in a way that doesn't demotivate you or the other. Superiors appreciate subordinates who take such initiative—when the initiative is in the pursuit of organizational objectives—and do not interpret such actions by the subordinate as signs of either disloyalty or disrespect.

Increasing Implementation Success Despite Skill Deficits

When we first describe the Developer model to managers, we frequently get some version of this wonderfully contradictory reaction: "I'm already doing all of that. Besides, to do it, I'd have to be far more skilled than I am or that is reasonable to expect from any manager!" Further exploration yields a response that could be used as a catalog of needed skills for an effective manager.

> But you are expecting a great deal from a manager! You are saying that they ought to be able to communicate clearly to subordinates and be able to draw them out; to listen well even when the subordinate may be saying things that the manager doesn't agree with; to be able to give and receive positive and negative feedback; to be influential without taking away the influence of others; to build a good working relationship even with somebody who has been difficult; to be able to negotiate out tasks so that organizational goals and individual interests are both met; to be able to handle conflict and, when necessary, change it from personal attacks to task disagreements; to be supportive without being condescending; to coach and advise without overcontrolling; to run meetings without dominating them; to develop the team while getting important tasks done; to be able to identify a goal that can challenge and excite all subordinates and to get them personally committed to this goal and not treat it just as rhetoric. That is a formidable list! How many managers have these competencies?

Unfortunately, too few managers could now successfully check off all these skills. On the other hand, each of these skills is presently used by many managers. None is new; what is new with the Manager-as-Developer model is the application of most, if not all, of these managerial skills within a developmental framework, which requires learning and a willingness to learn.

More than technical competence is necessary to achieve excellence; difficult human skills are called for. But these skills are not psychoanalytic or out of the range of managers who care about going beyond adequate performance.

If your job was to link up 12 disparate computers so that they could work interactively, would you be willing to say to your boss, "I'm not interested in learning how to make these computers work together; I am going to make the assumption that they are all alike and operate as I want them to act." We are not suggesting that you have to be a computer engineer who takes apart the circuits. It is not necessary to take computers apart to find ways of linking their capacities; similarly, managers don't have to "take apart" subordinates to develop skills in knowing how they work alone and in groups. In the jobs we've been discussing, people are the greatest cost and greatest potential resource, so people skills must be seen as worth mastering.

Although all of these development skills are tough to master, our training programs and consulting work have shown that managers who care about excellence can indeed master them. It isn't necessary to be a trained therapist to be able to listen, size another up, build a mutual relationship, and level with others about performance. A Manager-Developer does not have to be a T-group trainer to learn to watch how a meeting is going, to decide which issues can be decided by the whole team, to boost reticent members, to insist that tough issues be addressed without pushing for a predetermined solution, and to encourage members to confront one another on priorities, deadlines, and commitments. Finally, the Developer need not be a charismatic Pied Piper to speak forcefully and convincingly about goals.

We are convinced that all of these skills are learnable—and learnable by most people. Innumerable training programs teach communication, influence, negotiation, and team-building skills. Our own experience in developing a program for the Manager-as-Developer model substantiates our contention that managers, in a relatively short period, can successfully acquire at least minimal competence in these areas.

The belief that these skills can be readily learned goes against the common maxim that "personality is not change-able." However, we are not talking about *personality* change; we are talking about *behavior* change. A significant body of research and practice shows that most healthy individuals can change quite a bit of their behavior. Furthermore, in most cases, the objective is not to persuade people to give up existing behaviors but to help them acquire new skills, in addition to what they possess already. People tend to resist giving up behavioral actions—especially ones that have served them well in the past. But, as Deborah Linke found, most people get into trouble not because of some "bad" behavior, but because they overuse (or use at an inappropriate time or setting) something that could on another occasion be quite appropriate. Even the behaviors of the heroic manager (being concerned about control and having the correct answer) can be very important in some situations—trouble arises when the heroic response is the only managerial style available.

Why, then, does managerial behavior appear to change so infrequently? Some reasons were discussed in Chapter 5, where we identified the tendency of many managers not to try because they assume it won't work ("You can't teach an old dog new tricks," "That's the way Charlie has been for 10 years and will be for the next 20"). Related to this attitudinal problem is the fact that the person trying to change behavior often gives feedback in a totally inappropriate way—either by soft-peddling so the message doesn't get through or attacking the other's personality rather than focusing on the behavior. Finally, even when appropriate comment occurs, it may not be repeated, which completely ignores the fact that changing any habitual behavior usually requires persistent attempts. But, to close the circle, we must point out that the ability to help change a subordinate's (inappropriate) behavior is another crucial management skill that can also be learned!

After you realize that these skills can be learned, you still have to be willing to expend the effort to acquire them. Recently, as a speaker was stressing the developmental way to deal with subordinates, a manager exploded in anger: "Goddam, I have had a lot of superiors in my career; some have been good and others have been the duplicate of Attila the Hun. None of them asked *me* about my career goals or how they could assist *me* so that I could be more productive. It was always *my* job to change *my* style to fit *theirs*. Now you tell me that I should pay attention to what my subordinates want? That's not fair!" Irrespective of fairness, the problem of finding a way to achieve excellence remains. If that manager truly wants excellence, which requires making maximum use of subordinate abilities, we believe that he has no choice. Indeed, after his explosion, he agreed!

It is even interesting that this point draws dispute. For years it has been known that managers who have built high-performing departments have needed and used technical, administrative, *and* human-relationship competencies (Mann, 1965). Nobody would think of hiring a manager who said, "I'll take this position, but don't expect me to learn anything about our product." or, "I'll be manager but I don't know how to prepare a budget or even read a profit-and-loss statement, and I have no intention of learning." Managers frequently admit that they don't work well in groups, or that they have difficulty being direct with subordinates, yet somehow they expect that these limitations can be overlooked. No wonder merely adequate performance is so common when this three-legged stool has such a frail twig for one of its supports!

Although we don't want to soften our previous argument for the value of these developmental skills, some words of warning are in order. One must be wary of the possibility of substituting one heroic model for another. In the place of managers who have to have their hands on the helm at all times and answers to all problems, we could be seen as raising a new heroic manager who can solve all interpersonal and group problems that develop! Not only can this be felt as an awesome responsibility for a manager who is merely mortal, but it could cause managers to postpone introducing the Developer model because of what they felt were their skill deficiencies. Three points can put the issue of skills in their proper perspective.

First, there is real power in the concept itself of the Manager-as-Developer model. We have seen managers lacking most of the skills that we have described produce important changes just by having this postheroic model of leadership in mind. On several occasions, we have observed leaders substituting the Developer concept for the heroic model they had been using and finding they could relatively quickly modify their behavior. When their orientation was "How can I develop and utilize subordinate skills so that the problem gets solved?" rather than "What's the problem and how can I solve it?" a host of options emerged that would not otherwise have been considered. For example, a president of a small company recently accomplished a significant turnabout in style after a half-day discussion of the Developer concept. At his staff meeting that afternoon, he quickly shifted from his past "giving-the-answer" orientation to catching himself and questioning his subordinates: "What do you think the causes are? Do the rest of you agree? If so, how would you go about solving them?" Something as simple and basic as these few questions dramatically changed the tone of the meeting. Holding a new image of what the leader should do is probably more important than any of the particular elements of the model.

The second point countering the need for full-blown developmental skills is the central importance of risk-taking on the part of the leader. Taking personal risks can compensate for the lack of a lot of skills. Remember that Murray expressed the concern that he "wouldn't have the skills to implement this approach," but he found that he did have the skills, and "so long as I am willing to take the risks, this approach is effective." The people who had the least success were those who tried to avoid risks, who wanted to preserve their old forms of control, and who were not willing to confront others. As we mentioned in Chapter 7, risk-taking conveys to subordinates the leader's commitment and therefore increases their willingness to get involved.

The third reason that having all the management skills may not be required to be Manager-as-Developer is that the postheroic approach, by sharing the responsibility for departmental success, also shares the responsibility for development. The leader may *not* have all the answers or all the skills, but all the skills may be found collectively in the group. The Developer orientation builds a truly collaborative relationship between subordinates and superior, where subordinates are more willing to help their boss. When new Manager-Developers said, "I need your help to make this a better place," subordinates gave it.

Furthermore, a developmental approach means that the subordinates learn and the leader learns as well. For this approach to succeed, feedback must go up as well as down. For the team to continue to mature, open processing must continue on what went well and what needs improvement. As the successful coach helps the team learn from the successes and failures of last week's game (and learns something in the process), so the successful Developer learns by helping subordinates learn from the tasks they work on. Work then becomes a place for all—leader and members—to further their skill development. The situation does not require a totally skilled leader, but a leader who is willing to learn to become more skilled. If the manager can hold fast to that orientation, it is only a matter of time before most of these skills can be sufficiently developed.

GETTING PAST THE APPARENT NEED FOR SELFLESSNESS

There is real pleasure in galloping into a difficult situation and single-handedly resolving the difficulty; leaving the silver bullet (especially for those trained to be Lone Rangers) can be highly satisfying. What are the alternative rewards for the Developer that can compensate for the loss of these satisfactions?

Managers who are making the transition from directly performing the organization's work to managing it often report great difficulty in letting go of the hands-on work. As the head of an insurance-operations department poignantly put it: "How do I now prove I'm competent? Before, I could always prove my worth by jumping in and untangling the screw-ups.

I was secure then; my skills were irreplaceable. Now I have to depend on my general management skills, and there's nothing I can prove or demonstrate about my competence. I never have a nice, clean, finished solution to go home with." If there used to be job satisfaction for the untangled software program, successful sale, or engineering breakthrough, now there is only frustration (and/or interference in the domain of the subordinates) if the manager seeks the same rewards his former behavior brought. Managers who are interested in moving past heroic status need to find new kinds of gratification. Viewed as a challenge, managing as a Developer offers great potential satisfaction. The challenge that you used to find in a technical problem can be at least matched, and perhaps exceeded, by the challenge to build a way of working that not only brings out excellence in each individual, but also fosters an even higher synergistic output from members working together.

You can also look at the manager's task as a different category of "technical problem." Can the manager work with subordinates (who individually are more complicated than any computer and are also unique) and utilize their individual styles and abilities? Heroic satisfaction—at knowing more about the job than anyone else, or cleverly maneuvering people into doing their work—must be supplanted by the satisfaction of managing a process that builds an excellent organization. Making this transfer in source of satisfaction means that the manager must be more tolerant of ambiguity and uncertainty. The manager will be willing to accept the frustrations of the managerial role if problems are seen as challenges, not as unwelcome glitches in the administrative world that was supposed to be permanently in order.

A manager who understands why the transition is difficult—from doing the task to building and sustaining an organization—is better prepared to be successful and satisfied. The very nature of satisfaction is changed, to be more vicarious, or secondhand. The manager's situation is analogous to the parent's, who, from the passenger's side of the car, takes pleasure in the teenager's mastery of driving the family car. Mixed with satisfaction at the young person's new skills and greater independence are likely to be some other feelings of loss as well as worry—about whether the child will really know what to do when hazards come along, the weather suddenly changes, or adolescent passengers begin to act up. A wise, old manager beautifully captured these mixed feelings after watching a young leader manage a difficult discussion: "Watching you work is like seeing my son raise his children; I'm sure he's not doing it right and I think I could do it better, but it seems to be working and I've got to respect that."

Thus, a real challenge is to make good decisions continually about when to get involved with the work of subordinates and when to hold back. When is it appropriate to jump in and show the floundering subordinate how to do something, give direct advice or tips, or drop a few hints, and when is it better to bite your tongue and stay out of the way while the person struggles?

Managing any trade-offs that arise between short-term performance and development is a delicate and demanding task, with a strange inversion of psychological rewards. Often your best decisions, to hang back or to drop hints, will be least noticed and, therefore, least explicitly appreciated by your subordinates. You have to gain short-term satisfaction from self-appreciation; becoming known and appreciated for being a "good developer of people" is generally a gradual accomplishment over time.

Ultimately, however, the short-lived pleasure in personally solving a particular problem is less satisfying than seeing others grow in competence and the department perform at a higher level. These themes, reported here by Deborah Linke and Murray Garson, are echoed by managers who use the Developer approach.

A Developer leadership style does not require that the manager have a selfless ego, forever willing to stay in the background. A unit that consistently comes through gets recognized. It may be a subordinate who delivers a product, presents the report, or represents the department on an organization-wide task force, but if the department delivers, the performance pattern receives recognition for the manager.

When Bear Bryant retired as coach of the University of Alabama football team, the papers reported that he characteristically credited his staff for the previous night's final victory: "They won the game tonight in spite of me. I made few decisions." But that sharing of the glory did not diminish the accolades. A recent study shows that successful, innovative managers do share the glory rather than hog it (Kanter, 1983). They recognize that claiming all the credit would misrepresent reality, but more important, it would be a sure way to increase resentment and make the next round of accomplishment more difficult. When things are going well, there is plenty of credit to go around. In most organizations, managers who get a reputation for being good at growing other managers are highly valued. The rewards may be less dramatic than heroes are used to, but they are also likely to last longer.

SUSTAINING THE DEVELOPER STYLE

Anyone who has been around organizations awhile knows it is often far harder to sustain changes than to initiate them. The "program of the month" (or year) is often the butt of jokes from employees who know the department's history of momentary enthusiasms and waning interests. A new leadership style is particularly vulnerable to backsliding under pressure of deadlines, crises, unsympathetic bosses, or resistant subordinates.

Many workshop participants who wanted to try the Developer model worried about how to maintain momentum once they had begun. Deborah Linke raised a similar concern, even after change had been successfully achieved, about staying with her initial steps; she worried about her department's overarching goal becoming outdated. A prospective Developer considers the energy the heroic manager has to expend just to get adequate performance out and fears that it will take even greater effort to sustain excellence.

But on the contrary, day-to-day pressures and backsliding tendencies exert much weaker influence on the Manager-as-

Developer approach—especially when development has reached the point where subordinates start to feel responsible for the department's success and when the setting has been developed for them to exert influence in carrying out this responsibility.

What we have seen, time after time, is that once the leader makes the commitment to excellence and builds in conditions for subordinates to have influence in reaching that goal, subordinates start to pressure for improvement. What they tolerated before (in their own subordinates, in their peers, and even in their relationship to the boss) is no longer accepted. It is almost as if they say, "Oh, you really want things to be first-rate? In that case, we aren't going to tolerate Howard continually taking extended lunch breaks, Susan coming in with excuse after excuse for not delivering on time, or Bob dominating the meeting."

Not only have the standards been raised (especially if there is an overarching goal that stresses excellence); there now are legitimate mechanisms for subordinates to exert influence. If they start to feel a responsibility for the management of the department, they now consider that it is within their right to comment when their peers (and the subordinates of their peers) are not performing. As relationships become more open, feelings that were previously held back are now expressed. If the team starts to examine how it is operating and what can be done to improve, then comments will be made to offenders about inappropriate behavior or inadequate performance. As was true in Chuck's training department (described at the end of the last chapter), members become no longer willing to carry the substandard performer. In fact, the problem for the leader can change from getting movement from subordinates to running fast enough to stay ahead of them.

We recently worked with a manager whose experiences perfectly contrasted the stress effects of the heroic versus the Developer model. Six months previously, he had taken over a department under instructions to raise standards. He had done that in his own heroic way, but was facing increasing resistance from subordinates who saw him as dictatorial and punitive. He was not at the point of worrying about sustaining excellence; he was still struggling to get close to it. He complained that some of the supervisors under him wouldn't take initiative, supervise their subordinates strictly enough, or look beyond the narrowest definition of their jobs. When told that the Developer model could help him move far beyond his situation, he was skeptical but willing to try. In the ensuing weeks we worked with him to expand his style. He met with each of his subordinates and heard their complaints about how he had been managing. He agreed to modify his behavior in exchange for increased initiative from them and higher standards of performance. He then built a management team that took on more responsibility for managing the department. And he pushed more responsibility down, not only to his subordinates, but also to the level below them.

About two months later, he still had concerns, but they were of a very different nature:

> You know, I am worried about Sam [the supervisor he was initially most bothered about]. I am worried about the pressure the other supervisors are putting on him. They are all going to him and complaining when he doesn't come through or his subordinates goof up. I worry about whether he can take the pressure. Also, we are doing so much with so many projects starting that things are moving faster than I think I can handle. I feel like I am on a pair of racing skis going down the expert slope. I am struggling just to stay upright; my worry now is how to get to the bottom of the hill in one piece!

We suggested that he go to Sam, find out if he was feeling all of this pressure (he was), and explore what was going on that caused others to be on his case. In this discussion, it became clearer that Sam's job was ill-defined, which caused different and conflicting expectations among his peers. This problem was worked on in the next staff meeting. Subsequently, Sam's performance improved and friction between Sam and the others decreased.

When shared responsibility is introduced, many sources of pressure for improvement spring up. Sometimes this broad-based influence leads to clarification of the difficulties so that the difficult person improves; in many other cases, the substandard performer leaves: Having been brought into the department under old rules, he or she decides against playing in the new ball game. Since the Developer clearly states the new rules and helps all members be as successful as they want or can be, it is easier for the Developer to be perceived as fair with those who can't or won't respond and, in good conscience, to help them transfer out or leave for a new job.

We don't want to end this section without making sure that we have dispelled the image of the Manager-as-Developer and a pack of maniacal peers taking the place of the heroic manager breathing down a subordinate's neck. Although there are higher standards (and multiple pressures to achieve them) in the Developer model, there is also greater support. Members are more willing to pitch in and help each other with problems, but they are only willing to help the person who is committed to excellence. This dual emphasis on high standards and high support is the most vital ingredient for success. If the Developer model is seriously implemented, the team shares responsibility for maintaining momentum and for keeping a balance between pressure and support.

Finally, we do not want to downplay or discredit the very real problems that face a manager who has a negative work situation, a boss who espouses a very different leadership style, few interpersonal or group skills and is faced with sustaining the initial change effort. These real and valid difficulties are not insurmountable—they do not prevent a person from successfully implementing a developmental approach. Even though it isn't automatic, a willingness to risk, to lay yourself on the line (after careful preparation of your boss) and to allow your subordinates to help will move you toward excellence even if you are not so fortunate as to have almost all conditions just right.

I. DEALING WITH SUBORDINATES: ONLY ONE-THIRD OF THE MANAGER'S JOB

In writing a book about how to create excellence, we have told only part of the story. In order to do justice to the complexity of how to deal with subordinates, we have had to limit our discussion of dealing with peers and superiors to how the manager can gain the autonomy to use a Developer approach. But this emphasis is not meant to downplay the importance of these other key managerial issues. Departments and leaders do not exist in splendid isolation; it is the rare manager whose success isn't highly dependent on successful interactions with colleagues and superiors. In most cases it is impossible to create excellence without considerable skills in managing laterally and upwards, as well as down. These other players can have a major impact in terms of their willingness to share information, deliver resources, provide support, and cooperate in implementing decisions.

Furthermore, these three aspects of managing interact with each other so that success in one area influences outcomes in the others. Having clout with your boss gains respect from subordinates and peers; being influential with colleagues lets you deliver what your boss wants and your subordinates need; and high-performing subordinates increase your power sideways and upwards because you can deliver on your obligations and promises.

Although a full exploration of how to be more effective with these other two aspects of the manager's job is the subject for another book, it is worth noting that:

Many of the skills needed to get the most from subordinates are useful in dealing with boss and peers. For example, the ability to build common vision and compatible goals is important laterally and upwards. Skills in negotiation, confrontation, and joint problem-solving also apply to all three directions. You as a manager not only lead and have to develop your own team but are a member of your boss's team; group development skills are crucial in the latter situation as well.

The Developer model, once it is reasonably in place, frees you from many of the burdens of managing downward. If subordinates are genuinely sharing responsibility so that you do not have to carry all the weight on your shoulders, considerable time and energy are released for the work needed outside your unit. What we have seen with managers who operate under heroic assumptions is the extent to which their time and energy are consumed in putting out the constant internal brush fires that prevent them from adequately dealing with these external functions.

These points speak to a concern frequently raised by many of the managers who are considering the Developer approach. When we have taught the model, the response is often one of worry: "If I share my managerial responsibility with subordinates, won't that take away my job? Won't subordinates see me as superfluous?" With unemployment among middle managers an increasing phenomonon, many fear that the best way to justify their existence is to manage (downwards) in a more visible fashion.

However, the opposite is true. Creating a team that is committed to departmental success frees the manager to spend more time on those functions which often only the leader can do. This includes not only interfacing with other units in the organization but dealing with the powers-that-be. In an increasingly turbulent world, the leader has to manage the core processes of innovation and change. As Kanter (1983) has demonstrated in *The Change Masters*, leaders have to sense opportunities from above and outside, formulate new possibilities, build coalitions with peers to support cross-departmental change, and sell higher-ups on the ways these innovations will help achieve corporate goals. These are the ways in which effective middle and upper-middle managers get things done—and make themselves more valuable in the process.

All of that not only takes time but is difficult to deliver without a strong department and willing subordinates. The Developer model is useful insofar as it can ultimately free you to spend most of the time where your skills are ultimately needed and where the largest payoffs are.

II. MANAGER-AS-DEVELOPER: MAKING THE MOST OF YOUR IMPERFECT WORLD

We began this guide to achieving excellence by declaring that something is wrong with leadership in American organizations. In that initial chapter we reported some of the experiences of managers who did operate at an excellent level. In our consulting and training work, we frequently have posed the question, "What does it take to get excellence." We have raised this question in several ways and, to come full cycle from that first chapter, we want to describe a conversation we had with a group of savvy middle managers from some of America's leading companies.

We raised the following hypothetical issue: "How would you respond if the president of your organization came to you and said, 'I want you to take over Department X and make it perform at an excellent level. What would it take for you to do that?' " The managers in this session quickly agreed that they could deliver on the president's request if the following three conditions were met:

First, "Let me pick my own staff so that I can have highly competent people who will work well together."

Second, "Give me an exciting assignment that is important to this organization."

Third, "Give me a boss who doesn't interfere or tell me exactly what to do."

We then asked this group of managers how frequently those conditions are given to them; they laughed. If you can by skill, luck, or magic acquire these loaded-for-success conditions, life would be considerably easier than it is now. But one way to think about the message of this book is that it tells you how to build these conditions when they are not so fortuitously given to you. Few managers can completely pick their own staff—what we have shown is how you can develop high performers and a mature team with the individuals you presently have.

Few leaders in any organization are anointed by the president with just the perfect, crucial mission—what we have illustrated is how you can take the department's function and reconceptualize it into a challenging and exciting goal. Finally, few of us are blessed with the perfect superior—but we have given some hints about ways you can negotiate with your boss so that you can have the necessary autonomy and support.

III. SOME CONCLUDING PARADOXES

Rather than being dependent on those fortuitious but rare events when the perfect conditions are laid in your lap, this book is about how you can take control of what happens to you. By now, you should have a clear idea of how to go about countering the tendencies of organizational units to perform at levels far below what is possible. With determination, careful planning, and a willingness to risk doing things differently, you can produce excellence in the department you manage. You can make it a place where all the members are committed to the unit's goals, feel personal responsibility for its success, take initiative rather than wait passively for directions, and share a dedication to quality.

The experiences of managers who have begun using the Developer model show that it can work in a variety of conditions. Extra effort is needed when subordinates, superiors, or peers are resistant or unprepared, but these obstacles can be overcome. The key is to set up a process where you and your subordinates, working jointly, can discover the approach that best fits your specific situation. The act of sharing the responsibility for finding your ways to the shared-responsibility team is itself more important than following the model to a T.

Keep that paradoxical admonition in mind as you turn to our final words of wisdom, which we have formulated as a series of six paradoxes for postheroic managing.

PARADOX 1.   The Manager-as-Developer has to be both less active and more active than the heroic manager.

On the one hand, the postheroic manager has to back away from feeling solely responsible for solving all problems and managing the department. That obligation can be paralyzing at first, especially if you are used to achieving daily satisfactions from carrying the world on your shoulders. Although it is by no means appropriate to withdraw and go passive, you may not be able to see what else to do when you are trying to let go of heroic riding to the rescue. You might perceive heroism's apparent opposite as standing by while the damsel is run over by the onrushing locomotive.

Nevertheless, this dichotomy is false. We are not advocating management-by-absence; excellence can't be achieved by leader abdication. The Manager-as-Developer has to be quite active, but in a very different way from conventional heroics. While the traditional leader focused activity almost exclusively on solving task issues, Developers have to be active in managing procedural issues. Except when they have clearly greater expertise than their subordinates on that topic, Developers concentrate on managing the process so that full use is made of subordinate ability. The Developer's hard work and initiative are directed at seeing that the real issues are raised, arguments are joined, and commitments are made. Great activity is required of the Developer—to develop individuals and groups so that they can perform well in solving the problems and in sharing in the management of the unit.

Once a department is reasonably developed, there are fewer managerial demands on the Developers, but that hardly means that they have created their own unemployment. "Development" is not an end state in which the manager withers away. Improved performance just surfaces a new set of problems—redefined tasks, increased responsibilities, more complex issues. There will always be new people coming into the department who have to be integrated or changes in external conditions that require adjustments. And, as pointed out earlier, any time saved by the manager's not having to deal with internal issues can well be spent with the other crucial aspects of the leader's job: dealing sideways with other departments, upward with the boss, or outside the organization. The problem of having nothing to do or being reduced to watching the action from outside while longing to get into the game is not a problem in this postheroic world.

PARADOX 2.   The Manager-as-Developer must give greater autonomy to subordinates while establishing more controls.

To allow subordinates to share responsibility requires that the leader be willing to give up some of the conventional controls. The Developer must loosen the reins on problem solving, task assignment, and meeting agendas. Yet this loss of managerbased control is balanced by the increased controls that evolve when all subordinates are personally committed to departmental success. Collective acceptance of the same central overarching goal is a form of control. If members feel responsible for managing the unit, they will be more willing to pressure (exert control over) peers who are not coming through. If they accept the team as theirs, they will believe it is right for them to influence each other. All of this activity produces far more control than could be exerted by even the most watchful manager. Of course, these controls affect you as well as your subordinates; you become accountable to subordinates for commitments made, and they are more likely to push you to perform.

PARADOX 3.   Manager-as-Developers increase their own power by giving subordinates greater power.

Power and influence are not a fixed sum. In most organizations, there is too little power to produce excellence. Leaders who sense they are in low-power situations are hesitant about giving their subordinates increased influence in the decisionmaking process—in determining how the department is to be run and in deciding how best to carry out their assignments. Yet giving power begets power; subordinates who feel empowered and committed to the departmental goal are not only more motivated but are also more willing to be influenced by their peers and by you. People with low power most resist the power of others. The best way for you to increase your influence with subordinates is to increase their power with each other, with you, and with others outside the unit. This procedure is better defined as power-enhancement, rather than power-sharing.

PARADOX 4.   The Manager-as-Developer builds a team as a way to support member individuality.

Groups can be dangerous forces toward conformity in thought and behavior. Too many people experience their organizations as constraining. But groups can also support individuality. As a team develops, it moves from a collection of individuals who are suspicious of each other (and therefore want to limit differences among themselves) into a cohesive but consensual group where individual differences are valued and supported. A genuinely collaborative team can allow more diversity and autonomy than one that clings together for mutually distrustful motives.

In this vein, the Manager-as-Developer needs to hold meetings so that the team can develop to a point where fewer meetings are needed! So many present-day organizations support far more meetings than are necessary. The majority of unnecessary meetings are held because people don't trust each other or the manager is afraid that people will all march to their separate drummers. When the team has developed so that trust has developed and everybody is committed to the same goals, members know what to do and can usually act on their own in ways that are close to what the group and manager would have directed.

PARADOX 5.   The Manager-as-Developer model requires an optimistic faith in subordinate possibilities but tough implementation to work.

The Manager-as-Developer model is optimistic in several ways. First, the model is based on the premise that virtually everyone wants to do well—that no reason exists for basic incompatibility between what the organization needs (in its search for excellence) and what individuals want to produce (in terms of performing competently). Second, the model optimistically posits that most people basically do not seek to empire-build, play politics, and do each other in unless the organizational situation makes it difficult to accomplish anything otherwise. Nasty behavior arises mostly when members feel blocked from legitimate methods for getting their work done, not as a result of an innate component of personal nastiness. Finally, the model's optimism is revealed in its tenet that most people can change–their behaviors, not personalities. Under the proper conditions, which include a manager who functions as a Developer, a relatively high percentage of subordinates can learn and grow.

Many managers resist this optimism. There is a kind of comfort taken in cynicism—in hanging onto the beliefs that people are not to be trusted, are out for their own self-interest, and can't change. The developmental approach cannot be utilized without giving up this cynicism.

At the same time, the Manager-as-Developer model is basically a tough approach. It is tough in setting high standards (and holding people to them). It is tough in requiring that the manager hold subordinates' feet to the fire when they may want to avoid the difficult issues. It is tough in pushing for conflicts to be identified and worked through rather than smoothed over. It is tough in requiring that people be confronted (rather than shunted aside, or ignored) when they don't come through. And it is tough in demanding that the manager be willing to be open to confrontation as well.

Many managers avoid this toughness. Some are so concerned about being liked that they do not even raise the important issues. But even many of the managers who think themselves hard-boiled are not very tough in important dimensions. There is a difference between hardness and toughness. The manager can be hard by not listening to subordinate complaints, exploiting others for the sake of short-term productivity, or by showing a hard exterior to prevent subordinates from broaching difficult issues. Such hardness is not toughness. Being tough is fully listening to subordinates, acknowledging validity in their complaints, and still being able to take the difficult actions when appropriate. Toughness is not dropping bombs on distant, impersonal targets; insisting on performance despite closeness and caring is far tougher.

PARADOX 6.   Although the Developer model requires new behavior, the best way to improve your performance as a manager is to focus on the needs of others, rather than on yourself.

It is easy to become frozen by self-help books. Although we have tried to avoid detailed, step-by-step advice, we have drawn your attention to a lot of things at once, many of them involving changes in your attitudes, skills, and even behavior. This multi-faceted process can be like trying to learn how to play tennis by memorizing each motion in microscopic, sequential detail. By the time you remember how to hold the racket, where to plant your feet, how to line up parallel to the net, what to look at, and the angle of your arm, the ball is long since dead. At some point in your playing progress, you might benefit from minute examination of some aspect of your game, but only after you have the basic idea and rhythm of tennis to depend on. To build the idea and rhythm, you need to use the Zen tennis approach: Focus on the ball going back over the net and where you want it to land. Your swing and positioning will follow naturally.

Managing by a new style requires something similar to this attitude. You need to maintain your focus outward, on your subordinates and their needs, the nature of the tasks you all face, and the kind of results you desire. Too close attention to how you're doing—where your feet are planted (or how precisely you are executing the model)—only causes ungainly awkwardness.

Learning anything new requires a period of awkwardness, so don't let the prospect be discouraging. More important, even while checking once in a while to see how you are doing, don't become so self-conscious that you come to the fate of the centipede who was asked how he coordinated 100 legs: You can't move at all.

Remember, a long journey starts with small steps, even while your eye is on the guiding star. You have to do both at once. Happy trip.

APPENDIX

LEADERSHIP STYLE QUESTIONNAIRE

Name of your manager _____

Instructions:

Answer each question in terms of the extent to which it characterizes your boss. (We are using the terms "manager" and "boss" interchangeably to refer to the same person.)

Answer each question *twice*. First, put a circle ⃝ around the number that describes how your boss is *now*. Then put a square ☐ around the number that describes how you would like your manager *to be*. If it is the same, put the square around the circle.

Questions: To what extent . . . .

	Very Little				Great Extent
1. Does your boss have the necessary influence with his/her superior?	1	2	3	4	5
2. Has your boss helped you to plan your career opportunities in the organization?	1	2	3	4	5
3. Does your manager give you freedom to determine the details of how you go about doing your job?	1	2	3	4	5
4. Has your boss built a cohesive team of those people reporting to him/her?	1	2	3	4	5
5. Does your boss encourage feedback from subordinates on his/her performance?	1	2	3	4	5
6. Do the team meetings your boss runs deal with the important issues?	1	2	3	4	5
7. Does your manager give you challenging work assignments?	1	2	3	4	5
8. Does your boss shield your unit from excessive outside pressures?	1	2	3	4	5

Remember, answer each question twice. First in terms of how it is now and second in terms of how you would like it to be.

---

9. Does your boss have concern for you
and your professional well-being?   1   2   3   4   5

10. Does your manager allow you to have
influence on decisions important to you?   1   2   3   4   5

11. Does your boss encourage subordinates
to help each other?   1   2   3   4   5

12. Does your boss talk openly about any
difficulties the two of you have in work-
ing togther?   1   2   3   4   5

13. Is the purpose of each agenda item clear
at the meetings your boss runs?   1   2   3   4   5

14. Does your manager insist on high stan-
dards of performance?   1   2   3   4   5

15. Can your boss get his/her peers to coop-
erate when necessary?   1   2   3   4   5

16. Does your boss give you timely and
honest feedback on how well you are
performing?   1   2   3   4   5

17. Does your manager allow you latitude to
make and learn from mistakes?   1   2   3   4   5

18. Are all members of your boss's team
pulling together to achieve the same
goals?   1   2   3   4   5

19. Does your boss try to see the merits of
your ideas when they differ from
his/hers?   1   2   3   4   5

20. Do decisions made at the meetings your
boss runs get implemented?   1   2   3   4   5

21. Does your manager inspire you to give
your best efforts?   1   2   3   4   5

22. Is your boss effective in promoting departmental interests with others outside
your unit?   1   2   3   4   5

23. Does your boss coach you in ways that
help you perform better?   1   2   3   4   5

24. Does your manager encourage disagree-
ment with his/her ideas and proposals?   1   2   3   4   5

25. Does your boss foster team involvement
in solving crucial departmental prob-
lems?   1   2   3   4   5

26. Does your manager genuinely listen to
you and your ideas?   1   2   3   4   5

27. At meetings your boss runs, to what ex-
tent are decisions of high quality?   1   2   3   4   5

28. Has your boss articulated exciting or challenging department goals?	1	2	3	4	5
29. Can your manager get needed resources for the department?	1	2	3	4	5
30. Does your boss encourage you to develop new skills and abilities?	1	2	3	4	5
31. Does your boss allow you to take actions without having to check with him/her first?	1	2	3	4	5
32. Does your manager help team members constructively confront differences among themselves?	1	2	3	4	5
33. Does your boss give you all the information you need to know to get your job done?	1	2	3	4	5
34. At the meetings your boss runs, do members honestly express how they feel about the issues being discussed?	1	2	3	4	5
35. Is your boss enthusiastic when talking about the objectives of the department?	1	2	3	4	5

- -

A. What else does your boss do well as a manager?

B. What else does your boss do that prevents you and others from being as productive as you might be?

BIBLIOGRAPHY

Abdelnour, B., and Hall, D. T. "Career Development of Established Employees." *Career Development Bulletin*, 2(1), 5–8 (1980).

Adizes, I. *How to Solve the Mismanagement Crisis*. Homewood, Ill: Dow-Jones, 1979.

Argyris, C. *Personality and Organization*. New York: Harper, 1957.

Beckhard, R. "Optimizing Team Building Efforts." *Journal of Contemporary Business*, Summer 1972.

Berlew, D. E. "Leadership and Organizational Excitement." In D. A. Kolb, I. M. Rubin, and J. M. McIntyre (Eds.), *Organizational Psychology: A Book of Readings* (2nd Ed.). Englewood Cliffs, N.J.: Prentice-Hall, 1974.

Blake, R. R., and Mouton, J. "Power, People and Performance Reviews." *Advanced Management*, July–Aug. 1961, 13–17.

Cohen, A. R. "Crisis Management: How to Turn Disasters into Advantages." *Management Review*, Aug. 1982.

Cohen, A. R., Fink, S., Gadon, H., and Willits, R. *Effective Behavior in Organizations*. Homewood, Ill: Irwin, 1980.

Cohen, A. R., Fink, S., and Gadon, H. "Key Groups, Not T-Groups for Organizational Development." In D. Sinha (Ed.), *Consultants and Consulting Styles*. Delhi: Vision Books, 1979.

Cohen, A. R., Gadon, H., and Miaoulis, G. "Decision-Making in Firms: The Impact on Non-Economic Factors." *Journal of Economic Issues*, 10(2), (1976).

Deal, T. E. and Kennedy, A. A. *Corporate Cultures*. Reading, Mass.: Addison-Wesley, 1982.

Dyer, W. *Team Building: Issues and Alternatives*. Reading, Mass.: Addison-Wesley, 1977.

Fiedler, F. E. *A Theory of Leadership Effectiveness*. New York: McGraw-Hill, 1967.

Hersey, P., and Blanchard, K. H. *Management of Organizational Behavior* (2nd Ed.). Englewood Cliffs, N.J.: Prentice-Hall, 1972.

Hall, D. T., Bowen, D. D., Lewicki, R. J., and Hall, F. S. *Experiences in Management and Organizational Behavior* (2nd ed.). New York: Wiley, 1982.

House, R. J. "A Path-Goal Theory of Leader Effectiveness." In E. A. Fleishman and J. G. Hunt (Eds.), *Current Developments in the Study of Leadership*. Carbondale: Southern Illinois University Press, 1973.

Jones, E. E., et al. (Eds.). *Attribution: Perceiving the Causes of Behavior*. Morristown: General Learning Press, 1972.

Kanter, R. M. "Power Failures in Management Circuits." *Harvard Business Review*, 57(4), 65–75, 1979.

Kanter, R. M. *Men and Women of the Corporation*. New York: Basic Books, 1977.

Kanter, R. M. *The Change Masters: How People and Companies Succeed through Innovation in the New Corporate Era*. New York: Simon & Schuster, 1983.

Kidder, T. *Soul of a New Machine.* Boston: Little-Brown, 1981.

Likert, R. *New Patterns of Management.* New York: McGraw-Hill, 1961.

Livingston, S. "Pygmalion in Management." *Harvard Business Review,* July–August 47(4), 81–90, 1969.

Maier, N. R. F. *Problem-Solving and Creativity in Individuals and Groups.* Belmont, Calif.: Brooks/Cole, 1970.

Mann, F. C. "Toward an Understanding of the Leadership Role in Formal Organizations." In Robert Dubin, George C. Homans, Floyd C. Mann, and Delbert C. Miller (Eds.), *Leadership and Productivity.* San Francisco: Chandler Publishing Co., 1965.

Marshall Co. Series, A–J, Harvard Business School, ICCH 448-001-004/023-028, 1948.

McClelland, D. C. and Burnham, D. H. "Power is the Great Motivator." *Harvard Business Review,* March–April, 100–110, 1976.

Miles, R. E. and Ritchie, J. B. "Participative Management: Quality vs. Quantity." *California Management Review,* 8(4), 48–56, (1971).

Mintzberg, H. *The Nature of Managerial Work,* New York: Harper & Row, 1973.

Obert, S. L. "The Development of Organizational Task Groups." Ph.D. Dissertation. Case-Western Reserve University, 1979.

Ouchi, W. G. *Theory Z.* Reading, Mass.: Addison-Wesley, 1981.

Pascale, R. T., and Athos, A. G. *The Art of Japanese Management.* New York: Simon & Schuster, 1981.

Peters, T. J. "Symbols, Patterns and Settings: An Optimistic Case for Getting Things Done." *Organizational Dynamics.* Autumn 1979.

Peters, T. J., and Waterman, R. H., Jr. *In Search of Excellence.* New York: Harper & Row: 1982.

Pfeffer, J. "Organizational Demography." In L. L. Cummings and B. M. Staw (Eds.), *Research in Organizational Behavior,* Vol. 5. Greenwich, Conn.: JAI Press, 1983.

Rosenthal, R., and Jacobson, L. *Pygmalion in the Classroom: Teacher Expectations and Pupils' Intellectual Development.* New York: Holt, Rinehart, & Winston, 1968.

Sargent, A. G. *The Androgynous Manager.* New York: AMACON, 1981.

Vaill, Peter B. "Toward a Behavioral Description of High Performing Systems." In M. McCall and M. Lombard (Eds.), *Leadership: Where Else Can We Go.* Duke University Press, 1976.

Vroom, V. H., and Yetton, P. W. *Leadership and Decision-Making.* Pittsburgh: University of Pittsburgh Press, 1973.

Yankelovich, D. *The New Morality: A Profile of American Youth in the '70's.* New York: McGraw-Hill, 1974.

Yankelovich, D. "New Rules in American Life: Searching for Self-fulfillment in a World Turned Upside Down." *Psychology Today,* 16(Jan. 1982), 35–91.

INDEX